From Pr...
Acquie...

Political Movements of the

Paul Bagguley

MACMILLAN

First published 1991

Published by
MACMILLAN EDUCATION LTD
Houndmills, Basingstoke, Hampshire RG21 2XS
and London
Companies and representatives
throughout the world

Edited and typeset by Povey/Edmondson
Okehampton and Rochdale, England

Printed in Hong Kong

British Library Cataloguing in Publication Data
Bagguley, Paul
From protest to acquiescence? Political movements of the unemployed.
1. Great Britain. Labour movements, history
I. Title
331.80941
ISBN 0–333–53477–8 (hardcover)
ISBN 0–333–53478–6 (paperback)

From Protest to Acquiescence?
Political Movements of the Unemployed

Also by Paul Bagguley

RESTRUCTURING: Place, Class and Gender *(co-author)*

Contents

List of Tables and Figures   vii

Preface   viii

List of Abbreviations   x

1 Introduction   1

   1.1   The rise of unemployment during the 1980s   5

2 Theoretical Approaches To Politics and Unemployment   12

   2.1   Introduction   12
   2.2   Speculative Theories   12
   2.3   The neo-Marxist approach: Piven and Cloward   23
   2.4   The 'behaviourist' approach: Schlozman and Verba 29
   2.5   A British test of Schlozman and Verba: Marshall *et al.*   33
   2.6   Conclusion   36

3 The Structuring of Political Responses To Unemployment   37

   3.1   Introduction   37
   3.2   The unemployed and the state   38
   3.3   Organisational resources   45
   3.4   Cultural resources   56
   3.5   Community as a cultural resource   63
   3.6   Conclusion   70

4 Early Political Movements of The Unemployed   72

   4.1   The anti-Poor Law movement   72
   4.2   The Land and Labour League   76
   4.3   The Social Democratic Federation: 1880–1914   78
   4.4   The National Unemployed Workers' Movement   84
   4.5   Protest and the changing forms of unemployment relief: 1918–39   87

4.6   A messianic communism? The organisational and
      cultural resources of the NUW(C)M   98
4.7   Gender politics in the NUW(C)M   108
4.8   Conclusion   112

**5   Political Movements of the Unemployed
     in the 1980s   114**

5.1   Introduction   114
5.2   The TUC and centres for the unemployed   116
5.3   The unemployed workers' centre in Brighton   124
5.4   The campaign for a new centre   134
5.5   Conclusion   139

6   The Experience of Unemployment   141

6.1   Introduction   141
6.2   Perceptions of the disadvantages of unemployment   142
6.3   Perceptions of advantages of unemployment   150
6.4   Experience of the Unemployment Benefit and
      DHSS offices   155
6.5   Views about reasons for high unemployment   158
6.6   Conclusion   164

**7   Thatcherism, Class Consciousness and the
     Unemployed   167**

7.1   Thatcherism   167
7.2   Class consciousness and the unemployed   178
7.3   The political organisation of the unemployed   187
7.4   Class consciousness amongst the unemployed   191
7.5   Conclusion   200

8   Conclusion   201

Notes   204

Bibliography   208

Index   220

List of Tables and Figures

Tables

1.1 Unemployment rates by region and sex: Great
    Britain, 1985   7
1.2 Unemployment and vacancies by occupational class
    and sex: Great Britain, September 1982   8
1.3 Change in unemployment and unfilled vacancies by
    sex and occupational class: Great Britain, 1978–1982   10
3.1 Periodisation of state forms of unemployment relief   41
3.2 Ideal typical paradigms of political movements of
    the unemployed   51
4.1 Membership of working-class organisations amongst
    the unemployed in selected localities, 1936   102
4.2 Delegates from women's sections to NUWM
    Seventh National Congress   110

Figures

1.1 Total unemployment in Great Britain, 1978–90
    (May figures)   6
3.1 Ideal type of conjuncture of resources favouring
    mobilisation   67
3.2 Ideal type of conjuncture of resources blocking
    mobilisation   69
4.1 Trade union unemployment, 1870–1912   79
4.2 Unemployment rate, 1921–38   85

Preface

This book began as a D.Phil. thesis at the University of Sussex. It struck me when I began the work for the thesis in the early 1980s that it was rather odd that very little research had been carried out on the political responses to unemployment by the unemployed. There is still very little empirical research, and too much idle, ill-informed speculation. Although unemployment, as it is officially measured, has fallen from the high levels of the early 1980s, it has, during the middle of 1990, begun to rise again. I hope that what follows goes some way towards an understanding of political responses to unemployment both during the current period and in the past. I trust that the book will also be of some value to those interested in wider issues of social movements and contemporary social change.

Most of all, I would like to thank the many unemployed people who agreed to be interviewed for the the research reported in this book. Peter Saunders, my supervisor at Sussex, has provided endless encouragement and constant constructive criticism, not always heeded, throughout. I would like to thank the participants in several departmental and graduate student seminars in the Departments of Sociology at the Universities of Sussex and Lancaster who have commented on earlier versions of the work. Dan Shapiro, John Urry, Sylvia Walby and Alan Warde have commented on earlier drafts of several of the chapters below. The examiners of the original thesis, Huw Beynon and William Outhwaite, provided many detailed and useful comments. I would also like to thank Sue Penna and Kirk Mann for many detailed conversations about the content of what follows. Kirk Mann deserves special mention for having read no less than three versions of the text.

I am grateful to the staff of the libraries of the Universities of Sussex, Lancaster and Leeds for their assistance. The TUC and the Brighton centre for the unemployed were generous in providing documents upon which some of the analysis below is based. The Department of Sociology at the University of Lancaster kindly gave me an honorary research fellowship which enabled me to complete the writing up of the thesis from which this book has been developed. The departments at Lancaster and Leeds were also generous in the provision of printing facilities. The thesis and the book were written on an Atari ST using 1st Word Plus. I am especially grateful to the spelling checker! The research for the thesis, on which this book is based, was carried out with the aid of an ESRC research training studentship: number G00428222732.

Finally, I would like to thank the Department of Employment, Unemployment Benefits Section, for providing the means of existence during the last two months of the writing up of the thesis in the summer of 1988.

PAUL BAGGULEY
Department of Social Policy and Sociology
University of Leeds

List of Abbreviations

CEP	Community Enterprise Programme
COHSE	Confederation of Health Service Employees
CP	Community Programme
CPAG	Child Poverty Action Group
DE	Department of Employment
DHSS	Department of Health and Social Security
ILP	Independent Labour Party
LRC	Labour Representation Committee
MC	Management Committee
MSC	Manpower Services Commission
NGSW	Not Genuinely Seeking Work
NUAAW	National Union of Agricultural and Allied Workers
NUPE	National Union of Public Employees
NUW(C)M	National Unemployed Workers (Committee) Movement
OECD	Office of Economic Cooperation and Development
PAC	Public Assistance Committee
PC	Policy Committee
PER	Professional and Executive Recruitment
SDF	Social Democratic Federation
SERTUC	South East Regional Trade Union Congress
TC	Trades Council
TUC	Trades Union Congress
UAB	Unemployment Assistance Board
UWU	Unemployed Workers' Union
WEA	Workers' Education Association

1

Introduction

This book is concerned with a central social scientific issue of the 1980s. Why, with the widespread growth of unemployment in Britain over the past decade, has there been no mass political movement of the unemployed? In this introduction I shall lay out my principal arguments, and provide some general background to the sociological analysis of unemployment during the 1980s.

For most of the post-war period Britain had enjoyed 'full employment', with the unemployment rate consistently around 2 per cent. The rate of unemployment began to rise above these levels during the late 1960s, but reached unprecedented levels after 1979. By 1983, the unemployment rate in Britain was one of the highest of any advanced Western country, being over 13 per cent (Ashton, 1986, pp. 8–9; Therborn, 1986, p. 41). This dramatic change in the fortunes of the labour market generated not just major debates amongst economists as to the causes of high unemployment (Hawkins, 1984), but a major research effort aimed at describing, understanding and explaining the effects on the unemployed themselves.

There has been a range of studies concerned with the sociology of the labour market aspects of unemployment. These have usually focused on what have been seen to be problematic groups amongst the unemployed, such as the long-term unemployed (White, 1983), ethnic minorities (Smith, 1981), women (Walby, 1984) and young people (Ashton and Maguire, 1985; Roberts et al., 1985; Raffe, 1986). Some of the findings of these studies are discussed in relation to empirical data on the uneven distribution of unemployment in the second half of this introduction.

Numerous studies of the impact of unemployment on the non-economic aspects of the unemployed's lives have also been conducted. Considerable attention has been given to young people in these studies, concentrating on the break up of the previously 'normal' transition from school to work that has occurred with the rise in youth unemployment, and the emergence of extensive

1

government training schemes (Coffield *et al.*, 1986; Rees and Atkinson, 1982; Roberts, 1984a; Wallace, 1987). Broadly speaking, these studies conclude that changes in the position of young people have led to a divergence of lifestyle between the employed and unemployed, and that more diverse household structures were developing (Wallace, 1987, pp. 221–8). However, the traditional 'nuclear family' has remained an ideal to which most aspire, and the permanence of these changes could be called into question when, or if, full employment returns. Detailed research has also been carried out on women (Coyle, 1984), and the impact of unemployment on the family and gender relations more generally (Clark, 1987; Henwood and Miles, 1987; Jackson and Walsh, 1987; Laite and Halfpenny, 1987; McKee and Bell, 1986). Many of these studies found remarkably little change in such things as the domestic division of labour with the onset of unemployment. There were, rather, consistent attempts to maintain continuity, and researchers have found it difficult to disentangle the effects of unemployment from those of the life-cycle and relative poverty (McKee and Bell, 1986, p. 146).

Despite the broad conclusion of continuity in spite of change that emerges from many of these studies, it would be wrong to read this as meaning that unemployment has no consequences whatsoever. The other general conclusion is that unemployment leads to relative poverty (Cooke, 1987) and high levels of dissatisfaction with life generally. It is precisely because of these consequences, over which the unemployed themselves have relatively little control, that there is so much effort invested by many unemployed people in maintaining a degree of normality and continuity over those things which they feel they can influence.

For the purposes of my argument what is most striking about much of the research discussed above is its almost total lack of attention to the political responses of the unemployed themselves. In Chapter 2, I consider a wide variety of analyses and suggested explanations of the impact of unemployment on the political attitudes of the unemployed, and the structuring of protest by the unemployed. The accounts of Piven and Cloward (1977) and Schlozman and Verba (1979) are given more detailed attention. Although both are studies of the United States rather than Britain, they are the most developed theories of political response to unemployment that have been published, and, furthermore, are based on detailed empirical research. They also exemplify quite different methodological and theoretical approaches to the sociological analysis of politics. Piven and Cloward analyse a variety of political movements of the unemployed, unskilled workers and the urban poor within a neo-Marxist framework. In contrast, Schlozman and Verba operate within the dominant behaviourist orientation of political science, and their analysis is of individuals' political attitudes in response to unemployment. Whilst Piven and Cloward produce an account that is far too structural and deterministic, Schlozman and Verba's analysis is purely at the level of individual attitudes and responses to unemployment.

In Chapter 3, I construct a general analytical framework for the analysis of political responses to unemployment by the unemployed themselves. This not only draws upon some of the valuable insights gained from the literature discussed in Chapter 2, but draws critically upon wider accounts of working class politics. I shall be concerned to explain both protest and acquiescence, and there are three broad components to my account.

The first of these is to consider those institutions against which political movements of the unemployed, when they emerge, protest. I show that the changing *form* of the state's income maintenance system is central to understanding the structuring of protest. The broad preconditions of protest are democratically organised local decision-making over the forms and levels of unemployment relief. This form of state income maintenance in Britain has been found at its most 'ideal' for protest during the 1920s and 1930s. Subsequently, income maintenance systems have become centralised and bureaucratic, essentially sealing them off from the impact of collective action by the unemployed.

Secondly, for protest to emerge organisational resources are required by the protesting groups. Further, different kinds of organisational resources and forms of organisation generate quite different forms of collective action. I argue that for protest to emerge that actively involves the unemployed, it is crucial to examine the different kinds of organisational resources that the unemployed themselves wield. In particular, I show that only in those places and at those times where the political organisations of the working class have stressed decentralised collective action, as opposed to centralised and technocratic forms of action, have political movements of the unemployed been able to develop.

Consequently, attention to which sections of the working class become unemployed and which localities suffer from high unemployment is crucial to understanding the emergence, or lack of emergence, of political movements of the unemployed.

Thirdly, particular kinds of cultural resources also tend to either favour or block the development of political protest by the unemployed. Those cultural resources which consist of high levels of working-class solidarity, and belief in the efficacy of participation in collective action, provide the best basis for political movements of the unemployed. Ideological beliefs which obscure relations of domination, in contrast, will tend to retard the development of protest. However, I argue that fatalistic beliefs about the efficacy of collective action are more important than other types of ideological belief in blocking the emergence of collective action.

I then use this framework to analyse a variety of political movements of the unemployed between the 1830s and 1930s. I show that political protest amongst the unemployed is not simply determined by the level of unemployment, but is structured by their changing relationship to the state and the development of organisational and cultural resources.

Chapter 5 considers attempts to organise the unemployed in Britain during the 1980s. I examine the development of the Trade Union Congress's centres for the unemployed, and discuss the development of one centre, in Brighton, in more detail. I argue that these attempts have generally been unsuccessful when compared to, say, the 1920s and 1930s. This is because the state's unemployment relief institutions are highly centralised and sealed off from the effects of collective action by the unemployed. Further, the TUC has attempted, in a centralised and technocratic manner, to provide services for the unemployed rather than develop collective action. In this context the Brighton centre is an exceptional but interesting case study, since there was an attempt there to organise the unemployed locally for involvement in collective action. This case study also enables me to consider how the processes of mobilisation work out practically at the local level.

In Chapters 6 and 7, I present some results from a series of qualitative interviews with unemployed people which I carried out during 1983–4. These consist of two distinct samples, one of people involved in the Brighton centre for the unemployed, and the other of people who were not involved in the centre. This enables me to consider in some detail the differences in experience of and response to unemployment, and to examine the detailed patterns of cultural resources as they vary between the politically active and inactive groups.

1.1 THE RISE OF UNEMPLOYMENT DURING THE 1980S

Britain has had a relatively high level of unemployment during the 1980s compared to most Western countries. However, the measurement of both the level and rate of unemployment is highly contentious, both in statistical and political terms. This has been heightened by the fact that since 1979 no less than twenty-four changes have been made to the unemployment count, most of which have resulted in a reduction in either the level or rate of unemployment as it is officially measured (Unemployment Unit, 1988, p. 24).

Figure 1.1 presents data from two sources on the level of unemployment in Great Britain during the late 1970s and 1980s. The 'DE Count' consists of the series as it is officially defined, and the 'UU Index' is a series produced by the Unemployment Unit since 1983 which attempts to estimate the level of unemployment on the old official definitions. Figure 1.1 shows that unemployment rose rapidly during the early 1980s, and has fallen more slowly since 1986.

The discussion about the causes of high unemployment in Britain is a highly detailed and technical economic debate, and it would be out of place to deal with it in any detail here. However, Therborn's (1986) study comparing sixteen major OECD countries has produced some surprising and sociologically interesting results. Broadly speaking, Therborn argues that high unemployment results from how deeply embedded the value of 'full employment' is in a society's culture and political institutions. This shapes a country's response to international economic crises. During the mid 1980s unemployment rates have varied between 0.9 per cent and 14 per cent between the sixteen countries in Therborn's analysis (ibid, p. 41, table 3). He considered a wide range of economic variables in relation to the variations in unemployment rates between countries – economic growth, labour supply,

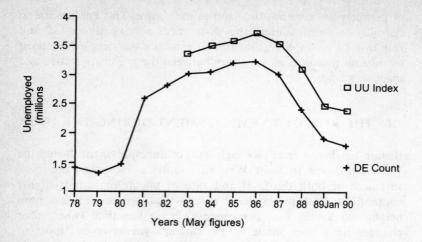

SOURCE Unemployment Unit Statistical Supplements and *Employment Gazette*.

FIGURE 1.1   *Total unemployment in Great Britain, 1978–90 (May figures)*

dependence on the world market, economic structure, inflation, labour costs, welfare state expenditure, taxation, and the level of unemployment compensation – none of which proved to be significant factors explaining the international variations (ibid, pp. 14–20). Furthermore, Therborn found considerable variations in the social patterning of unemployment; for example, it was by no means the case that women have been squeezed out of the labour market in most countries.

Within Britain there are considerable variations in the unemployment rate between regions.[1] Table 1.1 presents details. The rate of unemployment is much higher in the 'peripheral regions' of Scotland, Wales, the North, North West, Yorkshire and Humberside and the West Midlands. The differences are even more striking at a subregional level, however, with the sharpest differences between the cores of the older northern cities with high levels of unemployment and their rural hinterlands with quite low levels (Champion *et al.*, 1987, pp. 76–88).

The pattern of unemployment is strongly shaped by social inequalities of gender, class and 'race'. The data discussed here relate to the period from 1978 to 1982, and are based on the Department of Employment returns. This is almost a 'census' of all

Table 1.1 *Unemployment rates by region and sex: Great Britain, 1985 (percentages)*

Region	Men	Women	Total
South East	9.9	6.9	8.6
East Anglia	9.5	7.7	8.8
South West	11.0	8.6	10.0
West Midlands	15.7	10.7	13.7
East Midlands	12.0	8.7	10.7
Yorks and Humberside	15.3	9.9	13.1
North West	17.6	10.6	14.7
North	19.7	12.1	16.7
Wales	16.9	11.1	14.7
Scotland	16.6	10.7	14.1

SOURCE *Employment Gazette*, January 1987: S20–22, table 2.3: unemployment, regions. Reproduced with the permission of Her Majesty's Stationery Office.

those registered as unemployed, and the data are based on their statements about their previous occupation when they registered as unemployed.

Unemployment rates for particular occupational classes are not available for this particular set of data. However, the percentages in Table 1.2 present the class distribution of the registered unemployed based on their former occupation as it was reported when they registered as unemployed. Most unemployed people were formerly in manual jobs with over 55 percent of all unemployed people falling into the categories of 'general labourers' or 'other manual' occupational classes. Nevertheless, there are significant differences between the figures for men and women. Unemployed men are six times more likely to have been 'foremen or skilled manual' employees than unemployed women, and twice as likely to have been 'general labourers'. On the other hand, unemployed women were five times more likely than unemployed men to have been previously employed in 'clerical and related' occupations, and over four times as likely to have previously been working in other 'non-manual' occupations.

Table 1.2 *Unemployment and vacancies by occupational class and sex: Great Britain, September 1982 (percentages)*

Occupational class	Men		Women		All		Unfilled Vacancies		Unemployment/Vacancies ratio
	N		N		N		N		
Managerial and professional	219 146	10.7	102 027	12.8	321 173	11.3	15 603	13.7	20.6
Clerical and related	131 503	6.4	238 982	30.0	370 485	13.0	18 036	15.9	20.5
Other non-manual	68 401	3.3	118 201	14.8	186 602	6.6	18 237	16.1	10.2
Foremen and skilled manual	369 535	18.1	26 641	3.3	396 176	13.9	17 866	15.7	22.2
General labourers	704 444	34.4	131 036	16.5	835 480	29.4	3 334	2.9	250.6
Other manual	551 833	27.0	179 566	22.5	731 399	25.7	40 436	35.6	18.1
All occupations	2 044 826	100.0	796 453	100.0	2 841 315	100.0	113 512	100.0	25.0

SOURCE *Employment Gazette*, November 1982, calculated from table 2.12. Reproduced with the permission of Her Majesty's Stationery Office.

Generally, it appears that working-class people are much more likely to be unemployed than those employed in service-class occupations. This tendency is reinforced among the less skilled sections of the working class. Since it is not possible to calculate directly unemployment rates for the occupational classes, I have presented data on vacancies by occupational classes and calculated the ratio of the unemployed from each occupational class to the notified vacancies available in that occupational class (the U/V ratio). The U/V ratio is a crude measure of the number of unemployed people chasing each job. Since labour markets are segmented in such a way that, for example, general labourers are highly unlikely when unemployed to obtain employment in professional or managerial occupations, then the U/V ratio is also a crude measure of occupational class inequalities *within* unemployment. The one occupational class U/V ratio that is above the average is that for 'general labourers', a staggering 250.6 compared to the average of 25. The major qualification that must be added is that the U/V ratio for 'other manual' occupations is below the average at 18.1. This is largely explicable in terms of the sectors from which the occupational classes are drawn. General labourers largely come from the manufacturing sector, whilst other manual employees are largely found in the routine jobs of the private and public service sectors.

The U/V ratio says little directly about the gender divisions in unemployment. However, it is significant that the lowest U/V ratios are found for those occupational classes in which unemployed women are concentrated, especially the 'other non-manual' category, and unemployed women from manual occupations are concentrated in the 'other manual' occupational class (Table 1.2).

Further data showing the percentage changes in the number of people registered as unemployed between 1978 and 1982 by sex and occupational class are presented in Table 1.3. The percentage changes require careful analysis since the base Ns (1978) vary considerably between the occupational classes being compared. General labouring and clerical groups show relatively low percentage changes, whilst those for professional, skilled manual and others are higher than average. However, there has been a rapid decline in the number of general labourers' and skilled manual vacancies.

Table 1.3   *Change in unemployment and unfilled vacancies by sex and occupational class: Great Britain, 1978–82 (percentages)*

Occupational class	Men change		Women change		All change		Unfilled vacancies change
	N	%	N	%	N	%	
Managerial and professional	144 046	65.7	63 099	61.8	207 145	64.5	−23.3
Clerical and related	51 002	38.8	126 747	53.0	177 749	48.0	−82.0
Other non-manual	43 254	63.2	71 246	60.3	114 518	61.4	−15.0
Foremen and skilled manual	248 599	67.3	16 765	62.9	265 364	67.0	−245.9
General labourers	325 230	46.2	55 875	42.6	381 105	45.6	−233.0
Other manual	337 681	61.2	105 517	58.8	443 198	60.6	−110.7
All occupations	1 149 812	56.2	439 267	55.21	589 079	55.9	−103.6

SOURCE Calculated from *Department of Employment Gazette* November 1978, table 1, p. 129 and *Employment Gazette* November 1982, table 2.12. Reproduced with the permission of Her Majesty's Stationery Office.

One of the major features of contemporary debates about unemployment is the high level of unemployment in the black and Asian sections of the British population. Amongst men unemployment is highest for West Indian people, but for women it is highest for Asians. However, this generalisation does not hold for particular age groups since for both men and women unemployment is highest for the 16–19-year-old group amongst West Indian people (Brown, 1984, tables 83 and 84). The most important conclusion to draw from this data is that whatever sex or age category is considered West Indian and Asian people have higher rates of unemployment than white people. Research suggests that the reason for ethnic minorities' higher rate of unemployment is not so much the distinctive sectors of the economy in which they have been employed, their lack of qualifications, but discrimination in redundancy and at the point of recruitment (Smith, 1981, pp. 148–50).

The process of redundancy (operating on the basis of 'last in first out', and part-time employees before full-time employees) discriminates against young people (Raffe, 1986), and against women (Walby, 1984). Whilst this, along with reduction in recruitment, can provide an adequate account of unemployment amongst young people, the situation amongst women is more complex. Measures of unemployment for women are widely recognised to be imprecise, given their labour market situation. Broadly speaking, even allowing for the weakness of the statistics, women's employment during the recession has not been hit as badly as men's, because the jobs lost were concentrated in the manufacturing sector, whilst the service sector employing large numbers of women has grown significantly after a short decline. That is to say, women have been protected from the effects of the recession by their subordinate position in the labour market, which segregates them into the lower paying sectors of the service industries (Bagguley and Walby, 1988; Rubery and Tarling, 1988). It has been very much a men's recession.

2

Theoretical Approaches to Politics and Unemployment

2.1 INTRODUCTION

In this chapter I shall examine a number of approaches to understanding the political responses of the unemployed. The debates and literature are, rather surprisingly I think, relatively underdeveloped. I shall also discuss in more detail the work of Piven and Cloward (1977) and Schlozman and Verba (1979) carried out in the USA.

These constitute the two most developed theories of the politics of the unemployed backed up with extensive empirical studies. Piven and Cloward's work has generated something of a critical debate concerning their central claims (Castells, 1983; Gamson and Schmeidler, 1984; Hobsbawm, 1984; Jenkins, 1979; Roach and Roach, 1978), and Schlozman and Verba's work has been used to account for the political quiescence of the unemployed in Britain (Ashton, 1986, pp. 158–9). Furthermore, there has been at least one published attempt to replicate some of Schlozman and Verba's analysis in the British context (Marshall et al., 1988b) which I shall also discuss. But first I shall consider the wide range of more speculative literature which has been produced in the British context.

2.2 SPECULATIVE THEORIES

Jordan (1973) analyses the politics of the unemployed by trying to specify the objective economic interest of the poor and the

12

unemployed as distinct from those in work. He then links these interests to the development of political organisations of these groups. This account of the emerging conflict of interests between a stratum of 'paupers' and the rest of the working class is grounded in a simple version of dual labour market theory. In the primary sector are those highly paid workers organised in strong unions, and who are in technologically dynamic sectors with increasing labour productivity. In this primary sector of the economy productivity bargaining had not only resulted in some redundancies, but had also improved the security of employment of those within it. Those in the secondary sector work in labour intensive, low technology industries with low wages. In these sectors, Jordan asserts that productivity bargaining is not possible, and because of the inefficiency of this sector those employed in it are more likely to be made redundant (Jordan, 1973, pp. 4–7).

According to Jordan this labour market dualism is further reinforced by government policies, especially in the realm of social security. In particular, Jordan singles out the Family Income Supplement scheme, which he compares to the Speenhamland phase of Poor Law administration in the nineteenth century, arguing that both subsidise low wages. In the context of high inflation (he was writing in the early 1970s), the low-waged workers in the secondary sector will increasingly be forced to rely on state subsidies to supplement their incomes. For the ruling class, he argues, this is an eminently useful strategy since it effectively divides the working class so that the ruling class can maintain its dominance (ibid., pp. 8–11). Those in work seek to maximise their incomes and minimise the levels of taxation, whilst those out of work respond to the social security rules by seeking to avoid work and maximise their income through the benefits system (ibid., pp. 69–70). The Labour Party and the trade unions have sought to maintain the situation since they are part of the social order that created such affluence alongside state organised poverty (ibid., pp. 71–2).

The main problem with Jordan's account is the extreme economically reductionist nature of the proposed explanation. More specifically, it is logically incoherent in its own terms by conflating two distinct claims. The first is that as people *individually* become poorer, they protest and form a collective social and political force. The second is that as *more people become unemployed or poor* then protest emerges. These are two empirically distinct propositions that are implied in this emiseration thesis, but they remain unelaborated and in contradiction to each other in the core of the argument:

> There is a pauper sector already, and it is growing. All the economic trends are against it, and it is getting steadily poorer in relation to the rest of society. It is also increasingly more identifiable to itself and to others, as the government introduces more selective state benefits. Any movement which can begin to unite this class as a self-conscious interest group which identifies its own needs and expresses them in conflict with other groups, will only be giving shape to an entity whose existence will already have been recognised by its members and by those outside it. (ibid., p. 78)

It seems that for Jordan, any organisation merely gives expression to that which has already spontaneously emerged as a result of emiseration fostered by objective economic forces and state social security policies. The main organisational expression of this 'pauperisation' is the emergence of claimants' unions (a large section of the book is a detailed empirical account of the Newton Abbot claimants' union in which Jordan was involved), and they develop as a result of the increasing emiseration of the poor.

There is further ambivalence in Jordan's work which relates to the translation of the 'objective interests' of his putative 'pauper class' in a political movement. It would seem that such a movement should be 'fighting on two fronts': the first against the state's social security system, and the second against the established trade unions and their practices of productivity bargaining. However, most of the actual struggles that he describes in his account of claimants' unions are principally against the social security system (ibid., p. 85). One of my central arguments is that this struggle against the social security system is what gives political movements of the unemployed their specificity. Furthermore, in engaging in these struggles they frequently draw upon the resources of, or form alliances with, sections of the labour movement. Jordan tends to criticise the trade unions *en bloc* for productivity bargaining practices, thus failing to recognise the wide variety of politics found within the trade union movement.

What of value can be drawn from Jordan's work? Most significant is not his theoretical argument, but the general thrust of his empirical account of claimants' unions. In this he shows that *the principal axis of conflict and struggle is with the social security system.*

> Each union was autonomous, but several features were common to all; a membership consisting of people who were claiming Social Security; a concern for the welfare of all such people; a determination by members to support each others' claims and to fight against evasion, false information and intimidation by social security officers; and an opposition in principle to the wage stop and means test. (ibid., p. 26)

In contrast to Jordan, Jahoda argues that unemployment, through its deleterious psychological effects, breeds apathy. With a comprehensive welfare state system during the 1980s there is less of a connection between unemployment and poverty, and consequently less to protest about in comparison to the 1930s. The central plank of this argument revolves around the idea that there are a number of latent functions of paid employment, what might be called 'categories of experience', to which the unemployed are denied access. These latent functions are distinct from the manifest functions of employment to earn money, and include: a structured experience of time; regular social contacts; participation in collective purposes; social status which provides personal identity and regular physical activity (Jahoda, 1982, p. 39).

Jahoda's analysis is based on a discussion of several 1930s studies of the psychological impact of unemployment, *not on studies of political movements of the unemployed.* There is, therefore, no comparative element to her account whereby it might be possible to examine those circumstances where political movements did and did not emerge. Instead there is just the generalisation from a particular set of general studies of the psychological effects of unemployment.[1]

It appears that Jahoda is arguing against some putative emiseration thesis that she leaves unspecified (ibid., p. 6). Consequently, she fails to consider alternative explanations, which might be able to specify cultural and political factors as important conditions for the emergence of political movements of the unemployed. Therefore, she has no way of adequately explaining the fact that there was, as she puts it, 'some agitation' (ibid., p. 27).

Most importantly, Jahoda fails to examine the relationship between the unemployed and the welfare state, which is usually the focus for the struggles of political movements of the unemployed. This much is clear from Jordan's (1973) empirical discussion of claimants' unions, and the activities of the NUW(C)M during the inter-war years (Croucher, 1987; Hannington, 1977).

In the report of his study in Greenwich in the 1930s, Bakke (1933) argues that the political perspectives of the employed and the unemployed are essentially the same. This is because of their basically similar economic position, resulting in their support for the Labour Party in simply electoral rather than activist terms.

In part, at least, Bakke is correct in saying that the political views of the unemployed are basically similar to those of the rest of the working class. However, to generalise across the working class in this way fails to give any account of variations, especially those between regions and localities. To take account of this is crucial, since during the period of Bakke's study it is evident that political responses to unemployment varied markedly between different parts of the country. These variations resulted, as I shall show below, not from variations in unemployment, but from the high degree of cultural and political unity found in some working-class places, which provided the political and cultural resources for the political organisation of the unemployed.

More importantly, his claim that there is no real economic difference between the employed and the unemployed because of the income maintenance schemes is empirically incorrect. He provides no evidence to support this assertion. Research carried out in the 1930s shows that among the unemployed only 2.3 per cent of men and 5.2 per cent of women had incomes the same as or higher than those they received in employment (Moylan *et al.*, 1984, p. 3). The scales of unemployment relief during the 1930s were generally below Rowntree's 'human needs' minimum, with the average insured rates for men with dependants less than half the level of median wages at 24s 6d compared to 55s 6d (Thane, 1982, p. 182). There would appear to be no evidence of income equality to support Bakke's claim.

In a study of the media and attitudes to social security abuse, Golding and Middleton (1982) suggest that political unity and action among the unemployed are prevented primarily by massive daily doses of 'false consciousness' they gain from the media. This argument rests on a conception of a dominant ideology or central system of social values, which are *unproblematically* transmitted by the media to the public, who *unproblematically* internalise it and use it to interpret their situation (Abercrombie *et al.*, 1980). In contrast, Abercrombie *et al.* argue that theorists of the dominant ideology fail to consider in sufficient detail, or with any analytical precision, the following issues. What is the dominant ideology? What are its effects on the dominant class? What are its effects on the subordinate class? What apparatus transmits the dominant ideology? (ibid., pp. 2–4). Golding and Middleton do provide an account of the contents of the dominant ideology of welfare, but say almost nothing about its effects on the dominant class. In relation to the transmission of the dominant ideology of welfare, they provide an account of the way the media construct reports of welfare issues. However, the analysis becomes circular. They argue that the media report welfare issues in terms of popular beliefs, and yet it is supposed to shape those beliefs. In terms of the impact on the subordinate classes, Golding and Middleton rely on evidence from their own attitudes survey. They assert rather than demonstrate the link between the news and attitudes, and provide no empirical analysis of the way in which people 'take in' the news and discuss it. In short, there is no account of the centrally important process of the various ways in which news can be decoded and interpreted.

In fact their data indicate a much more complex situation with intra and inter class variations, and a recognition of a conflict between media representations and people's experiences. However, these not insignificant details seem to be absent from the main thrust of their argument. In other crucial instances their data do not support their argument. For instance, they use evidence showing that slightly more than one in ten of their sample thought unemployment benefits were too high, or that unemployment was largely voluntary, to assert that the substance of these views are 'general' (Golding and Middleton, 1982, p. 177).

A general hostility towards other claimants and the unemployed, produced by a dominant ideology, cannot be sustained as a putative explanation of the political quiescence of the unemployed for both theoretical and empirical reasons. Even if the majority did fit Golding and Middleton's stereotype, that would leave them with the problem of explaining away a potentially resistant minority. Their analysis can be seen as a variant of a wider thesis concerning the impact of 'Thatcherism' (Hall, 1982), and I shall also assess their argument in relation to my own empirical evidence.

Jeremy Seabrook (1982) argues that the unemployed, like the rest of the working class, are mesmerised by consumerism. Furthermore, the 'socialist victory' of the 'welfare state' has undermined traditional working class communities and their traditions of opposition and mutual support in the face of the consequences of capitalist crisis.

Superficially, this account has more plausibility than some of the others. It is also based on numerous carefully conducted taped interviews with working-class people, both employed and unemployed, but it remains journalism and not sociology. This gives little account of important regional, ethnic and gender differences in the changing experiences of the working-class that Seabrook seeks to chart over the past forty or fifty years. Diverse accounts of the subjects are placed alongside each other in the text, more it appears for their shock value than to facilitate understanding. Seabrook writes of a working-class culture which had socialist potential built into it, which has since been undermined by consumerism. No attempt is made to assess the possible positive aspects of this process. It might have facilitated new and diverse forms of cultural practices that have their own oppositional potential, as well as generally improved physical well-being. Most important of all, perhaps, Seabrook fails to consider the role of political organisations in providing the context for oppositional cultures and practices to emerge and be sustained.

One point that he makes, however, is significant. The emergence of a centralised welfare state is important, I believe, in understanding the historical variations in the politics of the unemployed. Although Seabrook misrepresents this, it is important to consider the changing relationship between the unemployed and the welfare state. Seabrook tends to portray the welfare state as an economic concession to working-class protest, which has been accepted by people undermining protest. However, most important is the degree of access to the state and control over levels of unemployment benefit locally. It is this loss of local control, rather then the mere existence of the welfare state, which is crucial for political protest by the unemployed.

An emphasis on perceptions of material standards is found in a re-evaluation of Runciman's relative deprivation thesis by Ditton and Brown (1981). They suggest that the unemployed, and the lower income groups in general, are involved in the informal economy which encourages political quiescence. They add a qualification to Runciman's perceptual account of politics based on economic inequality, which was that people only have accurate perceptions of the economic situation of those nearest to them in the economic hierarchy. Ditton and Brown argue that people will measure their visible and invisible incomes against only the visible incomes of those around them. People see themselves as the income equals of those just above them in the income hierarchy. Those who do not have an invisible income, on the other hand, will only have accurate knowledge of the invisible incomes of those nearest to them in the economic hierarchy (ibid., pp. 522–6). The result is intra-class antagonism rather than solidarity.

Ditton and Brown's argument, like many of the others considered here, identifies only one or two factors in their explanation. The diversity of political response to unemployment requires a more sophisticated analysis. More significantly for the specific claims of Ditton and Brown, there is good empirical evidence to suggest that the unemployed, in Britain at any rate, are not significantly involved in the informal economy. If anything unemployment is a significant factor preventing people from becoming involved in such economic activities (Pahl, 1984 and Economist Intelligence Unit, 1982). As Pahl (1984) has shown, access to work in the informal economy requires extensive and, in the case of the unemployed, trustworthy contacts through which to gain access to informal work. If the unemployed were to be involved in the informal sector on the scale suggested by Ditton and Brown's argument, then that would seem to imply considerable class solidarity rather than intra-class conflict.

Ditton and Brown's claims about intra-class conflict remain unspecified as to at what level this conflict is supposedly occurring. It is not clear from their account whether or not it is merely conflict of interpersonal relations at the level of a locality, for example, or if that conflict takes a more organised form. Without specifying this in more detail, it is difficult to see whether or not such intra-class conflict is merely trivial or a more fundamental axis of political conflict.

More generally, the relative deprivation theory proposed by Runciman (1972), to account for the political quiescence of subordinate classes in Britain, cannot be applied easily to the unemployed. Runciman's classic account of relative deprivation is essentially perceptual; he explicitly rejects accounts in terms of false consciousness (ibid., pp. 292–6). People compare their material condition with those who are materially and socially closest to them:

> we can roughly say that A is relatively deprived of X when (1) he does not have X, (2) he sees some other person or persons, which may include himself at some previous or expected time, as having X . . . (3) he wants X, and (4) he sees it as feasible that he should have X. (ibid., p. 11)

In relation to the unemployed relative deprivation theory simply will not work, for, in Runciman's definition, the reference group of the unemployed would include themselves when in employment either in the past or some putative future. Further, with reference to income, the unemployed, from their experience of employment, people they know with jobs, and the jobs they apply for, will be aware of the higher incomes of those who are otherwise like themselves. Moylan *et al.* (1984) showed both from their own data, and from an extensive review of similar studies, that only around 5 per cent of the unemployed receive the same amount or more in benefits than their wages when in employment. Relative deprivation theory, whether in Runciman's original account or in Ditton and Brown's modified version, does not seem capable of providing an account of the political quiescence of the unemployed in contemporary Britain.

Campbell's (1984, pp. 206–16) discussion of the politics of unemployment is one of the more useful and insightful, in that she compares the experience of the 1980s with that of the 1930s. In doing this she draws out comparisons of the different forms of unemployment relief, and of the different kinds of political organisations that have developed. During the 1920s and 1930s the local Unemployment Benefit offices and Boards of Guardians provided accessible local targets for political campaigns amongst the unemployed. However, today the social security system is a highly centralised bureaucracy over which local politicians have no control (ibid., p. 213).

Furthermore, the NUW(C)M of the 1930s was a locally organised movement of the unemployed rooted in the left of the labour movement. In contrast, the unemployment centres of today are more concerned with providing services for the unemployed funded by the MSC, rather than political organisation (ibid., pp. 207–13). With no influence over the welfare benefits for the unemployed, and tied to non-political work by the MSC, unemployment centres are faced with a 'confusion of purpose'; they want to do something, but it is not clear what they can do.

Campbell also points out one of the most obvious, but often overlooked factors affecting political activity amongst the unemployed, which is quite simply a *lack of material resources*. This includes not only money but the basics of any organisation such as typewriters, stationery, telephones, etc. (ibid., p. 18).

From the perspective I am developing here there are many problems with Campbell's approach. One general point is that she does not develop her arguments far enough. For example, I shall show below that there are other important implications of the bureaucratic administration of welfare benefits, and that it is important to highlight the role of political struggles in shaping their development. Furthermore, she says little about the social conditions which gave rise to the NUW(C)M, apart from noting the role of shop stewards.

Campbell also tends to slide over the issue of the nature of the relations between the organisations, that is, the possibilities of alliances between them. She also has a tendency to dissolve the issues around the politics of unemployment into the wider political problems of the 'labour movement' at large. This tends to undermine and belittle the impact of her arguments about the problems of the political organisation of the unemployed. The emphasis on material resources is also problematic, since organisational and cultural resources may be more important in developing collective action. Organisational and cultural resources are often the means through which material resources are obtained.

The question of class interests and unemployment has recently been raised by Van Parijs (1987). He argues that the unemployed form a distinctive class within the structure of contemporary Western capitalism. He analyses what he terms 'job classes', which are, broadly speaking, the employed and the unemployed. The division between the employed and the unemployed he sees as now being a permanent feature of the social structure of contemporary capitalist societies. Conventional class theory is inadequate in his view for it sees the unemployed only as potential workers, and consequently overlooks the emergent political divisions between the employed and unemployed classes.

Van Parijs bases his argument on the 'game-theoretic' approach to class analysis developed by Wright (1985). Consequently, Van Parijs theorises his job classes by hypothesising that employment constitutes a material asset by which the employed are materially better off than the unemployed. However, in line with the game-theoretic approach to class analysis, he has to show that the employed effectively exploit the unemployed through this uneven distribution of job assets. He argues that this occurs through the institutionalisation of the right to a job in the form of a right to strike and severance pay, which both result in unemployment becoming characteristic of welfare capitalism. Formally, the two job classes are defined in terms of the distribution of jobs, with the unemployed being 'exploited' by those with employment.

> One can accordingly define a *job exploiter* (a *job exploited*) as someone who would be worse off (better off) if job assets were equally distributed, with the distribution of skills remaining unchanged and all efficiency effects being assumed away . . . Like feudal, capitalist, skills and organisational exploitation, it denotes a way in which the unequal control over some productive forces generates inequalities in the distribution of material welfare. (Van Parijs, 1987, p. 468)

However, Van Parijs fails to complete his model since he argues that an adequate class theory must be able to show not only how the distribution of assets affects material welfare, but also that this distribution has major implications for the patterns of political consciousness and action within a society (ibid., pp. 456–7). He quite simply fails to provide any empirical evidence of what one would expect to be the political consequences of his account – widespread organised political conflict between the employed and the unemployed.

Indeed, he attempts to explain away this absence in terms of the social heterogeneity of the unemployed; that dole queues unlike factories are not conducive to collective action; that the unemployed cannot go on strike; that the organisers amongst the unemployed often obtain employment; and, what he regards as most important, the lack of ideological models amongst the unemployed to overcome job exploitation (ibid., p. 471). Now the first four of these factors are quite reasonable claims, and I shall expand on some of them in subsequent chapters. However, Van Parijs does not consider any real political movements of the unemployed, and consequently fails to perceive what is common to all of them, namely, that they struggle principally with the unemployment relief institutions of the state, not against the employed. Indeed, rather than struggling against the trade unions and their ideologies, which according to Van Parijs is what the unemployed ought to be doing, the unemployed, when and where they have become politically organised, have drawn upon the trade unions and their ideologies in their political actions.

2.3 THE NEO-MARXIST APPROACH: PIVEN AND CLOWARD

The central feature of Piven and Cloward's argument is that protest is shaped and directed by the institutions with which the protesters have most contact. In the case of the unemployed this is usually the state's income maintenance system. They assert that the poor only protest when there is a widespread economic, ideological and political crisis in these institutions. There are three main ways in which these institutions determine the form, immediate purposes and setting of protest. The everyday experience of deprivation and oppression is the first factor that gives rise to specific targets and grievances for lower class protests. They protest against the immediate administrators of their lives rather than senior politicians or businessmen. Their actions are directed against the people whom they deal with on a day to day basis. Secondly, the relevant institutions give shape to the collective base of the protest, either bringing people together or dispersing them, and moulding everyday group identities to create the setting for collective protest. Finally, the roles of the lower classes in the institutions define the strategies and tactics of any potential protest (Piven and Cloward, 1977, pp. 18–22).

Criticising other analysts for concentrating on the aspects of social life that protest exposes, they argue that protest should be seen as *the mechanism through which the lower classes obtain concessions from elites* (ibid., p. 23). However, the effects of protest are usually felt indirectly rather than directly, and that if the protestors have a central role in the institution, then their protest is more likely to be disruptive. The effects of the protest will be even greater if élites have a large stake in the institutions concerned. There are, however, limitations on the degree of institutional disruption that protestors can generate. Normally, such protest involves the withdrawal of the protestor's cooperation or contribution to the institution involved. The effects of the protest from this aspect depend on how crucial the protestors are to others, whether or not resources are available to make concessions, and the degree to which the protestors can protect themselves from reprisals (ibid., p. 25). From this argument it is clear that in Piven and Cloward's theory the poor are usually in a very weak strategic position. Put simply, their only option is to go out and have a riot. Here, argue Piven and Cloward, lies the explanation for the apparent spontaneity and irrationality of poor people's protests.

The weak strategic position of the poor not only gives rise to 'spontaneous' forms of protest, but it also means that political organisations of the poor are unstable, further reinforcing the tendency to 'spontaneity'. The lack of formal organisation is a link in the causal chain from strategic weakness to 'spontaneous' forms of protest. What few organisations there are, however, tend to be 'moderate' in order to retain 'legitimacy' in the context of the overall political system. The 'electoral-representative' system of politics is also significant, in the sense that the impact of political protest has to be most effective at this level, rather than simply at the level of the institution within which it occurs. Electoral politics thus 'mediates' the disruptive consequences of protest.

In Piven and Cloward's view, the efforts by élites to disarm protest are usually successful, partly through changing the movement itself and partly by changing the circumstances in which it operates. In these situations governments do not simply act to redress, but the concessions are usually granted in the context of or as extensions to established institutions and practices. Significantly for Piven and Cloward's argument, the major changes that do occur take place within the political context that gave rise to the movement in the first place, rather than important changes occurring within the movement. When protest subsides then the concessions may be withdrawn since there is no longer any disruption to placate, and there is no need for conciliation. Nevertheless, some reforms and concessions remain intact long after the threat of protest has subsided. In these instances, argue Piven and Cloward, such changes actually support, or at least do not contradict, ruling élite interests. For example, trade unions might be used to stifle rank and file action, welfare reforms could buttress consumption levels, stabilise economic fluctuations and have wider positive ideological effects (ibid., pp. 32–5). Therefore, Piven and Cloward conclude: 'What these examples suggest is that *protesters win, if they win at all, what historical circumstance has already made ready to be conceded*' (ibid., p. 36).

In summary, Piven and Cloward argue that a general acute economic, political and ideological crisis is *necessary* as a prior condition of protest by the poor. This protest is structured by the institutions that poor people are most in contact with, and these institutions create opportunities and targets for protest. However, the political impact of the protest depends most of all on the prevailing electoral conditions, on whether or not the elected representatives will lose votes as a result of mismanaging the protests. Poor people's protest is also brief and transient due to their basic lack of power, and their lack of access to legitimate political resources. Protest, therefore, emerges only when historical circumstances have *determined* that it is possible. Furthermore, poor people only have significant political effects indirectly through violent and deviant protest such as rioting. Finally, the central conclusion of Piven and Cloward's theory is that 'organising' the poor merely integrates them into conventional politics and their structurally powerless position. As organisations become 'respectable', external resources begin to be substituted for a mass base.

The most important problem with Piven and Cloward's approach is that it is *far too structural and deterministic*, and this problem has a series of serious consequences for their overall theory. There are three centrally important ways in which their account is too structural and deterministic.

First, the claim that the concessions won by protest are historically determined by intense social crises seems to imply that protest is not necessary. Protest seems to be a *functional process* which operates to restabilise the social system in times of severe crisis. In this sense they share much with the more general structural Marxism of authors such as Castells' (1976, 1977, 1978) analyses of urban social movements, and the more general political theories of Poulantzas (1978). The tactics and strategies of the protest movements seem to be irrelevant to the explanation, since these are simply part of the chain of causality from existing institutions and the general crisis. Social struggles do not seem to have any transformative impact independent of structural constraints.

Secondly, the claim that organising the poor simply reintegrates them into the legitimate political system assumes a fundamental structural inflexibility in the political system and the social system as a whole. It leaves one wondering how protest can possibly emerge under any circumstances, since any attempt at protest and organisation fails by Piven and Cloward's criteria, and, indeed, merely serves to reproduce the status quo. Any changes in the system in this scenario are merely the playing out of purely structural processes.

Thirdly, the objective interests of the poor are structurally determined, and, furthermore, Piven and Cloward see these interests as being *homogeneous* and coterminous with working-class interests as whole. There would appear to be no real differences of 'interest' among the poor and no genuine or real political cleavages among them. They are a homogeneous 'class-in-themselves', who, because of their structurally determined powerless position, are rarely capable of acting as a 'class-for-themselves'. This homogeneous conception is most clear in Piven and Cloward's formal definition of the poor:

a stratum within the working-class that is poor by standards prevailing in society at the time. Although the specific social origins of the participants in the movements examined have varied greatly – some were white men, some were black women; some were displaced southern agricultural workers, some were urban immigrant industrial workers – we consider that all of the protest movements we analyze arose among sectors of the working-class, including the protest of welfare mothers in the 1960s. (Piven and Cloward, 1977, pp. xii–xiv)

In their critique of Piven and Cloward, the Roaches note that most of those involved in one of the organisations that Piven and Cloward study (the National Welfare Rights Organisation of the 1960s) were black, and that this inhibited support from largely white organisations such as trade unions (Roach and Roach, 1978, p. 167). Others such as West (1981) and Gordon (1988) have pursued this line of criticism further. They have argued, using the evidence not only of the NWRO's social base among black mothers, but also the goals and arguments of its leaders, that it was a specifically black feminist social movement. The different constituents of the base bring to political protest different sets of interests, and different levels and forms of political and cultural resources. The patterning of these is crucial to explaining *where and in what form protest emerges*. Piven and Cloward largely ignore these issues.

There is a further aspect that Piven and Cloward ignore. Protest of the form under consideration here typically occurs at the local level, and it is dependent on the local conjuncture of social structure, local political organisations and local cultural resources. Hence protest in apparently similar general conditions of social crisis will occur in some places but not others within the same society. Therefore, the type of criticism directed at Piven and Cloward by those such as Schlozman and Verba (1979, p. 240), that they overestimate the mass support of unemployed movements by generalising from a few cases is, in part, misplaced. Piven and Cloward do overgeneralise, but the comparison of those places and times where protest does emerge is surely the only empirical way we have of testing theories about the conditions for the emergence of protest.

A major consequence of Piven and Cloward's structural and deterministic approach is that political organisations of the poor have no real impact. This is the central thrust of Hobsbawm's critique of their work. Hobsbawm (1984, p. 294) points out that there must be some form of organisation for the alternative policies to be formulated which may guide any protest. If the poor follow Piven and Cloward's prescriptions they will always be on the sidelines and at the mercy of the élites. This is also spelt out clearly by Castells in his brief discussion of Piven and Cloward's work:

the fate of the movements is predetermined by the stages of social evolution and the overall political framework . . . In this perspective, therefore, humankind is not the subject of its own history, but the actor of a play whose script has been written in advance (by whom?) and whose performance will invariably end up in bloodshed and co-opting. (Castells, 1983, p. 296).

These criticisms point to a central contradiction in Piven and Cloward's argument. Essentially, they argue that structural factors account for the emergence and form of protest by poor people and the concessions that they are able to obtain. On the other hand, they have an extremely voluntarist conception of the role of the élites who are, it appears, able to choose how to respond to protest, albeit within certain structural limitations. Most crucially, the state is seen to be structurally predetermined, to be used only by élites in a purely instrumental fashion. In Piven and Cloward's theory, the poor are at the mercy of structural imperatives and the decisions of the élites. The poor are 'outside' the system and unable to influence it directly.

The role of political organisations of the poor in Piven and Cloward's account is largely one of integrating the poor into the dominant political system. This subsequently leads to the failure of protest (Piven and Cloward, 1977, pp. 36–7). The central problem with this account is that they conceive of organisations purely in terms of the centralised bureaucratic mass membership form (Gamson and Schmeidler, 1984, p. 573). On the one hand, this overlooks the different forms that organisation may take (Offe, 1985; Offe and Wiesenthal, 1985), whilst on the other hand, it totally overlooks the crucial role of organisations in constructing and disseminating critical discourses and producing subjective perceptions of interests that may contribute significantly to political protest (Gamson and Schmeidler, 1984; Lash, 1984; Przeworski, 1986). In the following chapter, I shall argue that it is crucial to develop an account of the different organisational forms that the unemployed might possibly establish, and to consider the relationship between organisations and the development of cultural resources and subjective perceptions of interests which can contribute to protest.

Finally, there is a problem with the way Piven and Cloward conceptualise consciousness and ideology. Broadly speaking, it is clear that they operate with a version of dominant ideology theory (Abercrombie *et al*, 1980). The poor are integrated into society through sets of beliefs that systematically favour the interests of the dominant class, and these beliefs only come 'unstuck' in periods of profound crisis. In any case, Piven and Cloward's own empirical discussion demonstrates the falsity of their theoretical claims where they show that some people (political activists at the very least) are not integrated by the dominant ideology.

Perhaps the most valuable aspect of Piven and Cloward's theory is that dealing with the institutional structuring of protest. In my view they are entirely correct to emphasise the place of the state in unemployed people's lives, and consequently as the focus for political conflict around issues of income maintenance. However, their account of how pressure is exerted on the state and of how state institutions intervene in society is faulty.

In particular they assign a purely negative role to electoral institutions. The ability of political movements of the unemployed to obtain concessions from the state relies not just on an electoral crisis, but rather more on the political complexion of those elected. In contrast to Piven and Cloward, I shall show in the chapters below that the electoral control of the institutions of unemployment relief is a crucial, if uncertain, prerequisite for the emergence of political organisations of the unemployed. Piven and Cloward lack any analysis of the different *forms* that state unemployment relief may take. In later chapters, I shall be concerned to show how the move from an electoral form of state unemployment relief to a centralised bureaucratic one has had important consequences for the structuring of protest by the unemployed.

2.4 THE 'BEHAVIOURIST' APPROACH: SCHLOZMAN AND VERBA

The approach of Schlozman and Verba could not be in greater contrast to that of Piven and Cloward. Schlozman and Verba use quantitative measurements of attitudes of individuals in contrast to Piven and Cloward's narratives about specific protest movements based on secondary sources, newspaper reports and their own personal experiences. The strategy of Schlozman and Verba's research is to set up hypotheses and then proceed to test them systematically using standard survey research techniques, rejecting some hypotheses and retaining others. In contrast, Piven and

Cloward set up a theoretical model which serves more as an interpretative framework for their ensuing historical narratives. Both books consist largely of empirical data, one qualitative and the other quantitative.

Schlozman and Verba begin with what they term a 'riddle'. Why, with unemployment so high during the middle of the 1970s in the USA, is there no organised political response from the unemployed? Furthermore, other disadvantaged and previously unorganised groups, such as blacks and women, had in the recent past become highly organised and effective political agents, which further compounded their riddle. More generally, they thought an analysis of the issue of unemployment and political organisation should throw more light on the general question of how personal problems become politicised (Schlozman and Verba, 1979, pp. 3–7).

Schlozman and Verba develop a five-stage model of how personal problems, stress or disadvantage become politicised in the form of formally organised political movements, with clearly articulated goals and policy preferences. This model is set up as a temporal succession through which individuals pass, and sets up hypotheses about the characteristics of individuals for them to move from one stage to the other.

The first stage they identify is that economic strain in the form of unemployment creates a personal strain for individuals, and the second is that unemployment must be perceived by the unemployed as stressful and accompanied by a sense of dissatisfaction with being unemployed (ibid., p. 12). Thirdly, the problem of unemployment must become collectively politicised. Individuals must come to see government action as relevant to their problems, as distinct from private solutions that they could pursue themselves (ibid., pp. 13–15).

The fourth level of political mobilisation is where substantial numbers of a social group come to share realistic common policy preferences for government to pursue as a solution to their shared problem (ibid., p. 19). Finally, there is the moment of political mobilisation itself through protest, pressure groups or electoral politics, either individually or collectively. These five stages or levels in Schlozman and Verba's model are necessary but not sufficient factors for political mobilisation to occur (ibid.). However, they identify three sets of factors which might modify these hypothesised stages.

First, they argue that successful political mobilisation by a group of individuals will depend in part on the level of political resources they have at their disposal (ibid., pp. 19–20). Secondly, political mobilisation by some members of a group may affect the consciousness of others who are inactive. This would lead to wider than expected protest. Finally, political action on unemployment might be taken by people who are not unemployed. Schlozman and Verba note that increasingly in twentieth-century US politics such 'political advocacy' has become more widespread. Such political processes do not engage directly with the unemployed, and hence will not mobilise them as a political force in their own right (ibid.).

Overall, there are three interlocking themes to Schlozman and Verba's approach. Primarily, they are concerned with individual political responses to unemployment and how group political mobilisation may or may not emerge from individual responses. They are further interested in 'American exceptionalism', in the sense of the lack of 'class consciousness' and socialist politics in the USA, and the strength of the 'American Dream' of individual economic success amongst economically disadvantaged sections of the population. Finally, they deal with the politics of race and the relationship between 'race consciousness' and the politics of class and unemployment.

Broadly, their empirical findings did not support their hypothesised five-stage model of mobilisation. Although unemployment did produce economic and personal difficulties, there was no development of collective political consciousness or action amongst their unemployed respondents.

The question remains, what do Schlozman and Verba put in the place of their five-stage model of the political mobilisation of the unemployed? The resulting explanation is brief, *ad hoc* and eclectic, to say the least. There are three features to their reformulated explanation.

First, they lay more emphasis on the Olson 'free-rider' principle. The unemployed do not engage in collective action because they prefer to pursue their own individual job-seeking strategies. However, they note this can only be a partial explanation, since it cannot account for the lack of impact that unemployment has on political attitudes, voting behaviour and general ideological orientations.

Secondly, there is a general absence of class consciousness amongst the unemployed, and even where this is present it does not lead to any additional political activity. However, Schlozman and Verba note that the evidence about the unemployed expecting government intervention to help them (however incoherently specified) does not fit this particular explanation.

Thirdly, the unemployed lack the political, organisational, social and cultural skills and resources to develop a political movement. This is congruent with their evidence about the selective recruitment into unemployment and involvement in political organisations. Nevertheless, it cannot account for the lack of resources and skills in the first place and the failure, at the individual level, of the unemployed fully to politicise their personal stress (ibid., pp. 351–2).

The main problem with Schlozman and Verba's account is that it focuses on the attributes of individuals in a way that decontextualises them from the relevant social relations and organisations. They used a *national sample* of employed and unemployed. Now this is fine for a general descriptive account of the broad similarities and differences between the employed and the unemployed. But if the research question relates to political organisation, then surely one should be concerned with those unemployed who are actually involved with such organisations to compare with those who are not.

Given their interest in the development of political organisation amongst the unemployed, their decontextualised sample may not be the ideal methodology for other reasons. For example, they drew their sample from the largest US cities, but these have different political traditions and levels of organisation which will influence political responses to unemployment.

Further, they refer in their initial model of mobilisation to attempts to influence government policies. Yet which level of government, city, state or national, is not specified, and the unemployed will have varied levels of access to the different levels of the state. The state is conceived in classic pluralist fashion as open to all who are able to get themselves organised. The possibility that state institutions may not be 'open' to influence by the unemployed does not feature in their analysis. The whole question of the nature of the relationship between the unemployed and the state remains outside Schlozman and Verba's frame of analysis. Their survey methodology does not enable them to examine such issues very easily.

Within their mobilisation model there is no central role for political organisations as agents of political socialisation. This is due to its overemphasis on the individual as the unit of analysis (Marsh *et al.*, 1985, p. 356). Yet we might expect political organisations to have at least the potential for contributing to people's political response to unemployment, as they seem to influence people's wider political attitudes (Lash, 1984; Marshall *et al.*, 1988a). In short, their general model of mobilisation and political response is overeconomistic and overemphasises individuals who would somehow work out the political conclusions separately prior to organisation. Their own data show that prior political attitudes seem to be important in shaping political responses to unemployment.

Schlozman and Verba treat political behaviour largely as an individual phenomenon, one which is, furthermore, determined by individual attitudes (Marsh *et al.*, 1985, p. 356). They fail to show where those attitudes come from for the different social groups. However, they do show empirically, in a rather broad sense, that the unemployed have different attitudes from the employed due to the process of differential recruitment into unemployment. The major valuable empirical point that they make is that unemployment as a labour market condition does not have a massive impact on political behaviour, but that the social origins of the unemployed are more important in shaping political responses. However, Schlozman and Verba fail to give an adequate explanation of how this might work.

2.5 A BRITISH TEST OF SCHLOZMAN AND VERBA: MARSHALL *ET AL.*

Marshall *et al.* have attempted to replicate some of Schlozman and Verba's analyses for the the unemployed in Britain. They note, though, that in certain respects there are significant problems in doing this. For example, they argue that Schlozman and Verba's measures of dissatisfaction, class position and class consciousness are weak and poorly related to theoretical considerations. Further, the 'American Dream' in Schlozman and Verba's account may be seen as merely the pragmatic acceptance of the prevailing system. More fundamentally, Marshall *et al.* question how relevant Schlozman and Verba's account is to the current British context, given that British political ideologies have been more clearly structured by notions of class (Marshall *et al.*, 1988b, p. 198). Generally, Marshall *et al.* are critical of Schlozman and Verba's explanation for reasons similar to those I have outlined above.

Marshall *et al.*'s analysis deserves detailed consideration as it provides a quantitative 'benchmark' of the political attitudes of the British unemployed in the 1980s. Briefly stated, their results are as follows. The unemployed are relatively deprived and dissatisfied, seeing little in the way of distributive justice in the current social order. Preferences for changes in government policy to reduce unemployment were frequently expressed, and there were also high levels of 'class consciousness', the unemployed being very likely to describe themselves as working-class, unlike Schlozman and Verba's account (ibid., pp. 202–4). Most of the unemployed, like the other respondents in Marshall *et al.*'s sample, saw class politics in distributional rather than revolutionary terms.

Class was seen in terms of ascription rather than achievement. Consistent with this was the finding that few of the unemployed blamed individual or personal problems for high levels of unemployment, and structural or political explanations were most frequently given. The unemployed were highly critical of the Conservative government, being twice as likely as the employed to see a change of government as important in reducing unemployment. None of the unemployed saw women's increasing participation in the labour market as a reason for high unemployment, and only 1 per cent gave immigration as a reason (ibid., pp. 206–10).

Generally, Marshall *et al.* claim that unemployment has no clear consequences for changes in political beliefs and voting behaviour, except where policies specifically affect the unemployed. In particular, they show that the unemployed are much more concerned about changes in unemployment and social security benefits than are the employed (ibid., p. 218).

However, there are some important problems with Marshall *et al.*'s analysis. First, one of their central claims is that the unemployed are less involved in organised politics than are the employed. Whilst they show that the unemployed are less likely to vote in elections than the employed, their evidence for withdrawal from formal political actions is mixed to say the least. The proportions of people taking action against government decisions varied little between the employed (13 per cent) and the unemployed (11 per cent). Their evidence on the variations between the employed and the unemployed as to what kinds of action were taken is also ambiguous. Higher proportions of the unemployed than the employed had taken part in protest, written to their MP or councillor, written to the newspaper, been on a march or demonstration, or complained to a government department. Of particular note are the complaints to government departments – 46.7 per cent of those unemployed taking some kind of action compared to 9.7 per cent of the same group amongst the employed. In contrast, higher proportions of the employed than the unemployed had signed a petition, attended a public meeting, joined a campaign, changed their vote, changed to private service, complained to their local council, or done things privately themselves (ibid., p. 221, table 8.14). Furthermore, the unemployed were more likely to be involved in political parties, residents and similar associations, environmental groups, and other local and national pressure groups than the politically active amongst the employed. Not surprisingly, the activities of the employed were concentrated in trade unions, business associations and educational organisations (ibid., p. 222, table 8.16). In short, their generalisations about political inactivity require considerable qualification. From their evidence no clear pattern emerges, apart from the higher rates of complaints by the unemployed to government departments.

The second major problem with Marshall *et al.*'s analysis is that it fails to distinguish between social groups within the unemployed to examine the effects of the selective recruitment into unemployment which Schlozman and Verba quite rightly emphasise so strongly. Now this is for methodological reasons of sample size beyond Marshall *et al.*'s control, but it does mean that they should not lean so heavily on their evidence in making generalisations about the political attitudes and behaviour of the unemployed. They note that political beliefs are formed prior to unemployment, but they provide no account of how this takes place.

2.6   CONCLUSION

In this chapter I have discussed a wide range of rather speculative theorising about the relationship between unemployment and collective action, in Britain, in both the 1930s and the 1980s. I have also considered the main contributions to this issue from the USA and attempts in Britain to replicate Schlozman and Verba's study. I have found this literature to be deficient in many respects for the problem at hand, so what of value remains from this discussion?

From a variety of authors it seems that it is important to consider the relationship between the unemployed and the state in some detail as this is the axis of protest. Cultural and organisational resources are also important. It is necessary to examine in some detail what organisational and cultural resources the unemployed may have for collective action. It is to these considerations that I now turn.

3

The Structuring of Political Responses to Unemployment

3.1 INTRODUCTION

In the previous chapter, I examined a series of putative explanations of political responses to unemployment and found them deficient in varying degrees. However, despite the drawbacks of the various approaches three central themes have emerged – the relationship between the unemployed and the state, the organisational resources of the unemployed and cultural resources – which I shall develop in more detail in this chapter.

First, I develop a model of the changing relationship between the unemployed and the state's income maintenance system, which, in various ways in different periods, has structured political movements of the unemployed. Secondly, I discuss the contrasting forms of organisation that have developed and how these shape protest. I believe that it is important for analytical purposes to distinguish organisational from cultural resources. Organisational resources vary most significantly in their *form*, whilst cultural resources vary most importantly in their *content*. Finally, I outline the kinds of cultural resources which I think are necessary for a political movement of the unemployed to develop. In short, my argument shall be that *only when there is a temporal and spatial correspondence of a particular form of relationship between the unemployed and the state, particular forms of organisation and alliances, and a particular content to the cultural resources of the unemployed do political movements of the unemployed emerge.*

37

3.2   THE UNEMPLOYED AND THE STATE

The emphasis that I wish to place here is not on the content of the state's actions towards the unemployed, but rather on the *form* of the relationship between the unemployed and the state. My focus, then, will be on the changing *ways* in which state institutions are open to influence by the unemployed, on the one hand, and the form of unemployment relief, on the other. It often remains unclear against whom or what the unemployed would be able to protest. What social relations and social structures would such collective action attempt to transform? The simple Marxist answer would be 'capitalism'. However, I show below that historically, although the ideological rhetoric of political movements of the unemployed has often been 'anti-capitalist', their principal strategy has been to influence the state institutions with which they have most contact. On this I generally agree with Piven and Cloward who argue that the opportunities for protest are principally shaped by the institutions with which they are in contact. I shall try to develop this idea shorn of the deterministic and functionalist argument that Piven and Cloward cast it in.

The unemployed are dependent on the state for their means of existence, so it is the state's income maintenance system that they principally seek to influence if they become politically organised. However, this general abstract claim needs more concrete specification to be of use in empirical research. It is the *changing* forms of the state's income maintenance institutions that require some further more detailed analysis.

The state form is the institutional means by which social forces are represented in the state, the structure of decision-making and administration within the state, and the ways in which the state 'intervenes' in civil society and the economy. The state form has biased and asymmetrical effects on the political forces that are attempting to influence state policies (Jessop, 1982, pp. 228–30). Consider, for example, the extension of the franchise or the rise and subsequent decline of corporatism. With the extension of the franchise individuals in the working class and women were able for the first time to have some, albeit indirect, influence over parliamentary decisions. In the instance of corporatism, only those who were members of the functional organisations rooted in the division of labour, namely trade unions and employers' organisations, were able to have influence over state policies.

Further to this general claim about the state form, the institutions of the state are not some necessarily centralised, unified and smoothly functioning whole. The various levels and sectors of the state operate over different territories and in different forms. It is this phenomenon which the 'dual state' thesis attempts to capture in an ideal typical fashion, with the central state concerned with 'production' issues through a corporatist form of interest mediation, and the local state concerned with 'consumption' issues through a competitive pluralist form of interest mediation (Saunders, 1986, pp. 291–311). However, whilst the general point about the variety of functions and institutional forms of various levels of the state is well taken, this model is somewhat inadequate for my explanatory purposes here.

It is not clear that the income maintenance institutions of the state, with which the unemployed are most concerned, are clearly either 'production' or 'consumption' institutions. The terms 'production' and 'consumption' are highly problematic in themselves, since the unit of consumption is presumably the family/household within which there has to be considerable productive labour carried out in order to realise the use values of the goods consumed (Pahl, 1984; Walby, 1988, p. 220). Further, these state institutions intervene through their social security benefit programmes in both production by regulating the labour market, and consumption, or as I prefer civil society, by contributing to the maintenance of households. There are, therefore, contradictory 'pulls' on these forms of intervention. The current form in which this kind of intervention by the state takes place is through legally codified and bureaucratically administered cash benefits.

However, this form has not been historically constant, and its variations are part of the explanation for historical variations in political movements of the unemployed. Initially, in the early nineteenth century, for the unemployed to receive benefits, they either had to be part of a voluntary insurance scheme or had to accept 'relief' under the Poor Law, in which case they came into direct contact with the state. Such relief was in theory supposed to be given in the workhouse as 'indoor relief'. In practice, local political circumstances often determined that relief, to the unemployed at least, was not in the stigmatised workhouse (Knott, 1986). These institutions were not always offering legally codified cash benefits in a large-scale bureaucracy. Local state institutions under conditions of local democracy had some autonomy in setting the levels of benefit until the 1930s. This meant that they were 'open' to pressure from the local electorate and local social movements. However, after the effective centralisation of decision-making and its insulation from democratic control in the 1930s, *there was no effective way for political organisations of the unemployed to have clear access to the institutions with which the unemployed were in a day to day relationship.* This centralisation and insulation from democratic processes occurred in part through the successes of the struggles of the unemployed themselves. I shall examine this process empirically in the following chapter.

My periodisation of the forms of the state's institutions of unemployment relief are summarised in Table 3.1 below. Now this does some violence to the empirical details, but it does offer important analytical advantages. It enables the specification of the historical periods under which particular combinations of the various forms of the state's unemployment relief institutions provided the best conditions for the emergence of political organisations of the unemployed. Further, this classification also clarifies how the form of the state's institutions changed over time. It relates to each other the various relevant aspects of the forms of institutions, whether democracy is locally or centrally based, whether the franchise is limited or extensive; the degrees of development of decision-making in representative, corporatist, pluralist and bureaucratic modes; the form of intervention in either cash benefit or indoor relief modes; and whether or not insurance benefits were voluntary or state run.

During the early nineteenth century there were few if any political movements of the unemployed involving the unemployed themselves, although there was widespread opposition from the working class to the new Poor Law of 1834 (Knott, 1986). This is, in part at least, explicable in terms of the state form. Although the institutions were under the control of locally elected representatives, the franchise was limited, so there was little or no chance of working-class representatives sympathetic to any movement of the unemployed being elected. Most importantly, the recipients of

Table 3.1 *Periodisation of state forms of unemployment relief*

Features of State form	Early C19th	1880s–1930s	1930s–present
Democracy			
level	local	local	central
franchise	limited	extending	extensive
Decision-making			
representative	high	high	low
corporatist	low	low	medium
pluralist	low	low	medium
bureaucratic	low	medium	high
Intervention	cash benefits/ indoor relief	cash benefits/ indoor relief	cash benefits
Insurance	Voluntary	State/ voluntary	State

relief were excluded from the franchise even when it was slightly extended. The unions and friendly societies often ran their own voluntary insurance schemes, so there was little interest from those quarters in the unemployed who were not covered by insurance schemes (Mann, 1990).

The emergence of such mutualist alternatives constituted a distinctive form of class struggle by these fractions of the working-class, usually referred to as the 'labour aristocracy'. These fractions of the working class, with the organisational resources available for effective class struggle, also had the material resources to insure themselves against the privations of unemployment, ill health and old age. There thus emerged a significant division in the politics of welfare within the working class, which was codified into the division between insurance and means tested benefits (Mann, 1984, 1986, 1990). This division of material interest in the politics of unemployment was only really overcome to any degree during the inter-war period.

During the 1880s to 1930s period the franchise was extended, especially after 1918 when a large number of anomalies were eradicated and some women were allowed to vote (Blewett,

1966). Outdoor relief in the form of cash benefits without task work became increasingly common, gradually displacing the already limited indoor relief of the unemployed altogether after the First World War. Furthermore, the state took responsibility for the insurance schemes in the 1900s. The bureaucratic mode of decision-making tended to increase throughout this period as the state took on responsibilities for insurance benefits and their extension to more employees, on the one hand, and as the central state institutions attempted to exert more control over local representatives, on the other. Despite these changes local democracy remained extensive with an expanding franchise and continued, albeit limited, representative control over decision-making until the 1930s with the formation of the Unemployment Assistance Board (Deacon and Bradshaw, 1983, pp. 22–6). These are the factors arising out of the state form which enabled the emergence of the National Unemployed Workers Movement during the 1920s and the 1930s, the phenomenon of Poplarism (Branson, 1979) and the less well known 'agitations' amongst the unemployed by the Social Democratic Federation from the 1880s to the 1900s. What these social and political movements and struggles had in common was a central concern with the forms and levels of relief for the unemployed. Now this is not to place all the explanatory weight on changes in the state form, since other changes in the organisational and cultural resources of the wider labour movement enabled these political movements to develop. All this assumes, of course, that the sheer size of the problem of unemployment meant that something would happen. However, precisely what depends, in my view, much more on these other factors. The sheer scale of unemployment alone is insufficient as an explanation.

During the contemporary period, the form of state institutions responsible for unemployment relief means that the conditions for a political movement of the unemployed are now more limited than in the past. The democratic aspects of the institutions governing unemployment benefits are now entirely centralised. Local state institutions have no role in their administration. The process of decision-making is dominated by formal bureaucratic procedure, with civil servants and appointees, rather than elected representatives, taking the central role in the details of levels of benefit etc. since the middle of the 1930s (Whiteley and Winyard, 1987, pp. 63–7). The role of appointees even has all but disappeared since the abolition of the Supplementary Benefits Commission in 1980, and benefits now tend to be fixed in the midst of the government's budget in general. The dominance of bureaucratic and legal procedure means that political organisations which can respond in similarly detailed legalistic ways are more likely to influence policy. Hence the centralised organisations of neo-corporatism such as the TUC and the CBI have been more able to influence policy. Furthermore, since the 1960s there has been a proliferation of lobbying organisations in relation to social security benefits forming the pluralist mode of decision-making. These centralised pressure groups, such as the Child Poverty Action Group or Shelter, staffed by middle-class professionals, influence policy by making a detailed documented case for reform on behalf of client groups who may or may not be members of the pressure group concerned (Whiteley and Winyard, 1987). Into this category I would also place bodies such as the Institute of Directors or the Institute of Economic Affairs, which, although quite different kinds of organisations politically from the poverty lobby, essentially seek to influence policy in the same way as the more conventionally understood poverty lobby through the pluralist mode. Currently, it would seem that these pressure groups of the 'New Right' have more influence than any other sections of civil society over social security policy (Penna, 1990).

During the late 1970s and early 1980s, the few remaining features of local discretion were exploited by representatives of the poor and the unemployed, but in a legalistic fashion. Local DHSS officials still had some discretion over exceptional needs payments, although these were tightly bound by centrally determined rules (Prosser, 1981, pp. 148–9). Organisations such as the Child Poverty Action Group and some claimants' unions were able to extract considerable sums of money for individual claimants. However, these gains were for individuals rather than the unemployed or claimants as a whole, so it was difficult to present them as incentives for wider collective action. In any case, the Fowler reviews of the mid 1980s replaced the remnants of local discretion, and the scope for successful welfare rights action, with the more tightly regulated social fund, which gave loans rather than grants (Penna, 1990).

In this sense, there is *structural bias* built into in the form of state institutions. They systematically favour different kinds of political strategies and different forms of political organisation and mobilisation in different historical periods in the influence of policies. Currently, the structural bias for outside influence is towards centralised pressure groups, rather than collective action by the unemployed. However, this structural bias of the state form is the product of social struggle. I consider this in more empirical detail in the following chapter. However, the historical evidence is quite clear that a principal reason for setting up the Unemployment Assistance Board in the 1930s was to remove the administration of relief from local democratic control as part of the more general aims of rationalisation and modernisation (Miller, 1974). Conceivably, it could have been modernised without the loss of local democratic control (Briggs and Deacon, 1973). Young, the Minister of Health responsible for this at the time, wrote in a Cabinet memorandum comparing the 1930s innovation of the UAB to the 1830s reforms of the Poor Law, commenting that Parliament could ignore the demand of those in receipt of poor relief since they did not have the franchise (PRO, CAB27/501, Memorandum, 16 December 1932, quoted in Miller, 1974, p. 184).

There are two further aspects of the relationship between the unemployed and the state that require consideration. The first of these is the *individual* rather than *collective* relationship between the unemployed and the state. The relationship between the unemployed and the state is totally unlike class relations at the point of production for example, which are normally collective in character and provide a material basis for the collective political organisation of classes, albeit in considerably varying empirical forms (Beynon, 1984; Burawoy, 1979, 1985; Offe and Wiesenthal, 1985). This relationship to the state is an instance of the 'isolation effect', or 'serialisation' of social relations, discussed by authors as disparate as Sartre, Poulantzas and Foucault (for an insightful comparison see Jessop, 1985, pp. 315–20). However, this individualisation is mediated by the patriarchal form of households, or rather the way in which the practices and legal codes of the income maintenance institutions presume that men are the single sources of income for households. In so doing, through the rules relating to cohabitation, the state contributes to the maintenance of such household forms. Unemployed women are subjected to the disciplines of the state's social security system in a quite different way from men (Gordon, 1988). So the state does not have a simple straightforward 'isolation effect' on social relations as authors such as Poulantzas suggest (for example, Poulantzas, 1978, pp. 130–37). There is a systematic gender bias in the individualising practices of the state in relation to the unemployed[1].

Secondly, this relationship is not all one way with the state's institutions dominating their unemployed 'subjects'. This much should be clear from my discussion of the importance of forms of decision-making above, but there is a further element of this I would like to clarify here. In relationship to the state the unemployed have certain legally codified *citizenship rights*, and the contestability of these changes over time and varies between categories of claimants. For example, men would tend not to be questioned in detail about their personal lives in order to prove cohabitation. This contestability may be conceptualised as an instance of what Giddens (1982, pp. 197–8) has termed the 'dialectic of control': 'in any relationship which may be involved in a social system, the most seemingly "powerless" individuals are able to mobilise resources whereby they carve out "spaces of control" in respect of their day to day lives and in respect of the activities of the more powerful'.

The contest over these legal rights forms the content of most political projects of movements of the unemployed, albeit shaped by the institutional forms of the state. Further, this 'dialectic of control' has been systematically restructured in the context of social struggles, so that there is currently less space now than say in the 1920s and 1930s for social struggles by the unemployed. The details of the citizenship rights during the 1920s and 1930s were open to contestation at the local level, whilst they are now much more tightly codified in technical legal discourses which are less open to influence by popular social movements. Consequently, this places contemporary political organisations of the unemployed in something of a dilemma. If they can no longer *collectively* influence the levels and forms of unemployment benefit, what indeed can they do on a day to day basis in terms of political struggle?

3.3 ORGANISATIONAL RESOURCES

Several discussions of the political quiescence of the unemployed note that they lack the resources to organise effectively. However, this rather general claim is never unpacked in any detail, and it is assumed that 'resources' here means simply material resources. For example, Marshall *et al.* (1988b, p. 224) merely assert without further comment that the unemployed lack the 'material resources to organise collectively from the grass roots'. In other words, the unemployed simply lack the money, typewriters and photocopiers, etc. that are required to communicate political arguments effectively and efficiently (Campbell, 1984, p. 18). Others, such as Schlozman and Verba (1979), again simply listing things in this way, argue that the unemployed lack these organisational resources because they are disproportionately recruited from the lower socio-economic sections of the population (Schlozman and Verba, 1979, pp. 244–6). However, something more sensitive than simply saying that the groups from which the unemployed come lack the resources to organise effectively is required for a more detailed explanation. What is needed is some account of *how and why the unemployed from different groups and places have varying kinds of political and organisational resources at different times*. There are variations in terms of social structure, place and historical context to be taken into consideration.

Furthermore, these versions of resource mobilisation theory tend to stress material economic resources following McCarthy and Zald (1977) and Tilly (1978). A materialist instrumentalism is what characterises Tilly's approach. For him what matters is control over labour power, weapons, goods, etc. (Tilly, 1978, p. 7). For McCarthy and Zald the emphasis is on formal bureaucratic resources for the organisation of a social movement. My account in contrast stresses the different *forms of action* that various kinds of organisational resources may give rise to.

By *organisational resources as forms of action* I mean, most abstractly, the knowledge of organising and mobilising people politically. Consequently, knowing how to do this, the possession of this social 'skill', may provide access to the material resources that others have seen as so important. Over and above this level of organisational resources there is a second level, that of alliances. Political movements of the unemployed will develop where there are alliances between these movements and more permanently organised institutions of the labour movement. Further, these alliances can work in two ways, either to the advantage or disadvantage of the autonomous movement of the unemployed.

Political movements of the unemployed, I wish to argue, flow out of the existing organisations of the labour movement.

Organisational resources come in different types, rather than just the formal bureaucratic and professional forms discussed by McCarthy and Zald. There are different ways in which to mobilise people politically and, furthermore, these are logically connected to different kinds of tactics and strategies. They therefore constitute what Offe (1985, p. 820) has termed 'political paradigms', which I shall discuss below. Organisational resources are unevenly distributed throughout society both in terms of social structure and spatially. The different kinds of resources give form to the 'interests' of social forces in different ways, so that some kinds of resources are more compatible with particular state forms than are others. Briefly, compare the different kinds of organisation required to make a well-researched case to a civil servant on some issue, on the one hand, with the resources required to mobilise a large number of people in street demonstrations to influence locally elected officials, on the other. Locally elected officials might well ignore a detailed technical report, whilst a professional civil servant would probably be inclined to read it in some detail. The civil servant would most likely ignore some local disturbance many miles away, but the locally elected officials would probably pay some attention to the same large angry crowd outside their offices! Depending on the institutional form of the state, then, different sets of organisational resources will vary in their effectivity. Furthermore, 'successful' strategies, tactics and modes of political organisation will tend to be replicated and reproduced, and where they 'fail' they may well cease to have any widespread support.

Organisational resources exist not only in terms of the knowledges and practices of the political organisation of social groups, but also in terms of the *allies* they are able to mobilise. My general claim here, to be elaborated below, is that *the political mobilisation of the unemployed only occurs where and when the appropriate organisational resources and organisational allies exist for them to influence, to some visible degree, the state's income maintenance institutions*. Without the appropriate political resources and allies there can be no political movement of the unemployed. What, then, are these organisational resources and political allies?

The generic notion of resources that I am employing here is rather different from Giddens' concept with which many will be familiar. He ties his concept of resources logically to notions of power at the level of social action, and the concept of domination at the level of social structure. Resources for Giddens consist of 'transformative capacities' in relation either to material objects (allocative resources) or people (authoritative resources) (Giddens, 1984, pp. 258–62). Organisational resources in my analysis refer principally to *the knowledge and skills that social groups can draw upon in order to realise their transformative capacities, in relation to both material objects and people.* They are thus separate from and independent of any transformative capacities that a social group may have. Further, Giddens' concept of resources prevents one having any notion of the ways in which different kinds of resources might influence the way, or degree to which, a social group's transformative capacities might be realised. Put another way, different kinds of organisational resources shape people's perceptions of their interests and how those interests may be furthered.

Addressing this issue requires a detailed discussion of the kinds of organisational resources that might be available to the unemployed. At the outset I shall criticise one very recent empirical discussion of these issues, that of Whiteley and Winyard (1987), before considering Offe and Wiesenthal (1985) and Offe's (1985) analyses of the logics of collective action and political paradigms, and prior to elaborating my own model of organisational forms, resources and alliances that may be available to the unemployed.

Whiteley and Winyard classify the 'poverty lobby' in terms of their aims, support and strategy. The aims of organisations can be either lobbying or service relationships with the groups with which they are concerned, while support is classified as either promoting or representing the interests of those groups. Finally, their strategies can be focused on either a particular level of the state or other institutions such as the press, or on seeking to influence many levels of the state and other institutions (Whiteley and Winyard, 1987, pp. 26–31). Further to this classification of organisational characteristics, they also briefly mention alliances which may be either short-term opportunistic affairs or longer-term relationships mediated through umbrella organisations (ibid., p. 34).

The analysis presented by Whiteley and Winyard is limited by the fact that it is based simply on an empirical generalisation across the organisations they happened to choose for their sample. It is therefore restricted to the consideration of these kinds of organisations. However, I wish to consider historical variations as well, so a more general and broader account of organisational resources is required. Although they discuss the aims of organisations, Whiteley and Winyard fail to take into consideration what *degree* of change in the social security system the different organisations seek. That is, are the organisations merely seeking quantitative changes without challenging the basic structure and logic of the system, or are they seeking a qualitative transformation of the whole system? Further, there is no explanation given as to why particular sets of organisational characteristics might tend to go together and reinforce each other.

A more useful approach can be developed from the work of Offe and Wiesenthal (1985). They show how the material differences between capital and labour mean that they have different logics of collective action. Capital can merge to larger firms, cooperate informally and form associations, whilst labour, consisting of individuals, can only associate after it has been organised in the first place by capital. Labour has to defend itself against capital by aggregating individual interests, material resources, and, most crucially, by redefining collective identities to overcome the subjective assessment of the costs of collective action, usually referred to as the 'free-rider' problem. Furthermore, Offe and Wiesenthal maintain that political conflicts occur not only between labour and capital, but also within labour between what they term 'monological' and 'dialogical' forms of political organisation (ibid., pp. 170–205).

Monological forms of organisation occur when discussions of policy and action occur at the leadership level; power is exercised through the leadership; communication is in terms of technical imperatives; and the actions are legitimated in terms of the general interest. Dialogical forms of organisation involve the rank and file in decision-making; power is exercised through the actions of members; communication is in terms of normative claims; and these claims are legitimated in particularistic terms in relation to the beneficiaries. The monological model of trade union organisation is further extended by considering two different ways in which its development is encouraged. First, through corporatist forms of interest mediation such as the involvement of leaders in national policy making processes. Secondly, through the unions pursuing a strategy of *opportunism*. Priority is given to short-term accomplishments and quantitative rather then qualitative criteria of success. Above all, opportunism involves an all-encompassing commitment to the means of political representation, for example corporatism, over and above any longer-term goals (ibid., pp. 214–15).

These themes in Offe's work re-emerge in his recent writings on 'new social movements'. At a superficial glance, the new political paradigm of new social movements corresponds to the ideal type of dialogical forms of organisation, whilst the old political paradigm of class politics corresponds to the ideal type of monological forms of organisation. Analysing a political paradigm involves specifying the values and issues of collective action, who the agents are and how they become organised, and what are the institutional forms, tactics and practices of the movement. The old political paradigm was concerned with economic growth, distribution and security mediated through institutionalised interest groups and political parties, with collective bargaining and party competition as the key mechanisms of conflict. The new political paradigm is concerned with territory, spaces of action or 'life-world', that is, with issues such as sexual identity, neighbourhood and the physical environment. Collective agents are constituted through informal modes of action. The new social movements lack sanctions over their members and do not rely on traditional modes of identification, but on categories such as gender, age, or locality. The important social bases of the new social movements are the new middle class, the old middle class and what Offe refers to as 'peripheral' and 'decommodified' groups such as the unemployed. These groups share, according to Offe, lives shaped by visible authoritarian bureaucracies, and time with which to engage in political activity (Offe, 1985, p. 834).

Offe seems to have a somewhat 'romantic' view of the political potential of these peripheral groups. It seems that the old politics no longer has any 'dialogical' elements. With some reworking of Offe's ideal types, it should be possible to provide some kind of framework with which to identify the political paradigms of political movements of the unemployed. Following Offe, then, two principal paradigms can be identified and the elements of these are summarised in Table 3.2.

Table 3.2 *Ideal typical paradigms of political movements of the unemployed*

	Monological	Dialogical
Goals	quantitative gains	qualitative changes
Form of action	centralist and technocratic	decentralised collective action
Relations of representation	organises *for* the unemployed	organisation *of* the unemployed
Level of state	national	local
Sources of finance	state/charitable/ membership	membership/charity/ allies
Cementing discourse	formal rationality	substantive rationality

This ideal type can be both generalised from Offe's papers – by effectively dissolving his implicit distinction between dialogical forms and the political paradigm of the new social movements – and made more specific – by relating it directly to political movements of the unemployed. His implicit distinction between the new social movements' political paradigm and the dialogical form of class politics, essentially the shop-floor movements of the trade unions, is largely a false one since they only really differ in the *issues that they address themselves to*. Shop-floor movements are principally concerned with autonomy (job control), have informal modes of action within the movement ('democracy' and accountability to the membership) and are cemented by powerful 'us/them' ideologies (compare Offe, 1985, pp. 825–32 with Beynon, 1984, pp. 101–61). The only differences, albeit crucially important ones, are the issues and the substantive content of the cementing ideologies of the two types of movement. The distinction between monological and dialogical forms of organisation that I am developing here cuts through the division between the new and old political paradigms that Offe discusses.

The distinguishing criteria of the two forms of organisation are, first, that monological organisations aim for short-term quantitative gains without changing the basic parameters and assumptions of the system they are dealing with. Dialogical organisations tend to challenge the basic assumptions and parameters of the system, but they may also use quantitative demands in the short term to retain some kind of continuity in action. Compare, for example, the Child Poverty Action Group with the Claimants' Unions in this dimension. CPAG seeks increases in benefit or changes in the rules, without challenging the fundamental logic of the income maintenance system. The Claimants' Unions seek to remove the whole system and replace it with a guaranteed minimum income for all under democratic control (Rose, 1973; McCarthy, 1986).

Secondly, the forms of action of monological organisations tend to be centralist and technocratic, with a central national office of professionals seeking to influence policy through carefully researched and detailed alternative proposals to be presented to governments. The principal mode of action that tends to be favoured by dialogical organisations is decentralised and collective. The aim is to mobilise as many members from the social base as possible in a collective manner, which often necessitates a local focus for action given the difficulties of achieving this nationally. National action may, of course, occur but it does not necessarily enter into the routine of the organisation. The CPAG and Claimants' Unions are again instructive as illustrative examples. CPAG is well known, if not respected by civil servants in central government, for its well-researched and argued cases. However, the Claimants' Unions are notorious among the same civil servants for being interested in 'bad publicity' (Whiteley and Winyard, 1987:, p. 130). The Claimants' Unions focus on fighting the local grievances of claimants through collective representation, which aims to transform the participants' consciousness as much as to achieve material gains for individuals (Jordan, 1973, pp. 24–68).

Thirdly, there is the way in which the group the organisation seeks to represent is practically involved within the organisation, what I have termed the relations of representation. The crucial division here is between providing services for the unemployed, in contrast to the unemployed being actively involved in collective action. This is crucial to understanding the politics of centres for the unemployed, since there has been a major struggle over this particular key aspect of the organisational form. Whether or not the unemployed would have effective control over the centres and do things for themselves, rather than be *served* by paid staff, has been central to the political struggles within the centres. What kind of organisational form results depends on the different kinds of organisational resources that are brought to the centre by those who form it, and the outcome of the subsequent struggles between these groups.

Fourthly, monological and dialogical organisations seek to influence different institutional levels of the state. This follows from the discussion of the different levels and forms of the state earlier in this chapter and how they structure political protest, and also from the discussion of forms of action above. Monological organisations attempt to influence the central, national institutions of the state, whilst dialogical organisations try to influence local state institutions. Monological organisations, with their preference for quantitative gains through centralised technocratic forms of action, are well placed to influence state policies where bureaucratic forms of decision-making are found. In contrast, dialogical organisations are perhaps better suited to influencing state policies when they are most directly under the control of elected representatives, and this is most likely to be the case, though not necessarily so, at the level of the local state. Their preference for consciousness transforming participatory forms of *decentralised* collective action also tends to push dialogical types of organisation towards the local state. Therefore, this dimension of the differences between monological and dialogical organisations can be seen to be influenced by the state form, on the one hand, and the values embedded in the types of action preferred by the different kinds of organisation, on the other. This dimension is perhaps most important for purposes of historical comparison of the dialogical tendencies of the NUWM during the 1920s and 1930s, compared to the more monological forms of organisation that predominate amongst contemporary centres for the unemployed.

The fifth dimension is one which Offe tends to overlook, but to which Whiteley and Winyard pay more attention, namely, sources of finance. In relation to political organisations of the unemployed in particular, this is a crucial variable to consider given the lack of material resources amongst the unemployed. Monological organisations for the unemployed frequently rely on state funding and this has enormous implications for their possible political acti... s. i examine this in more detail below, but suffice it to say that if an unemployed centre is dependent on state funding, it is effectively barred from attempting to organise the unemployed as a political force. This also has enormous implications for the relations of representation, since if a centre takes state funding the unemployed users of it *are not allowed to have control over its resources*. In such centres services are provided *for* the unemployed, controlled by a local microcorporatist structure of trade unionists and local authority officials (for more details see Chapter 5). By employing people to run centres this arrangement also effectively 'incorporated' potential political leaders among the unemployed themselves. In contrast, those centres, such as Brighton, which do not take state funding rely on resources from the membership, charitable donations and material support from allies.

Finally, there are the cementing discourses of the two types of organisational form. Monological organisations tend to use a formal rationality to cement and legitimise their support, whilst dialogical organisations tend to have a substantive rationality cementing and legitimising their support and actions. These discourses seek to provide 'cement' for the members of the organisation, on the one hand, and legitimacy in the eyes of others, on the other hand. They thus have a dual function, but the most critical one is in relation to the membership and supporters *since these discourses seek to constitute their interests as a group* (Przeworski, 1986, pp. 70–2; Offe and Wiesenthal, 1985). The organising principles of these discourses, that is, how they constitute the membership's subjective perceptions of their interests, can be roughly characterised as claims about formal rights, on the one hand, and substantive rights, on the other. This distinction is grounded in Weber's discrimination between formal and substantive rationality (Weber, 1964, pp. 184–6), and his related separation of formal legal ideologies and substantive natural legal ideologies (Lash, 1984, p. 64).

These cementing discourses connect back directly to the distinction between the different aims of organisations – quantitative versus qualitative changes. Cementing discourses characterised by the formal rationality of legal ideologies constitute the members' interests *within the law as it stands*. In contrast, those discourses characterised by the ideologies of substantive natural rights constitute members' interests in terms of *how the law ought to be*. The former stresses formal equality before the law, whilst the latter stresses an equal distribution of resources, the right to work, etc. Formal rationality as a cementing discourse encourages members to measure the 'success' of the organisation in terms of calculable quantitative gains. If the cementing discourse is one of substantive rationality, then members act in the expectation of some wider qualitative transformation. The formal legal discourse propounded by monological forms of organisation are also congruent with the formal legal citizenship rights of the state.

The six characteristics of the two forms of organisation are mutually reinforcing and interlocking. Furthermore, the kind of organisations that develop amongst the unemployed will to some degree be influenced by the organisational forms and cultural resources of their allies. If the allies tend to be monological organisations, then the unemployed organisations will also be pushed in this direction in order to continue the alliance. This is precisely what has happened with many of the contemporary centres for the unemployed, principally because of the characteristics of the financial relations of the two sides of the alliance.

The most important allies of political organisations of the unemployed are the wider organisations of the labour movement, namely, trade unions, the various local, regional and national levels of the TUC, and socialist political parties and their branches. Alliances here are to be understood as relationships between organisations rather than classes or fractions of classes. These alliances can take three general forms.

First, they might be *alliances of dependence*, where one of the organisations, say an unemployed centre in the 1980s, is crucially dependent on the allies for organisational and material resources, as well as support in political campaigns. In short, the dependent organisation would soon cease to exist without the support of its allies.

Secondly, there might be an *alliance of reciprocity*. In this instance organisations can survive without each other, but there are advantages to both in continuing the alliance since both would be more likely to achieve their goals by so doing.

Finally, there might be the situation of *autonomy/isolation*, where an organisation has few or no allies, or where alliances are very short-lived and marked by severe conflict and mutual hostility. Clearly, for any one organisation these possibilities are not mutually exclusive, for example, in being isolated from some organisations, and having reciprocal relations with, yet being dependent on, others. In the empirical chapters which follow, I shall examine the importance of the changing relationships between labour movement organisations in understanding the politics of unemployed movements.

3.4   CULTURAL RESOURCES

In this section, I shall consider the different kinds of cultural resources that the unemployed may draw upon in the development of protest. I shall be engaging with three large areas of analysis in the sociology of the British working class – the analysis of class consciousness, theories of ideology and analyses of working-class communities. My aim is to develop a set of general categories through which comparisons can be made over time, between different places and between different groups of the unemployed in the remaining chapters.

The political quiescence and reformist character of one of the best formally organised working classes in the West, the British working class, has been perhaps the major research programme of British sociology since the Second World War. The explanations of the consciousness of the British working class that have emerged from the research efforts of the 1950s, 1960s and 1970s (for a selection see Bulmer, 1975) have been conventionally divided between those which emphasise the *heterogeneity* of the working class, and those which highlight its *incorporation* into the dominant values and ideologies of society (Marshall, 1988, p. 99). However, Marshall has argued that such a distinction is positively misleading, since most accounts include elements of both heterogeneity and incorporation. In contrast, he shows how survey-based empirical research had, by the early 1980s, reached an impasse between explanations in terms of ambivalence and those stressing working-class instrumentalism (ibid., pp. 100–3).

Marshall's critique of the class consciousness literature, both neo-Marxist and neo-Weberian, is wide ranging and devastating, challenging its substantive claims, interpretation of empirical evidence and methodological procedures. The theories of working-class heterogeneity and incorporation come in for particular criticism. The ontological status of class consciousness remains obscure, eliding the distinction between cognitive and evaluative dimensions, and effectively ignoring the many diverse aspects of working-class consciousness. The sources of consciousness are not explored, so there is no account of the way in which various aspects may come from different sources. The relation between consciousness and action is not discussed, since the extent to which action is structurally constrained is overlooked, resulting in an overly voluntaristic explanation of action in terms of individuals' values. Consequently, the nature of class action is unclear. The question of precisely what does constitute radical class consciousness is not faced up to, since all too often mere 'sociability' has been taken for class solidarity. Class consciousness has been conceptualised in an ahistorical way, with little attempt to consider the impact of experiences of and involvement in collective action. This has followed largely from the mechanical use of ideal types such as those proposed by Lockwood (1975). Finally, Marshall argues that surveys are inappropriate techniques for analysing the immediate context and interaction of action, consciousness and structure. Most of the work he discusses, based on these quantitative studies, has inappropriately decontextualised the phenomena it seeks to explain (Marshall, 1988, pp. 105–7).

Theories of working-class ambivalence and instrumentalism also cut across the neo-Weberian/neo-Marxist divide. According to Marshall, these accounts are far too structural. The Marxists put too much emphasis on the internal structure of ideologies, ignoring any analysis of whether people actually take in what the media feeds them. The Weberians are too structuralist for a different reason. They essentially make the elementary ecological error of generalising from groups to individuals. Instrumentalist accounts are flawed for generalising along one dimension of people's lives – their relationship to the market. Structural locations – technology, work situation and occupational communities – have too frequently been claimed to generate class imagery (ibid., pp. 108–14).

Furthermore, I would add that these attempts to explain working-class consciousness and action (or rather inaction, since the agenda, either explicit or implicit, is to explain the non-revolutionary character of the British working-class) suffer from an over preoccupation with generalised forms of consciousness.

They fail to specify, theoretically, ideological mechanisms at the level of discourse and beliefs which may tend to conceal the putative relations of class domination. Finally, they tend to overlook the role of the forms of organisation of collective action in the shaping of class consciousness. Although Marshall does not quite put it this way, he hints at the problematic concentration on generalised forms of consciousness when he criticises instrumentalist modes of explanation, for simply making the obvious point that in a market economy workers are primarily interested in higher wages (ibid., p. 111).

This says nothing about what it means to the individuals concerned, and according to Marshall we should consider the ethical and evaluative aspects of high wage demands. In short, we should examine the content of the beliefs informing people's behaviour rather than concentrating on its inevitably monetary form. What Marshall fails to do, however, is to indicate in what way such beliefs may be ideological in the sense of practically concealing sectional interests and relations of domination (Giddens, 1979; Thompson, 1984; Urry, 1981). Such a drawback is common to most accounts found in the class consciousness literature; they largely fail to specify how putative ideological beliefs work, concentrating instead on the generalised forms of consciousness and their structural sources.

An adequate account of working-class consciousness and culture should therefore indicate some distinction between cognitive and evaluative aspects. The more detailed content of the beliefs should be related to the role of organisations as producers and disseminators of critical class discourses, as suggested by Parkin (1971, p. 99) and Lash (1984) amongst others. Class organisations should also be taken account of in the structuring of different forms of collective class actions – distinguishing between monological and dialogical forms of organisation, as discussed previously. The structural context for class consciousness and action should also be clearly elaborated. For collective actions of the unemployed I have argued that the changing relationship between the unemployed and the state is the most important structural context. Finally, the historical context is also important, not only at the level of showing how the various elements structuring collective action relate to each other in different ways at different times, but also whether or not the content of class consciousness is seen as 'modern' (building the future) or as 'traditional' (preserving the past). The former is more likely to have an optimistic transformative character.

Much of the debate on ideology in British sociology during the 1970s revolved around Althusser's theory of 'interpellation'. Ideology in these accounts became a functional prerequisite for the existence of capitalism. More recently, however, the 'critical' concept of ideology has been resurrected (Giddens, 1979; Thompson, 1984, 1987, Urry, 1981). Rather than attempting to develop generalised accounts of the functioning of ideology as a level of a social formation which constitutes individuals as subjects, these authors have sought to specify particular kinds of ideological mechanisms which operate to conceal relations of domination.

In Giddens' account, three kinds of ideological mechanism are identified: first, sectional interests may be represented as universal interests; secondly, the denial or transmutation of contradictions; and thirdly, the naturalisation of the the status quo or reification (Giddens, 1979, pp. 193–6). In contrast, Urry attempts to specify no less than six different ideological mechanisms. These are the inappropriate isolation of practices; the inappropriate conflation of practices; the eternalisation of practices; the naturalisation of practices; the obscuring of the interrelations between practices; and the concealment of interests (Urry, 1981, p. 61). These beliefs must operate through concealment to the benefit of the interests of dominant groups.

A similar account is given by Thompson (1984), and he specifies four ways in which beliefs can have ideological effects. The first of these is *legitimation* in Weber's sense (i.e. rational, traditional or charismatic). Secondly, ideological effects may occur through *dissimulation* whereby relations of domination are concealed. Thirdly, beliefs may *reify* social relations, representing historically specific conditions as transhistorical or natural. Finally, discourses may operate through *fragmenting* oppositional groups (ibid., pp. 130–1; 1987, pp. 518–21).

These recent attempts to resurrect a critical theory of ideology are more sophisticated than previous ones in a number of respects. First, they do not involve a simple listing of beliefs and ideas that earlier theories of dominant ideologies frequently did (Abercrombie *et al.*, 1980, p. 4). Secondly, they do not rest on a simple science/ideology dichotomy, since they recognise that discourses are open to diverse and challengeable interpretations (e.g. Thompson, 1984, pp. 137–42), and that any particular discourse or belief may only be partially ideological (e.g. Urry, 1981, pp. 61–2) or become ideological under new relations of domination (e.g. Giddens, 1979, p. 197). Thirdly, they recognise that ideologies are not just structural characteristics but are produced under specific relations of domination. As Thompson puts it, meaning has to be 'mobilised':

> different individuals or groups have a differential capacity *to make meaning stick* . . . Relations of domination are sustained by a *mobilisation of meaning* which legitimates, dissimulates or reifies an existing state of affairs; and meaning can be mobilized because it is an essentially open, shifting, indeterminate phenomenon. (Thompson, 1984, p. 132)

However, there are three particular problems or gaps in these recent theories of ideology. First, they fail to account for the production, dissemination and patterning of what may be termed 'counter-ideologies', or critical beliefs, which do not reproduce relations of domination. Secondly, they fail to identify fatalism as an ideological mechanism, which, empirically, is central to the reproduction of relations of domination in many societies (Abercrombie *et al.*, 1980, pp. 166–7; Marshall *et al.*, 1988a, p. 165). Thirdly, they pay insufficient attention to the relationship between beliefs and collective action, especially those kinds of action which challenge relations of domination, and the impact collective action might have on beliefs.

In relation to the first point about the production and dissemination of critical beliefs, it is part of the 'common sense' of studies of electoral behaviour and political attitudes in Britain that membership of trade unions correlates with 'socialist' attitudes and voting behaviour.[2] A wide variety of sociologists recognise the importance of political organisations in generating and transforming beliefs. These range from Marshall *et al.*'s bland assertions that 'organisations matter' (Marshall *et al.*, 1988a, p. 193), via Parkin's discussion of the role of political parties in systematising and disseminating the 'radical value system' (Parkin, 1971, p. 99), to Gramsci's discussion of 'organic intellectuals' (Gramsci, 1971, pp. 15–16) and Lash's more sophisticated account of trade unions as institutional bearers of critical substantive natural rights ideologies:

worker militancy is not primarily determined by objective variables, but by political parties and trade unions as agents of socialization. That these organisations, and particularly parties, are, to a greater or lesser extent, carriers of ideologies of substantive natural rights which workers, to a greater or lesser extent, will adopt [*sic*]. (Lash, 1984, pp. 235–6)

To the account of the ideological mechanisms of beliefs and discourses we need to add a consideration of critical beliefs. In what ways are they critical? What is the organisational 'infra-structure' of such beliefs? I have previously outlined the different forms such organisational infrastructures could take, and how they relate to critical belief systems – cementing and legitimising collective action.

Returning to the second problem of the new critical theories of ideology, their failure to specify 'fatalism' as an ideological mechanism, it might be argued that this is just an example of Urry's 'eternalisation' or Thompson's 'reification'. If this was the case fatalism would be a rather peculiar example of these mechanisms, for whilst it appears to fit the 'eternalisation/reification' category in the sense that fatalistic beliefs assert that social relations cannot be changed, fatalism is *always necessarily critical and informed about those social relations*. My argument here is that fatalistic beliefs are essentially rationalisations of inaction in terms of processes and social relations over which individuals or groups believe they have no control. It is analytically distinct from reification, for example, as a category of belief. People who express fatalistic beliefs do so with the knowledge that things are wrong and should be different. An eternalising or reifying ideology would not allow for such an alternative conceptualisation to be so central to the particular belief.

A variety of theorists have discussed fatalism, but in a rather brief way which does not do justice to its empirical importance as a phenomenon which blocks or retards collective action by subordinates against relations of domination. Gramsci, for example, noted briefly that 'fatalism is nothing other than the clothing worn by real and active will when in a weak position' (Gramsci, 1971,

p. 337). This basic notion of fatalism is reflected in Mann's discussion of 'pragmatic acceptance' where working-class people, although taking cognition of social inequalities and having a negative evaluation of them, do not conceive of a realistic alternative (Mann, 1983, p. 375). The theme of fatalism is again central to the approach of Abercrombie *et al.* who argue that there is no evidence of widespread acceptance of a 'dominant ideology'. However, subordinates acquiesce in the face of the 'dull compulsion' of economic relations, the interdependent character of the division of labour and the coercive apparatuses of the state (Abercrombie *et al.*, 1980, pp. 153–68). Furthermore, for Abercrombie *et al.* a radical class consciousness does not develop because of the success of 'reformism' in producing real tangible benefits, internal divisions in the working-class and the 'negative demonstration effect' of the Soviet Union as an alternative model of society (ibid., p. 153). Most recently, Marshall *et al.* (1988a, p. 165) have made a similar argument on the basis of large-scale survey data for the 1980s, arguing that although people perceive and disapprove of social inequality, they are fatalistic about the prospects for radical change and instead direct their dissatisfaction into instrumental collectivism. Moreover, some of these authors fail to make a clear distinction between fatalism as an informed belief in the immutability of social relations, and reification where apparently fatalistic types of belief are grounded in ideological claims about 'human nature'.

Fatalistic beliefs operate centrally on the relationship between beliefs and action. In Lukacsian terminology people may have 'true consciousness' at the level of both cognitive and evaluative perceptions of the class structure, but be 'falsely conscious' in their beliefs about the efficacy of collective action to change that structure. This merely reinforces the strictures against analysing ideology in terms of crude 'true/false' or 'science/ideology' dichotomies. Fatalistic beliefs combine both critical and ideological 'moments'. They contain a cognitive and evaluative critique of relations of domination, *but then use that understanding to rationalise inaction.* Thus although other ideological beliefs may be drawn upon further to rationalise the inaction, the 'essence' of fatalism is *the mobilisation of critical meaning to rationalise the failure to act in rational accordance with those beliefs.* The problem of 'objective' and 'subjective' interests is not a real problem for this account of fatalism. It is founded on the idea that people have a negative evaluation of the social order, so they presumably know, to some degree at least, that it is in their 'subjectively' perceived 'objective' interests for the social order to change. The problem is why people do not act in accordance with those beliefs even when they have a clear subjective notion of their interests.

This kind of understanding of fatalism begins to throw light on the problematic relationship between consciousness and beliefs and action, especially collective action against relations of domination. Beliefs may be transformed or reproduced by involvement in collective action against relations of domination. This bears directly on Lash's account of the sources of worker militancy, and on my account above of the characteristics of dialogical forms of political organisations of the unemployed, in which involvement in collective action is seen to have positive 'consciousness raising' benefits (Lash, 1984). However, in relation to fatalism this is the crucial point. *Involvement in unsuccessful collective actions will tend to reinforce fatalistic beliefs.* The socialising benefits of involvement in dialogical forms of organisation and collective action therefore cuts both ways. It can enhance agents' critical penetration of relations of domination, but at the same time reinforce their beliefs about the immutability of those relations. In contrast, monological forms of organisation (presumably 'reformist' in other terminology) will be more able to deliver some of the goods in the short term. This does not, however, preclude the unemployed using a dialogical organisation in a 'reformist' manner, i.e. to achieve short-term ends, as was arguably the case with the NUW(C)M.

3.5   COMMUNITY AS A CULTURAL RESOURCE

As a sociological concept community has had a very unhappy history, having been subject to such devastating criticism during the 1970s in Britain (Bell and Newby, 1971), that the very idea of researching 'communities' has all but died among many sociologists. However, in the light of the resurgence of sociological interest in localities (Bagguley, *et al.*, 1990), the debate on how to analyse local social and political processes has been renewed. In this context I shall argue that the concept of community, properly theorised, can have a central place in understanding political mobilisation. The notion of community that I wish to develop and draw upon here is based on Cohen's recent formulation of it as a *symbolic boundary*. 'The quintessential referent of community is that its members make, or believe they make, a similar sense of things either generally or with respect to specific and significant interests, and, further, that they think that that sense may differ from one made elsewhere' (Cohen, 1985, p. 16).

The 'members' of the 'community' share the symbol of the boundary that they ascribe meaning to, but members sharing the same symbol ascribe different meanings to it. For Cohen this symbolic conceptualisation of community is not a mechanism of social integration, but rather a mechanism of aggregation. Further, Cohen sees this notion of community as a cultural resource; it provides people with the means with which to produce new meanings. In this process of production of new meanings people draw upon references to the past, or rather some putative past (ibid., 1985, p. 103). People with diverse material or social interests can find those interests aggregated in the symbolic representation of a boundary. If these boundaries are in some sense threatened, then the symbol provides the cultural means by which that threat can be resisted. A recent dramatic example of this process would be the way in which individuals in mining areas spoke of the defence of the community during the 1984–5 miners' strike, partly in terms of the resurrection of the mining communities' lost historical patterns of mutuality (Samuel, 1986a, pp. 9–10). Whether or not the patterns of resistance were really like that, or whether or not the past was really like people claimed, does not matter. Rather the fact that many people *believed it was so* was an important *cultural* resource for political resistance aggregating interests within the struggle.

This reworking of the notion of community is especially valuable in the sense that different political projects and different 'interests' can tend to hegemonise the symbols of community. Contemporary examples of local working classes defending their communities need not take the particular political forms that the miners' strike did, resurrecting images of 'little Moscows'. Pahl and Wallace (1988, p. 137) note how the defence of 'community', articulated around workplaces, can take the form of resistance against picketing by other workers, a not unreasonable account for many Nottinghamshire miners' actions in 1984–5. In short, local working-class organisations can mobilise different kinds of meanings in the process of hegemonising local symbolic communities.

Symbolic communities are not necessarily 'local' in character, they could be nations and 'races' (Gilroy, 1987). However, my claim here is that where the occupants of a locality do develop a strong symbolic sense of community, especially around some distinctive occupation or industry, and where this tends to be hegemonised by particular socialist political practices, then this provides a crucial cultural resource for the unemployed to draw upon. This notion of a localist symbolic community articulated around particular kinds of socialist politics goes some way, at least, to understanding the highly localised and geographically uneven character of the NUW(C)M during the inter-war period. This symbolic sense of community, when oriented around the work-place, enables the political practices of the workplace to be more easily translated into the political realm 'outside' which was crucial in the development and activities of the NUW(C)M. However, if the symbolism of working-class community becomes increasingly 'nationalised', then this tends to undermine the cultural resources for specifically 'local' political action.

How can these wider issues of class consciousness, ideology and community help with elaborating a general model of the varieties of cultural resources that are available to the unemployed? At the most general level, I shall make an idealtypical distinction between those resources which tend to block political mobilisation and those which favour it. Further, I wish to claim that the principal producers, bearers and disseminators of these resources are political organisations. I am concerned also with identifying different kinds of cultural resources which may cement the support of a political movement of the unemployed, and legitima-tise it in the eyes of others, especially allies, and with how these cultural resources work.

Additionally, my concern is to specify different kinds of class consciousness, in terms of their various cognitive and evaluative dimensions, and to outline how these are then connected to different ideologies of 'rights' (i.e. formal versus substantive natural rights). These are then related to forms of collective social action both through a transformative dimension implied in these beliefs, and through their connection to distinctive organisational forms of collective action. Through the actions of such organisations these discourses can hegemonise symbolic communities. In contrast, class consciousness can also take the form of fatalistic beliefs, and I shall argue that these tend to be articulated to cement and legitimatise monological forms of organisation through ideologies of formal rights. These can also hegemonise symbolic communities through political organisations. Finally, I shall briefly outline various ideological mechanisms which tend to conceal relations of domination as a further set of cultural resources which tend to block political mobilisation. However, my claim here, largely on empirical grounds, is that the fatalism model is the principal explanation of political inaction at the level of cultural resources. I shall not detail these empirical grounds here, since several extensive discussions of this issue are to be found elsewhere, and I have already discussed these above (Abercrombie *et al.*, 1980; Mann, 1983; Marshall *et al.*, 1988a).

The two general idealtypical kinds of cultural resources are summarised in Figures 3.1 and 3.2 below. Figure 3.1 shows the idealtypical conjuncture of cultural resources which tends to favour political organisation of the unemployed, whilst Figure 3.2 shows the idealtypical conjuncture of cultural resources that tends to block mobilisations through fatalistic sets of beliefs. I should emphasise again that these are ideal types of *outcomes*, hence the reference to 'conjunctures'. With these ideal types I am attempting to capture the cultural dimension of the essential prerequisites for the political mobilisation of the unemployed. I am using them to cut into one 'moment' in the ongoing structuration of social life. In the sense of Giddens' analysis of this 'moment', I am examining here the resources (in Giddens' terminology 'media') that are drawn upon in social action (Giddens, 1979). Empirically, these ideal, typical resources would be the products of past social action. In particular, they would be the *outcome of past social struggles*.[3]

Class consciousness in these models has two dimensions – cognitive and evaluative. Within the cognitive dimension the features referred to, or rather the putative class identities and explanations, can either be features of the distributive order, social relations in production or a generalised model of social relations. Each of these possible aspects in the cognitive dimension may be evaluated in up to five possible ways. First, through discourses of substantive natural rights; secondly through discourses of formal legal rights; thirdly, they may be evaluated fatalistically; fourthly,

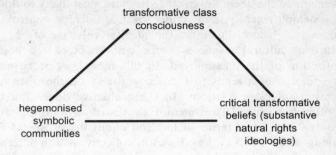

FIGURE 3.1   *Ideal type of conjuncture of resources favouring mobilisation*

they may be legitimated by ideological beliefs; or, finally, they may be reified by ideological discourses. If the recent survey results reported by Marshall *et al.* are accurate, then it would seem that those in the British population who are class conscious are principally conscious of class as a *distributive* phenomenon, and evaluate this in terms of fatalism and formal legal rights. Marshall *et al.* argue that this leads to fatalism allied to instrumental collectivism in class organisations and actions. This broadly corresponds to my model in Figure 3.2 below.

In the idealtypical conjuncture favouring mobilisation, class consciousness will either be referring to production relations or generalised relations of class in the cognitive dimension, and will evaluate these relations in the form of a substantive natural rights ideology. Further, these evaluative beliefs entail a strong belief in the efficacy of class actions. To the extent that such claims hegemonise symbolic communities, those symbols form a further cultural resource for the political organisation and mobilisation of the unemployed. Hegemonised symbolic communities are an important link in the causal chain in that they frequently (though not necessarily) entail a localist geo-social referent. Therefore, if the cultural resources of the workplace can hegemonise the local symbols of community, they will further inform political practices outside the workplace which makes political pressure on the local state more likely. This is crucial for the practices of political movements of the unemployed since they are most likely to flourish when unemployment relief is under local democratic control.

Figure 3.2 below illustrates the idealtypical case of the conjuncture of cultural resources which tend to block the political mobilisation of the unemployed. In this model, as noted above, class consciousness tends to focus cognitively on the distributive dimensions of class relations. In the evaluative dimension there may often be a critical assessment of the distributive order, but this assessment will be in terms of fatalism about the prospects for it changing, and a belief in the efficacy of collective action in terms of formal rights and short-term quantitative gains. For collective political action the fatalism tends to lend credence to monological forms of organisation. These organisations pursuing a strategy in terms of formal legislative and/or quantitative gains for individuals, rather than global changes for subjectively perceived interest groups, fail to achieve widespread changes, thus reinforcing the fatalistic belief in the immutability of the distributive order.

Where such beliefs and political practices tend to hegemonise local symbolic communities, then political organisations of the unemployed tend to take a monological form, if they develop at all. Furthermore, it can also be reasoned that wider legitimating, dissimulating, fragmenting and reifying beliefs are more likely to occur in these conditions, since there are no established critical cultural resources embedded in dialogical forms of political organisation and practice.

It should be stressed that these are idealtypical models which aim to isolate the peculiar features and major causal processes. Hence for any real, concrete instance there will be a mixture of the two extremes, often instantiated in the struggles between different political forces. These are *ideal* types of the outcomes of previous political struggles, both within the working-class (see Offe and Wiesenthal, 1985; Przeworski, 1986) and between the working-class and other classes, which provides the resources or medium through which the unemployed are able to become politically organised. Since the actual causal processes are to do with social struggles, they can only really be fully grasped through concrete empirical analysis.

Nevertheless, the ideal types enable historical and geographical comparisons to be made. For example, I would claim that part of

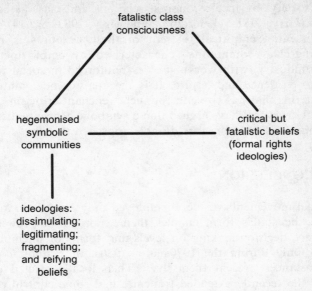

FIGURE 3.2 *Ideal type of conjuncture of resources blocking mobilisation*

the explanation for the strength of the NUW(C)M in particular areas, and its existence during the politically and culturally specific inter-war period, can partly be explained by the existence of localities where the conjuncture of cultural resources most closely approximated the ideal type in Figure 3.1. As previously mentioned, the ideal type in Figure 3.2 is now much more frequently found.

Part of the explanation for this lies in the decline in the organisational resources which tended to pursue dialogical forms of struggle more generally in the realm of 'class politics'. Further, the material bases of such cultural and organisational resources have also been undermined or, rather, restructured. The material bases of such cultural resources, forms of organisation and collective action have been analysed in terms of, on the one hand, Lockwood's (1975) ideal typical 'traditional proletarians'.

On the other hand, there are analyses in terms of the structuring of 'civil society' by local economic relations and class-based social forces (Urry, 1981; Abercrombie and Urry, 1983, pp. 141–2). The quintessential empirical referent of these accounts is the 'old working-class community' characterised by employment in a single industry, with workplace ties reinforced in social relations of kin, residence and leisure. It is the analysis of community in these terms that has come in for such trenchant criticism over the years. However, I have argued that a symbolic conceptualisation of community is a much more durable approach to take.

3.6 CONCLUSION

Political movements of the unemployed only emerge on any scale where the state's form enables them, more or less directly, to influence decision-making on levels and forms of unemployment relief. Only during the 1920s and 1930s, in Britain, did these circumstances present themselves. Then locally elected officials under the recently extended franchise had some control over the levels of relief.

Political movements of the unemployed do not simply spring from the dissatisfaction with unemployment; they have to be built. Unemployment itself provides no clear sense of identity comparable to that of class, occupation or locality, but rather these cultural resources may be found amongst those who are 'recruited' into unemployment. These movements have to be constructed using the available organisational resources and grounded in the culture of the people they seek to mobilise, if they are to retain their support and maintain alliances with other sympathetic organisations. Furthermore, different kinds of mobilisation and political consequences are dependent on the various forms of organisational resources that are available. Those forms which approximate to the dialogical model above, with decentralised forms of participative collective action, require discourses asserting the substantive natural rights of the unemployed as part of an ascendant working class. In contrast monological organisations, which are arguably more suited to influencing the contemporary form of state, draw on more formal and fatalistic discourses of class consciousness and workers' rights.

Clearly, organisations alone are insufficient. Their membership needs cementing to the organisation's goals and actions through beliefs which generate a sense of common interest amongst the participants. In the 1920s and 1930s, the state could still be influenced by the unemployed building on the organisations and culture that had already developed in workplaces and locales. Relatively few places, however, had these characteristics. By the 1980s, the state had effectively been closed to pressure by the unemployed on levels and forms of relief, in part as a result of the 'successes' of earlier struggles in the 1920s and 1930s. Monological forms of organisation are now even more widespread than previously, and the material bases of dialogical organisations and a critical, transformative modernist working-class culture had been eroded by forty years of deindustrialisation. These organisations, rather than building the future, are defending a stereotyped 'traditional' past. The organisational and cultural resources that produced the NUW(C)M during the inter-war period are now largely nowhere to be found.

The conditions for the collective action of the unemployed are quite different in the 1980s in comparison to the 1920s and 1930s. There are limited forms of organisation and collective action in the 1980s. However, these are significantly different from those of the past. They cannot orient themselves so directly towards the state's unemployment relief, having to rely instead on the more tightly drawn legal welfare rights field with gains for individual cases rather than masses of local people. The resources they tend to draw upon are the formal organisations of trade union movement, more concerned with controlling the activities of the unemployed than with encouraging collective action. The cultural resources for collective action remain in the beliefs and practices of trade union activists who, as during the inter-war period, have formed the basis for today's centres for the unemployed.

4

Early Political Movements of the Unemployed

4.1 THE ANTI-POOR LAW MOVEMENT

During the nineteenth century there were a number of social movements associated with unemployment relief. The first of these, the anti-Poor Law movement of the 1830s is not strictly a movement *of* the unemployed, but rather a political alliance of sections of the middle classes and the early trade unions in the north of England. The unemployed were noticeable by their *absence* from the struggles around the 1834 Poor Law Act (Knott, 1986, p. 274). However, it deserves some brief attention as a proto movement of the unemployed, in that it demonstrates the importance of the availability of organisational and cultural resources. It was also centrally concerned with the levels, forms and local control over unemployment relief. Further, since it is an attempt to influence relief prior to the the extension of the franchise later in the nineteenth and early twentieth centuries, an examination of the anti-Poor Law movement is a useful comparison with later movements in relation to the claims I have made previously about the importance of state forms in structuring political protest by the unemployed.

The anti-Poor Law movement of the 1830s emerged in response to the attempts by central government to implement the 'New Poor Law' of 1834. This involved the 'policing' of local Boards of Guardians by a new Poor Law Commission. During the late 1830s the commissioners set out across the country to amalgamate the existing Poor Law unions into larger units, and to ensure that local Guardians were not being too lax in granting outdoor relief. The Act and its implementation has usually been seen as the successful

72

application of the principles of Benthamite political economy to the labour market. Essentially, those without work, the 'able-bodied paupers', were not to be granted outdoor relief as was apparently common at the time, but were to be taken into the workhouse under the principle of less eligibility. The aim was to enforce a rigorous labour market discipline (Brundage, 1978; Novak, 1987).

The new commissioners met some opposition in the rural areas of the south of England, but it was in the north, especially Lancashire and West Yorkshire, where opposition was organised most thoroughly (Edsall, 1971). Many towns in the north had a cyclical industrial labour market by this time, with full employment followed by slumps and unemployment. This was quite different from the labour market conditions in the rural areas and London, where seasonal employment and casualism prevailed. However, perhaps the most distinctive feature of the northern towns at this time was the ability of unions to organise more or less permanently, providing a base for a variety of radical popular movements (ibid., p. 53; Knott, 1986).

The anti-Poor Law movement flowed largely out of the agitation for the factory acts, since, after the passage of the 1833 Factory Act, campaigners were looking for a new issue around which to agitate. All but one of the prominent leaders of the anti-Poor Law movement were supporters of factory reform (Edsall, 1971, p. 58). The movement as a whole was an uneasy alliance of local middle-class ratepayers and trade unionists, with various independent radical politicians of often nonconformist religious persuasion, rather than of the poor or the unemployed. Middle-class rate-payers, especially in the north, resented the loss of control over local affairs, and believed that the proposed extension of indoor relief would prove more costly than the traditional outdoor relief in times of recession, thus putting a strain on the rates (Rose, 1988, pp. 82–3). The different labour market conditions prevailing in the north, where the able-bodied poor were often regularly employed as skilled textile workers in normal times, were used to claim that the New Poor Law was inappropriate to local conditions there (Edsall, 1971, p. 64).

The anti-Poor Law movement, however, had no clear alternative to the New Poor Law other than a return to the old established Poor Law practices. In some rural counties in the south of England the poor did oppose the implementation of the New Poor Law, but this was short-lived. These rural southern protests were quite different from the stronger more resilient opposition of the industrial north. The rural opposition was concerned to preserve the traditional moral economy of agricultural society, and collective action took the form of the pre-industrial riot (Knott, 1986, pp. 65–84).

The geographical base of the anti-Poor Law movement was the industrial north. Its tactics involved petitioning Parliament to repeal the new law, contesting the elections to the Boards of Guardians, and local opposition to the Poor Law commissioners when they came to implement central government policies. However, the principal tactic was the public meeting (Rose, 1988, p. 87). Throughout 1837 and 1838 many townships in the north held their own public meetings, which were extensively reported in the northern radical press of the time. Furthermore, many pamphlets were produced attacking the New Poor Law and its principles. These reveal that the central arguments and 'rationality' of the movement depended as much on a religious culture as a clearly articulated separate and secular class culture.

> The campaign was portrayed as a crusade for the 'divine rights' of the poor against the 'Devil King Law'. Orators and pamphleteers used the most glowing, violent language they could muster, and relied more on Biblical than statistical evidence. 'The Bible containing the will of God – this accursed Act of Parliament embodies the will of Lucifer. It is the Sceptre of Belial establishing its sway in the Land of Bibles DAMNATION ETERNAL DAMNATION to the accursed Fiend' cried Oastler. (Rose, 1988, p. 88)

The cultural resources drawn upon, then, were principally those of nonconformist religion, whilst organisationally the movement emerged from the trade unions and the alliance behind the factory reform movement. There was no permanent organisation either locally or nationally, the local activities being coordinated by *ad hoc* committees of political radicals (Edsall, 1971). Here there was a dialogical form of organisation, but not one asserting the interests of the unemployed or the poor in any direct way, since there is no evidence of them being directly involved in the organisations.

Paupers took almost no part in protests against the 1834 Poor Law. It is true that in the south of England some recipients of poor relief had demonstrated their anger over the new regulations by mobbing relieving officers and setting fire to workhouse extensions, but such activities were exceptional. What characterised most anti-poor law protests was the total absence of paupers. (Knott, 1986, p. 274)

The contest of elections to the local Boards of Guardians was largely disastrous for the anti-Poor Law movement. Few people had the franchise, so those who were most immediately affected by the New Poor Law were effectively sealed off from exerting any significant influence. In some places there were attempts to boycott local elections, but these were largely unsuccessful. Popular pressure was seen to fail in a widespread way, and politicians shifted their attentions to the question of the franchise as a prerequisite to changing the Poor Law, since the groups they sought to mobilise lacked influence without it. The anti-Poor Law movement fed into the 1840s Chartist movement. In many respects, frustration over the failure of the anti-Poor Law movement to achieve total victory was a key trigger behind the Chartism of the 1840s. Furthermore, Chartism was an issue that split the anti-Poor Law movement's alliance between radicals and conservatives (Edsall, 1971, p. 185; Rose, 1988, p. 90). The actual operation of the New Poor Law was less of a disaster than many of the northern middle classes had feared, and, in the context of local/central compromises, many details were still left to local discretion. Their active opposition was thus defused (Rose, 1988, p. 91). The implementation of the Act was by no means a decisive victory for the Benthamites, since for most of the nineteenth century 80 per cent of the poor remained on outdoor relief, a reflection of the continuing strength of local control (Brundage, 1978, p. 184). This can be seen as a significant set of local victories for the anti-Poor Law movement.

The experience of the anti-Poor Law movement emphasises the centrality of unemployment relief to social struggles around unemployment. Further, the insularity of the state from working-class influence, due to the limited franchise, is central to understanding the movement's failure. Hence the move to Chartism by several of the movement's leaders. Most striking is the lack of active organisation by the unemployed themselves. This is accounted for by the relative lack of organisational resources.

The response to this situation by the better-off sections of the working class, conventionally known as the 'labour aristocracy', was to extend mutualist forms of provision. Mann (1984, 1986) has shown how the friendly societies developed rapidly after the early 1830s, as a pragmatic response to the New Poor Law among these better-off sections of the working class. Class struggle did not simply disappear, but it took a different form in relation to unemployment relief which the working class could not influence because they were excluded by the limited franchise. However, this pragmatic mutualist strategy of the 'labour aristocracy' was to give rise to further problems in the later mobilisations of the unemployed, by creating deeper divisions within the working class (Mann, 1984, 1986, 1990).

4.2   THE LAND AND LABOUR LEAGUE

Political organisations agitating on the issue of unemployment also emerged in the late nineteenth century, with the formation of the Land and Labour League in October 1869 (Harrison, 1965, p. 215). Primarily concerned with land reform, the League was formed by men influenced by the writings of Marx and the politics of the First International, but other influences emanated from contemporary republican trends in English politics. Some of the membership had also been involved in Chartist and Owenite socialist organisations and the currency reform movement (ibid.). Besides land reform in general, the League was also concerned with the implications of land reform for Ireland.

However, where the League was specifically innovative in its politics, for the purposes of this discussion, was that it broke with the traditional attitude of the trade unions of the skilled working class towards the unemployed. From the perspective of the League, the unemployed were a section of the working class to be organised into a political force, and they were not to be excluded from the concerns of working-class organisations and politics (Harrison, 1965, p. 220). The organisation of demonstrations on behalf of the unemployed by the League in the early 1870s was, according to Harrison, synchronous with the emergence of the word 'unemployed' in both everyday language and more formal political discourse (ibid., p. 245). Although the League cannot be attributed with the distinction of having introduced a new word into the English language, its members did organise the first recorded political demonstration against unemployment in Britain, which actively involved the unemployed themselves, in Trafalgar Square, in London, on Good Friday 1870 (ibid., p. 223).

The economic background to this demonstration was that 1 032 000 people were in receipt of poor relief in 1869 – the highest figure for more than twenty years, and that the East End of London was considered to be the worst affected area. Furthermore, the number of jobs in shipbuilding and marine engineering in London fell from 27 000 to 9000 between 1865 and 1871. The Land and Labour League's proposed solution to this problem was one that was to permeate debates about unemployment among socialists for many years to come, namely, to employ and feed the surplus labour on state financed cooperative farms in rural areas (ibid., pp. 221–3).

Apart from the demonstration called for the afternoon of Good Friday in 1870 (*The Times*, 12 April 1870), little seems to have been achieved according to Harrison's account, although a debate in Parliament on unemployed labour took place on 17 June 1870. The League itself broke up in the early 1870s over divergent views about the Paris commune, and over how to respond to J. S. Mill's proposed compromises about land reform promoted through the Land Tenure Reform Association. Moreover, unemployment was falling throughout 1871 and 1872 and slipped from wider public concern as well as that of socialist radicals (Harrison, 1965, pp. 239–41). Some League members, however, did become involved in organising casual labourers in the East End of London from 1872 onwards and achieved some notable wage increases for dockers (Harrison, 1965, pp. 232–4).

By and large, the Land and Labour League was ineffective, but it did introduce, in a way unknown before, the idea of the unemployed as not just a 'common-sense', economic category, but also as a social collectivity that could be potentially mobilised around politically constructed sets of interests. Its work amongst the unemployed and unskilled workers of London prefigured that of the Social Democratic Federation in the 1880s. The League was not an organisation *of* the unemployed, its activities in relation to the unemployed were clearly a case of 'opportunistic' political activity around a short-term issue, which was not central to *their* main concerns with land reform. This opportunism was also to be a feature of later political activities amongst the unemployed pursued by the Social Democratic Federation.

4.3   THE SOCIAL DEMOCRATIC FEDERATION: 1880–1914

The Social Democratic Federation's (SDF) agitations amongst the unemployed were somewhat more consistent and long lasting than the activities of earlier groups. They also attempted to involve the unemployed themselves, although it seems that the casually employed poor who made up most of the 'unemployed' on these demonstrations did not take an active part in their organisation. The agitations of the SDF were also part of wider action by the labour movement of the time on issues of unemployment, so there was the possibility of alliances between the different organisations. However, only the SDF was strongly committed to the active involvement of the unemployed over any length of time.

Figure 4.1 presents data on the changing proportions of the workforce who were unemployed between 1870 and 1912. Data for this period are notoriously unreliable, being limited only to trade union returns, and almost certainly underestimate the true levels of unemployment, as we might understand it today, to a considerable degree. They are, however, the best available estimates of the basic trends (Harris, 1984, pp. 371–3). The graph shows a remarkably sharp cycle roughly every ten years, with 'peaks' in the late 1870s, the mid 1880s, the early 1890s, and the early and late 1900s. Between 1870 and the mid 1880s there were, as far as I am aware, no political protests by the unemployed. However, unemployment peaked in this period during the late 1870s. The broad trend of protest is if anything towards a peak in the early 1900s. Although it is not possible to quantify this, it does seem that changes in the level of unemployment do not automatically result in protest, but that political resources are required to provide a response.[1] There was no protest by the unemployed until organised by the SDF.

I shall discuss the activities of the SDF in terms of the framework developed in Chapter 3 initially considering the

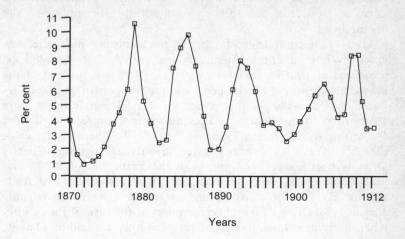

SOURCE Harris, 1984, P. 374, table 2.

FIGURE 4.1 *Trade union unemployment, 1870–1912*

changing form of the state, followed by some examination, albeit limited by the quality of historical sources for this exercise, of organisational and cultural resources.

The most important aspect of the changes in the forms of the state was undoubtedly the extension of the franchise under the 1867 and 1884 Reform Acts, and most crucial of all, for the effectiveness of political agitation on unemployment relief, was the abolition of property qualifications for elections to the Boards of Guardians under the Local Government Act of 1894 (Brown, 1971, p. 15; Harris, 1984, p. 145; Thane, 1984, p. 878). For local elections some women had the vote, but there were major anomalies in the various franchises and their administration, which excluded many working-class people. During the 1900s, less that 30 per cent of all adults were on the electoral register for national elections. This was due to the exclusion of specific groups, (most importantly those in receipt of poor relief), the specific qualification requirements of the regulations, such as regular payment of rates, and the extremely complex process of registration (Blewett, 1965, pp. 31–3). The extension of the franchise was by no means an unproblematic advance from the perspective of a putative organiser of the unemployed.

Matters are complicated further by the forms in which relief was given. Whilst unemployment, to the extent that it could be measured accurately, was generally rising towards the end of the nineteenth century, ablebodied outdoor pauperism declined between 1871 and 1891 as the 'principles of 1834' were applied more stringently, so the Poor Law became a minor source of relief for the unemployed (Harris, 1984, pp. 53, 148–9). The major sources of relief were private charity, often through the detested Charity Organisation Society, champions of the 'principles of 1834', and mutualist organisations such as the friendly societies and trade unions. By far the most important of these were the friendly societies, which had 5.6 million members at the turn of the century when trade union membership numbered only 1.2 million (Thane, 1984, p. 878).

With those sections of the working class with some degree of organisation effectively making their own provision for unemployment, there was little direct material interest in organising for higher levels of state relief (Mann, 1984, 1986, 1990). Those who did come into contact with the Poor Law were, by and large, the casually employed of large cities, such as London and Manchester, and they had little in the way of their own organisations as well as being largely excluded from the franchise (Kidd, 1984; Stedman-Jones, 1984; Thane, 1984). The changes in the form of the state enabled some local Boards of Guardians to be influenced to some degree by groups from working-class organisations, as indicated by the early phases of Poplarism in the 1900s (Ryan, 1978, pp. 57–62).

The late nineteenth century saw a proliferation of more permanently organised working-class political institutions. The TUC was formed in 1867; the SDF appeared in 1883; the Independent Labour Party was formed in 1893; and the Labour Representation Committee was formed in 1900, to become the Labour Party a few years later (Brown, 1971, p. 15). Furthermore, the 1880s also saw the emergence and growth of general unions attempting to organise the less skilled, casually employed sections of the working class (Hobsbawm, 1974). In general, more sections of the working class were coming into contact with organisations which were attempting to promote their interests and disseminate oppositional ideas. The SDF in particular presented a crude class against class ideology, and, more generally, the new unions were the product of local working-class discontent combined with the work of the new socialist organisations (ibid.). These organisations were not drawing on some clearly worked out 'tradition', but were creating new 'modern' forms of working-class politics.

However, there were deep divisions between and within these organisations, especially on the issue of how to deal with unemployment. The friendly societies and some of the trade unions had a vested interest in not being in favour of further state intervention in unemployment relief (Thane, 1984). They were then given a corporatist role alongside employers' organisations, running their own state subsidised insurance schemes under the Liberal National Insurance legislation of 1911 (Harris, 1984). There was widespread opposition to the idea of National Insurance from many sections of the organised labour movement for a wide variety of reasons. These varied from the worries about its demoralising effects by the Fabians, to the arguments against its failure to redistribute resources from the rich to the poor by the ILP and the SDF.

Since the late 1880s a wide variety of schemes to reduce unemployment had been discussed within the emergent labour movement, including labour colonies in rural areas, and extensive relief works in cities. All were attempted in a limited fashion, and all were deemed to be failures (Brown, 1971; Harris, 1984). The National Insurance option probably won through because the state incorporated the strongest sections of organised labour and capital in the running of the scheme, and it avoided the loss of citizenship and voting rights for the recipients (Langan, 1985). Further, the National Insurance scheme was also limited to particular categories of employees. Neither organised labour nor organised capital had a clearly worked out policy on unemployment[2] which the state could implement. If anything the state was the agent of organisation, with the emergent professional civil servants playing a central role in working out both the financial and political aspects of the legislation (Harris, 1984). The state thus effectively incorporated those sections of the working class most likely to have the resources for effective class struggle. The 'labour aristocracy's' forms of mutualist provision, earlier developed as the main response to the Poor Law, were successfully imitated by the state, thus reproducing debilitating divisions within the working class and among the unemployed (Mann, 1984, 1986, 1990).

The actual organisation of the unemployed was largely left to the Marxist SDF, which engaged in significant if sporadic agitations from the 1880s to the 1900s. These were concentrated in London and Manchester where the SDF was strongest. Historical opinion is divided on the issue of the effectiveness of these demonstrations with Harris tending to see them as largely irrelevant (despite citing evidence which suggests the contrary, see, for example Harris, 1984, pp. 152–3; 272), and others seeing them as more central to the policy process (Brown, 1971; Gilbert, 1966; Stedman-Jones, 1984). However, Kidd (1984) has emphasised the more important point that what characterised these demonstrations was *their local and decentralised character*. They most clearly did wrest concessions in the form of relief and relief works at the local level, but they did not affect the substantive content of national policy (ibid.).

The local and decentralised character of the SDF's demonstrations was a result of their policy of seeking short-term 'palliatives', and their recognition of the ease with which locally run, quasi-democratically accountable institutions could be influenced by public protest. However, by and large they failed to develop a permanent organisation of the unemployed.

Throughout their agitations the SDF attempted to combine elements of what I have characterised as monological and dialogical forms of organisation. They sought to mobilise the unemployed themselves, and were partially successful at this, but did so through committees composed of SDF members and others who were not necessarily unemployed. Some committees of the unemployed themselves, though rather short-lived, rejected the interventions of the SDF, as in Salford in 1904 (ibid., p. 346). The typical mode of organisation was to form a committee of labour movement leaders to lead the agitation.

In 1902, for example, the ILP convened a conference to establish a permanent organisation to coordinate activities *on behalf* of the unemployed. The resulting National Unemployed Committee consisted of middle-class reformers and official labour movement figures from bodies such as the Fabians and the LRC. This organisation never achieved anything, since it disappeared amidst major disagreements amongst its members in 1904 (Brown, 1971, pp. 21–41). The SDF was hostile to this, not for any principled reason, but simply because it had not been consulted. It had again been forming its own front committees to launch agitations in 1902–3 often using full-time party workers. These campaigns frequently led to violence, further alienating the SDF from potential allies in the labour movement (ibid., p. 24). A further factor holding back the more permanent organisation of the unemployed by the SDF was their fitful interest in the issue. They only seemed to become interested when there was a rise in the official trade union unemployment figures.

The SDF, although its membership was concentrated in working class neighbourhoods (Kidd, 1984, p. 341), included a rather ostentatious upper-class element which played a leading role (Hobsbawm, 1974, p. 233). Its membership seemed mostly to be amongst artisans, and its trade union strength was concentrated in the London Trades Council. Although winning some places on Boards of Guardians, especially in London, the electoral field of the left was dominated by the ILP and the LRC. The SDF's attitude towards trade unions was somewhat schizophrenic, some activists being centrally involved in the rise of the 'new unionism', whilst the SDF at times had a deeply sectarian attitude to other labour movement organisations. Nowhere, either geographically or organisationally in trades unions, did the SDF have widespread or deep support. Furthermore, its ideas were rather alien to those it sought to mobilise through its 'front' committees:

> there was an unwillingness to be exploited for political ends by an organisation with whose politics very few workers agreed, and the SDF made things worse for itself in this respect by its hostile and sectarian attitude towards trade unionists. This explains why it so often tried to work through what can best be termed 'front organisations'. (Brown, 1971, p. 167)

In short, the unemployed lacked the organisational and cultural resources to mobilise in any more permanent way from within their own ranks, so they were organised from without by the SDF. Although the state form was to a limited degree 'open' to influence at the local level on issues of unemployment relief, as witnessed by the phenomenon of Poplarism (Ryan, 1978), and the SDF made the most of the opportunities here, paupers did not have the vote and the franchise was still limited by various bureaucratic hurdles. Also of importance was the strong division between those who were in mutualist forms of unemployment insurance schemes and the rest who relied on private charity and poor relief (Mann, 1986). This division of immediate practical material interests in relation to unemployment generated deep divisions over the precise details of any labour movement policy for unemployment.

4.4   THE NATIONAL UNEMPLOYED WORKERS' MOVEMENT

A more detailed discussion of the National Unemployed Workers' Movement is possible due to the extensive archive materials left behind by the movement, and autobiographical accounts, especially those of its national organiser Wal Hannington (Hannington, 1967, p. 1977). Consequently, there are a number of accounts by historians, usually focusing on the hunger marches of the 1930s and the threat they posed to public order (Hayburn, 1972; Stevenson and Cook, 1977, pp. 145–94; Turnbull, 1973). There is also a rich variety of secondary sources providing local accounts, for example, of localities in South Wales (Francis, 1984; Macintyre, 1980); Manchester (Frow and Frow, 1976, and no date; Hayburn, 1970); Sheffield (Moore, 1985); localities in Scotland (Macintyre, 1980); Brighton (Trory, 1974); Liverpool (Garrett, no date); Birkenhead (Kelly, 1987); and Nottingham (Wyncoll, 1985). There are, furthermore, national overviews of the movement as a whole (Croucher, 1987), the hunger marches in particular (Kingsford, 1982) and the women's sections of the NUW(C)M (Bruley, 1980, pp. 220–48). The bulk of these are not particularly analytical, usually being historical narratives or personal recollections. The main scholarly debates amongst historians are over the putative success or failure of the activities of the NUW(C)M (see, for example, Turnbull, 1973, p. 142 and Stevenson and Cook, 1977, p. 194 for the 'failure' view and Croucher, 1987, pp. 202–10; Deacon and Briggs, 1973; Miller, 1979 for evidence and arguments for 'partial success'). There is, then, a wealth of secondary material from which to construct a more analytical account of the

NUW(C)M, and this is what I shall attempt in the rest of this chapter.

The unemployment rate for much of the period under discussion here is illustrated in Figure 4.2. Unemployment peaked in the early 1920s and the early 1930s. Although making strict comparisons would be rash, the level of unemployment peaked higher in the 1930s than between the 1870s and 1900s. As in the earlier period, there is no clear correlation between the level of unemployment and the level of protest. The most widespread protests took place in 1935 around the creation of the UAB, *several years after the peak of unemployment in 1932.* It was policy changes in the levels and administration of benefits, not the level of unemployment, which provided a reason for protest.[3]

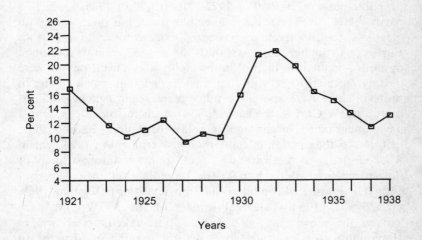

SOURCE Beveridge, 1960, p. 47, table 1.

FIGURE 4.2   *Unemployment rate, 1921–38*

The history of the NUW(C)M can be usefully divided into four phases: formation and consolidation (1920–3); initial decline (1924–7); plateau (1928–35); final decline (1936–40). The NUW(C)M grew out of a widespread series of protests by the unemployed in 1920 which in many ways emulated the activities of the SDF in the 1900s. Local committees were formed to put pressure on local Boards of Guardians for out relief and higher levels of relief to supplement National Insurance (Croucher, 1987, pp. 23–31; Hannington, 1977, pp. 15–27; Kingsford, 1982, pp. 13–32). These committees sprang from a range of sources, but especially from unemployed servicemen and engineers, and the centre of the movement, like the agitations of the 1900s, was in London. The movement itself was formed at a national conference of local committees on 15 April 1921, where three former engineering shop stewards, Wal Hannington, Percy Haye and Jack Holt, were elected to the key positions (Croucher, 1987, pp. 40–1). Unlike earlier movements, however, these were organisations of the unemployed, defining and pursuing their own interests.

The period from 1924 to 1927 saw an initial drastic decline in the activities of the NUW(C)M. Membership, for example, fell from a probable peak of 100 000 in 1922–3 to 10 000 in 1925–6 which is partly related to the decline in unemployment, but there was by no means a tenfold decline in unemployment over that period. Further, Croucher suggests that the more general economic optimism created by the fall in unemployment meant people were putting more effort into finding work rather than participating in protest. There were also the genuine increases in benefit obtained by the NUW(C)M in the early 1920s, which to some degree must have undermined incentives for collective action. Beyond these factors was the election of the Labour government in 1924, which, when elected, was met with a wave of optimism amongst many of the unemployed (ibid., p. 67). The Labour government subsequently fell amidst the scandal of the Zinoviev letter (Klugman, 1969, pp. 369–72). Finally, several leaders of the NUW(C)M were leaving the movement or had their time taken up elsewhere. Hannington, for example, spent several months in Moscow in 1924, in 1925 he spent a year in gaol (Hannington, 1977, p. 137), and his work for the Minority Movement generated complaints at the 1926 conference of the NUW(C)M (Croucher, 1987, p. 76). The initial decline, then, was brought about by a range of independent but mutually reinforcing factors.

The plateau period from 1928 to 1935 also coincides with a rise in unemployment, but, like earlier changes in the activities of the NUW(C)M, cannot be simply read off from the changing levels of unemployment, since the peak of activity was in 1934–5 when unemployment had been falling for some time (see Figure 4.2 above). The basis of the movement, furthermore, shifted from London to Scotland and Wales. Now this is not simply a consequence of the regional variations in unemployment, although they are obviously an important part of the explanation, since some areas with very high unemployment in this period, such as Lancashire, were comparatively barren areas for the NUW(C)M (Walton, 1987). The victimisation of Communists in mining areas after the general strike is an important factor explaining the resurgence in activity, and is epitomised by the 1927 march of 300 unemployed miners from South Wales (Croucher, 1987, pp. 87–90; Kingsford, 1982). Further, the more general rise in unemployment after the 1929 crash and the subsequent changes in benefit, such as the 10 per cent cuts of 1931, gave the NUW(C)M more issues to take up (Croucher, 1987, pp. 119–21).

After 1935, however, the movement went into terminal decline, unemployment was not only falling but was largely eradicated by the Second World War.[4] The NUW(C)M now concentrated principally on individual casework regarding unemployment benefits and on 'stunts' to attract attention to the unemployed. Most historians account for this in terms of the fall in unemployment and the coming of the Second World War. Moreover, some point to the importance of the Spanish Civil War, where several key NUW(C)M activists lost their lives, and many more were involved in the aid for Spain movements (Croucher, 1987; Francis, 1984; Kingsford, 1982, p. 225). Also of importance was the changing form through which the state delivered unemployment benefits. Since the formation of the Unemployment Assistance Board in 1935, there had been no effective way of influencing the levels of benefit for whole groups of people at the local level through collective action. In this area the NUW(C)M was left only with casework for individuals.

4.5 PROTEST AND THE CHANGING FORMS OF UNEMPLOYMENT RELIEF: 1918–39

The unemployment relief system changed many times during the inter-war period, with no less than twenty Acts of Parliament on unemployment insurance alone during the 1920s (Deacon, 1977, p. 15). In terms of the ideal type of the periodisation of forms of unemployment relief outlined in Chapter 3, four sets of issues require further discussion: the changing character of the franchise and central/local dimensions of democracy; the changing form of decision-making; changes in the character of intervention; and changes in the extent of insurance as distinct from non-insured benefits. The inter-war period has characteristics of two of the periods I identified in Chapter 3. Until 1930–5 there was some local democratic control through an extensive franchise, with decision-making by directly elected representatives monitored by some central bureaucratic control. Intervention in the form of outdoor relief cash benefits became almost universal after the early 1920s, and the insurance scheme was extended to more occupational groups, albeit with more centralised bureaucratic control. After the abolition of the Boards of Guardians in 1929 and the creation of the Unemployment Assistance Board in 1934–5, locally elected representatives had no say in unemployment relief, and decision-making became overwhelmingly bureaucratic and subject to more detailed legal criteria. Although the detailed institutional forms have since changed, the generic form of this kind of administration of relief remains today. I shall discuss the impact of these changes on the structuring of social protest by the unemployed. This aspect of these changes has received little or no attention by historians who have concentrated on the explanation of the institutional changes (for example Briggs and Deacon, 1973; Deacon, 1977; Miller, 1974, 1979).

Extensions of the Franchise

Prior to 1914, there had already been criticisms of Boards of Guardians who were willing to operate a more liberal regime in poor relief towards the unemployed, and this was seen to emanate from the extension of the franchise. This came both from the Royal Commission on the Poor Laws and from Beveridge.

> Under the present method of direct election...there is no security that the Guardians elected will be those who are most suited to the position. The work is tending more and more to fall into the hands of persons who...direct their administration more towards the attainment of popularity than towards the

solution of the real problems of pauperism. We shall recommend that in future the members of the Local Authority shall be largely nominated from amongst men and women of experience, wisdom, and unselfish devotion to the public good. (Majority Report of the Royal Commission on the Poor Laws, Vol. 1, p. 145, quoted in Novak, 1987, p. 104)

Many of the 'undeserving' unemployed, undeserving that is of anything better than a rigorous Poor Law, are voters, to whom it would be ruinous policy to allow electoral control over any public relief agency by which they hoped to benefit. (Beveridge, cited in Novak, 1987, p. 137)

The franchise for the elections to the Guardians prior to 1918 was determined by the 1888 and 1894 Local Government Acts. The franchise consisted of all parliamentary electors as well as those eligible for local elections, but without the parliamentary franchise, such as some women. In 1918 paupers were allowed to vote, because it was thought that they would be constituted mainly of the 'deserving poor' such as widows and the elderly. Consequently, after the 1918 Act, the number of people eligible to vote in the Guardians' election increased from just over 8.3 million in 1915 to over 21.3 million in 1918 (Deacon and Briggs, 1973, p. 358). Although in some wards paupers might constitute up to 60 per cent of the electorate, this was not the sole reason for the transformation of the Guardians that followed, since the Labour Party was now better funded and organised than ever before to contest these elections on the issue of the levels and forms of relief (ibid., pp. 359–62). This resulted in a situation where:

persons on relief were able to participate directly in the selection of those who heard their cases for relief and decided how much they should receive. Moreover, it was still usual for Guardians to hear cases arising from their own wards, despite the attempt of the Local Government Board to stamp out the practice before 1914. Since many of the wards covered a small area the result was a quite unique degree of community involvement in social security administration. (ibid., pp. 347–8)

Subsequently, both the levels of pauperism and expenditure mushroomed, with an increase in the number of paupers from

450 000 in November 1918 to 1 519 829 in November 1921. This was largely due to the growth in unemployment generally. However, levels of pauperism varied between areas, not so much by levels of unemployment as by levels of relief, and whether or not task work was required (Briggs and Deacon, 1973, p. 45). Where the Guardians were not inclined to raise levels of relief they were put under direct pressure by the emergent NUW(C)M. This was in part an imitation of the tactics of the SDF in the 1900s,[5] but it was also encouraged in the press by Lansbury, the leader of the Poplar Guardians, who were themselves subject to pressure from the local NUW(C)M (Hannington, 1977, pp. 53–4). Briggs and Deacon describe one such example of the pressure that was placed on the reticent Bristol Guardians:

> The gates of St. Peter's Hospital, the office of the Guardians, was stormed (sic): the police were pelted with stones and wood paving blocks and struck with the banner poles of the demonstrators, who carried red flags. The police made a baton charge but the crowd, escaping through Bridge Street, broke most of the shop windows and used the road repairing material as ammunition. (Briggs and Deacon, 1973, p. 46)

The usual pattern was to compare the local levels of relief with those elsewhere (invariably somewhere could be found with higher levels of relief), and then organise public meetings and a committee to go to the Guardians with demands for higher relief and no task work. If no concessions were forthcoming the crowd outside was apt to react violently. Indoor relief was unrealistic, because in most places the workhouses were too small to take in the large numbers of unemployed.[6]

In the context of 'Poplarism', where socialist Boards of Guardians exploited the system to liberalise relief, and the concessions achieved from less sympathetic Boards of Guardians by the early protests of the NUW(C)M, central government discussed the reform of the Guardians continually throughout the 1920s (Deacon and Briggs, 1973; Deacon, 1977). The Board of Guardians (Default) Act empowered the Minister of Health to appoint commissioners to replace recalcitrant Boards of Guardians. Furthermore, the Audit (Local Authorities Act) enabled Guardians to be disqualified for five years for illegal expenditure (Briggs and

Deacon, 1973, p. 47). In relation to the franchise, its withdrawal from paupers was considered seriously in 1927 and 1928, when unemployment and especially protest were at a low ebb. However, in both instances the government drew back from disenfranchising paupers due to the large number of ex-servicemen amongst them. This was deemed to be politically unacceptable when the franchise was being extended to even more women (Deacon and Briggs, 1973, pp. 355–6).

The drastic measure of disenfranchisement was avoided by the even more fundamental reform of abolishing the Guardians and replacing them with Public Assistance Committees (PACs), operated by county councils, in 1929. This was preferred because it avoided the politically messy alternative of selective disenfranchisement. It was thought by central government that the PACs with their geographically wider franchise (there were only 146 PACs compared to 635 Boards of Guardians) would be much less susceptible to left-wing 'takeovers' (Briggs and Deacon, 1973; Deacon and Briggs, 1973).

Unemployment Insurance

The unemployment insurance scheme ran under a different institutional form. Under the 1911 Insurance Act central government had control over levels of benefit in the form of the Ministry of Labour. Local committees of representatives of employers and employees and an independent chair, *all appointed by the Ministry*, adjudicated claims for unemployment insurance benefit. As Harris has shown (1984, pp. 289–330), this was a kind of state orchestrated corporatism but in a decentralised form. Furthermore, Mann (1984, 1986) has shown that it also incorporated those sections of the working class who had developed mutualism as a response to the Poor Law in an earlier period.

Central government policy on unemployment insurance has been aptly described as a combination of coercion and concession during the 1920s (Deacon, 1977). This does not imply that central government had some clear overarching strategy – nothing could be further from the truth. If anything the government's response was largely in terms of crisis management (Offe, 1984). The concession aspect is exemplified by the extension of insurance to employees earning less than £250 a year (excluding higher level white collar workers and agricultural workers) in 1920; the extension of the period covered by benefit from fifteen to forty-seven weeks in 1921 (effectively undermining the actuarial basis of the scheme); the introduction of dependants' allowances in 1921; benefit was eventually allowed to be drawn continuously for an indefinite period after 1922; and the rates of benefit were increased in 1924, 1928 and 1930 (Thane, 1982, pp. 172–3). Between 1920 and 1930 the state's subsidy of the unemployment fund increased from 3.1 million to 37 million, or from 3.4 per cent of social services expenditure to 37 per cent (Deacon, 1977, pp. 9–10). The cumulative effect of all these changes on the real value of benefits for a family of four was an increase of 240 per cent between 1920 and 1931 (Thane, 1982, p. 173). The latter in particular must have had a dulling effect on the ability of the NUW(C)M to mobilise large numbers of people as the decade progressed. The reason for all this would appear to be the desire of the central government to subdue protest in the early 1920s, which exemplifies the crisis management character of the responses. As Deacon summarises:

the unemployment insurance system was extended in the early 1920s because Ministers were convinced that such a concession was essential if a serious threat to political stability was to be avoided. Several reasons for this belief can be located, most obviously the extent and violence of the unrest and the manner in which information upon it was transmitted to the Cabinet. The perceptions of Ministers of events in Continental Europe after the Armistice, however, were also important. (Deacon, 1977, pp. 10–11)

The central aim of government policy remained the lowering of public expenditure on relief, and this is where the coercive aspects of unemployment insurance policy come to the fore. To this end, the governments of the early 1920s introduced two particularly coercive measures in the unemployment insurance legislation, which were to be a major focus for later social protest – the not genuinely seeking work (NGSW) clause and the means test. The NGSW clause was introduced in April 1922 and in particular excluded otherwise eligible married women from insurance benefits (Thane, 1982, p. 174). For five years, until 1927, the NGSW clause was ignored in Parliament because the parliamentary Labour Party thought that 'scroungers' should be chased up. The NUW(C)M largely ignored it because they thought it only applied to married women (Deacon, 1977, pp. 20–1). Their activities amongst women were non-existent after the early 1920s (Croucher, 1987), and their view is consistent with the early domination of the NUW(C)M by engineering shop stewards. The engineers were notorious for their exclusionary practices towards women in employment (Summerfield, 1984; Walby, 1986). Further, Bruley (1980, pp. 220–1) cites oral evidence of Hannington and other engineering workers leading the NUW(C)M at the time of having attitudes typical of skilled engineers towards women. Indeed, the test did affect married women in particular, but others were affected too, and this became increasingly visible as central government instructed the local committees to make more use of the clause later in the 1920s (Deacon, 1977, pp. 20–4; Thane, 1982, p. 174).

The other major coercive measure was the family means test introduced in 1922. Again, this was to be increasingly used by the authorities as the decade progressed, but, unlike the NGSW clause, it was widely opposed as soon as it came into effect (Deacon, 1977, p. 16). The means test was briefly removed by the 1924 Labour government, only to be replaced by the following Conservative administration (Thane, 1982, p. 175). Together these two measures increasingly accounted for the disqualification from benefit of claimants, increasing from 5 per cent of claims in 1922 to 20 per cent by the end of 1927, and in some places over 30 per cent of claims were refused (Deacon, 1977, p. 10; Thane, 1982, p. 174).

The Structuring of Protest

These changes in the form of the state's unemployment relief had immediate consequences for protest by the NUW(C)M. First, the increases in the real value of insurance benefits for many meant that collective action was more difficult to organise, since many short-term demands had been met. Further, the issues in relation to insurance benefits were not so much concerned with collective material interest in the levels of benefit, but increasingly with *individual* grievances against its coercive features. These might well come from groups, such as married women, which the leaders of the NUW(C)M were not positively inclined to help at this stage. Secondly, the growing central control over the Boards of Guardians meant that the NUW(C)M would be less able to influence these. In short, the 'successes' of the NUW(C)M in the early 1920s were beginning to undermine the conditions for its own collective action to obtain further successes.

At the end of the 1920s and the beginning of the 1930s unemployment again began to rise, but further short-term changes in the form of state unemployment relief also produced more issues for the NUW(C)M to mobilise around, again with mixed 'success'.

The concessions of the early 1920s began to be eroded in 1927, when those who had been unemployed for so long as to have exhausted their entitlement to insurance benefit, were placed on a new 'transitional benefit'. Abolition of the NGSW clause in 1930 lead to an increase in married women's claims, and this was dealt with under the more specifically discriminatory Anomalies Act of 1931 (Deacon, 1977, p. 27). But the 'big bang' of unemployment relief came with the cuts of the new National government in September 1931. These involved an increase in contributions to the insurance fund with a 10 per cent cut in benefit. But crucial for the later successful mobilisation of the unemployed, those on transitional benefit were subject to a family means test, and came under the jurisdiction of the *locally accountable PACs, and also involved a significant loss of rights under the insurance scheme* (Croucher, 1987, pp. 119–20). However, Croucher fails to see the significance of this move. Overnight 400 000 people on transitional benefit were placed in a position where they could influence directly, through local elections, those who could be on the committees that would assess their benefits. Most writers on this change seem to have overlooked this partial reversion to the conditions of the early 1920s, and the new opportunities it provided for protest. It was not just the rise in unemployment that mattered, but also the restructuring by the state of the conditions for collective action.

Consequently, 1931 and 1932 saw a resurgence of local activity geared towards pressurising local PACs not to implement a stringent means test and to pay higher levels of benefit. In places such as Manchester and Birkenhead where there was some degree of organisation, but unsympathetic local PAC's 'riots' broke out (Croucher, 1987, pp. 121–36; Kelly, 1987). In the case of Birkenhead, the local PAC increased the allowance for a married couple from 22s to 28s 9d, an increase of over 30 per cent (Hannington,

1940, p. 59). However, the capacity of local PACs to pay above the official scales was limited by the fact that the rates bore the burden of the surplus, and local PACs in the distressed areas could not afford this, just as they could not afford many other welfare innovations of the 1930s (Webster, 1985). It seems clear that for local PACs to pay the maximum scale, or to go above it, local organisation and protest by the unemployed were necessary, sympathetic councillors and perhaps the electoral instability of the local council as well (Miller, 1974, p. 170). Sometimes the protesters and the councillors were one and the same, as in the case of Lewis Jones who was an NUW(C)M activist in the Rhondda. Their activities were monitored by central government:

> the tendency of of the Relief Sub-Committees in the Area was to grant the *maxima of the scale* ... This tendency was accounted for in part by Communistic activity in the Area and particularly by the activity of Mr. Lewis Jones a Communist who has recently been elected a member of the County Council for the Tonypandy division. Mr. Jones has set himself out to educate his constituents as to their rights to Public Assistance. This he does in various ways. He has for example a motor van with a loudspeaker by means of which he broadcasts to all in doubt as to their rights and invites all with a grievance to report their cases to local communist agents whose names and addresses are given; the agents pass on the particulars to Mr. Jones who then gives advice. He also holds crowded meetings every Sunday night in the Judges Hall, Tonypandy at which he makes such statements as that there are hundreds of people in the Area not receiving the assistance to which they are entitled and advises them how this may be rectified. (Asserted Laxity in the Operation of Public Assistance and a Description of the Activities of Mr. Lewis Jones. PRO. MH. 79/312. Quoted in Webster, 1985, pp. 229–30)

Again, this demonstrates the importance of there being locally elected representatives who had some control over the levels of benefit which provided a *realisable collective goal for local protest*. As in the 1920s, central government was concerned about these local deviations from what they considered appropriate levels of relief. Central government's 'final solution' to the problem of local autonomy, and, indirectly, protest by the unemployed, was the creation of the Unemployment Assistance Board (UAB) in 1934 (Briggs and Deacon, 1973; Miller, 1974, 1979).

The UAB was designed by the Cabinet of the National government during 1932–3 in the context of conflict between the Ministry of Labour and the Ministry of Health over the details. Some accounts stress the role of this high-level conflict in determining the details of the new UAB (Miller, 1974). Whatever the details of these debates the basic aims of this major reorganisation were eventually achieved. The aims were severalfold. The most immediately provocative aspect, which was the cause of much of the subsequent protest, was nationalisation of benefit scales which meant increases for some, but decreases for the majority.

The determination of levels of benefit and the general administration of the scheme were also to be taken out of local democratic control and organised into a centralised bureaucracy. At the apex of this bureaucracy was to be the UAB itself, appointed by the Minister of Labour, and which decided on levels of relief and policy. Local offices were initially run by staff transferred from the PACs, and appeals were to be made to local appeals tribunals modelled on those of the insurance scheme, i.e. appointed by the Ministry.

Finally, there was a recategorisation of the unemployed. Prior to the UAB, there were basically three categories of unemployed claimant: those on insurance benefits; those who had exhausted their insurance benefits and had been moved on to transitional payments; and those who had never been eligible for insurance benefits and relied on poor relief. In September 1932, there were 1.3 million, 1 million and 170 000 in each of these categories respectively. Under the UAB those on transitional payments would be lumped with those on poor relief to form one category of unemployed ineligible for insurance benefits and subject to the same means test.

The debate on the UAB in Parliament, in December 1934, passed without major opposition. However, when the new scales of relief were announced in January 1935 there was widespread and apparently spontaneous protest. In the last week of January and first week of February public demonstrations developed in most large towns and cities in the north of England, Scotland and Wales. South Wales in particular saw extensive protests with 300 000 taking part over the weekend of 2–3 February. The government responded with a Standstill Act which proposed a change back to the old local PAC scales within a few weeks. On 6 February, a demonstration of 30 000 in Sheffield ended in a 'riot' in front of the town hall which resulted in an immediate restoration of the cuts (Miller, 1979; Moore, 1985). Miller for one describes the UAB crisis as resulting from a spontaneous protest of the distressed areas (Miller, pp. 346–7), but as Moore has shown in the case of Sheffield, and Francis in the case of South Wales, for example, several months of preparation by the local NUW(C)M and its local allies went into organising protests against the introduction of the new scales (Francis, 1984, pp. 68–71; Moore, 1985). Further, the protest occurred in those places where the scales had been 'bid up' through local political agitation, whereas they were a welcome improvement in other areas. 'The unemployed of Bakewell and district for example, welcomed the new scales for the simple reason that they had not had any organisation strong enough to force their PAC to give the kind of rates "enjoyed" by the Sheffield unemployed' (Moore, 1985, p. 6).

However, the basic administrative machinery remained in place and over the next three years the UAB scales were gradually introduced piecemeal, but with some modifications. More important perhaps were the consequences for collective action by the unemployed, for, now given the isolation of decision-making over levels of relief from direct political control through the local state, there was little or no collective gain to be had through local protest.

At the beginning of the 1920s, the conditions for collective action by the unemployed in terms of the form of state unemployment relief were at their peak, but by the end of the 1930s these conditions had been swept away in a series of centralising reforms. On all the dimensions I have specified the form of unemployment relief had been transformed.

In terms of electoral accountability, this had been extended dramatically by the 1918 Act which rationalised and extended the franchise. Local working classes and their organisations found that they had a level of access to the local Poor Law decision-making machinery greater than ever before. With the abolition of the Guardians in 1929 this was partially lost, but the local PACs were still capable of being influenced through some form of local representative democracy. With the creation of the UAB in 1935 the role of locally elected representatives in decision-making on the levels and conditions of unemployment relief came to an end. Bureaucratic forms of decision-making came to predominate, and later the corporate interest organisations of labour and capital, and the pluralist pressure groups of the poverty lobby operating at the centre (Cawson, 1982, p. 98; Whiteley and Winyard, 1987), came to have more influence than either locally organised protest groups or local councillors.

4.6 A MESSIANIC COMMUNISM? THE ORGANISATIONAL AND CULTURAL RESOURCES OF THE NUW(C)M

In my account of the forms of organisation and organisational resources in Chapter 3, I specified six dimensions to distinguish between monological and dialogical forms of organisation. I shall now consider the characteristics of the NUW(C)M along each of these dimensions. The NUW(C)M largely exhibited dialogical characteristics, especially in those localities where it was strongest. This was due largely to the role of engineering and later mining shop stewards, but the movement, especially at national level, developed several monological aspects subsequently in the 1930s.

Goals

It is the failure to make a distinction between short-term and long-term goals that leads some writers on the NUW(C)M (for example, Stevenson and Cook, 1977) to dismiss it as a failure. They assess it purely in terms of its long-term 'revolutionary' goals. In respect of these the NUW(C)M certainly was a 'revolutionary' organisation and usually stated this explicitly. At the sixth national congress it was declared: 'Capitalism is the system which inevitably creates unemployment, we declare therefore that our movement shall keep before itself the ultimate goal of working class power for the overthrow of capitalism and the establishment of the Workers Socialist Republic (NUW(C)M, 1929, p. 7).

However, this is only one of eight 'main objects', whilst the others included aims to change aspects of the unemployment relief system, and to involve the unemployed in the defence of their claims against the authorities. Beyond this there were several 'immediate demands' relating to increases in the levels of benefit and the removal of various administrative features of the relief system such as the NGSW clause. The NUW(C)M always made a distinction between the longer-term aims and the shorter-term goals of everyday campaigning (Hannington, 1935, pp. 4–5).

Forms of Action

The aims and demands in the conference reports of the NUW(C)M also give some insight into the forms of action the organisation engaged in. These involved local collective action for higher levels of relief, centrally coordinated hunger marches to London, and local and national casework on individual claims. The hunger marches are the best known forms of action, but I believe that they were not the most important for mobilising the unemployed and securing their commitment to the NUW(C)M, in terms of the everyday activities of the movement or of achieving any of its goals.

Commitment to the NUW(C)M flowed not from involvement in the hunger marches, but from three other major sources. First, from a wider commitment to socialist politics, secondly, from the stipulation that any individual receiving advice on benefits must first join the movement, and finally, from the collective benefits of pressure put on locally run forms of unemployment relief. Those chosen to go on the hunger marches were selected for their prior commitment to the movement (Kingsford, 1982, pp. 176–7). So the ability to organise a large march in the first place depended on the success of the local organisations. In achieving the goals of the movement the hunger marches had a limited role when compared to the success of local agitations for higher collective levels of relief: Only in the case of the modifications of the UAB regulations, in 1936, can Kingsford demonstrate any clear connection between a hunger march and a concession (ibid., 217).

The individual casework of the NUW(C)M was seen as being subordinate to the 'mass' collective actions and not its principle form of activity.

The chief task of the movement is the systematic planning and development of mass agitations against unemployment and the conditions of the unemployed. The defence of claims before the Court of Referees, Labour Exchange and Public Assistance

Committee is a very necessary part of the practical everyday work of our movement and must be developed as such, but it must never be regarded as the main work of the Movement. It is valuable only in so far as it gives protection to our members against unjust administration of the Unemployment Insurance and Poor Law Authorities and thereby draws the mass of the unemployed closer to our movement for participation in our mass agitations. (Resolution on defence of claims, Report of the Seventh National conference of the NUWM, 1931, p. 11)

Local collective action was the principal form of agitation of the movement, with other activities either dependent on that form of action or in support of it, but always subordinate to it.

Relations of Representation

Membership of the NUW(C)M was open to all unemployed workers who agreed with its aims. There were categories of associate membership for the employed, but any part of the organisation was limited to only one-third associate members. National conferences elected full-time officials, whilst a national administrative council of representatives from each district took major decisions between conferences (NUWCM, 1929, Report of Sixth National Conference, pp. 3–8). The basic unit of the movement, however, remained the local branch which was the focus of activity, and where the unemployed themselves ran the show. It was at this local level that a radical participatory democracy ruled, often ignoring the circulars of the central full-time officials as constant exhortations to branches indicated (Hayburn, 1970, p. 621; Croucher, 1987). In the localities where the NUW(C)M was strongest, this participatory democracy was part of the organisational culture of the labour movement. It was the fundamental assumption of all organised politics.

A democratic thread ran through the life of labouring communities and played no small part in their conviction that they possessed a popular legitimacy. Industrial activities, co-operative societies and other organisations were all constituted on the sovereignty of the membership . . . It was a pragmatic, and at times primitive, democracy that prevailed in the labour movement. The preference was for making decisions openly and collectively, at public meetings or in open air. Moves to take democracy out of the public arena were resisted as inimical to popular sovereignty. (Macintyre, 1980, p. 172)

This local popular democracy in the localities[7] where the NUW(C)M was strongest was at odds with the detailed bureaucracy laid down in the formal rules. Further, Croucher presents evidence of a growing resentment among branches against the 'rule of comrade Gestetner' – the endless circulars from the national office (Croucher, 1987, p. 104). This suggests a strong tendency to develop monological forms of organisation at the centre, whilst retaining dialogical aspects in the local branches. Overall, however, the emphasis was on locally organised collective action.

Orientations to Levels of the State

The movement saw itself as directing pressure on the issue of unemployment towards both the central and local state, acknowledging as one of its roles: 'To lead and direct the struggles of the unemployed against the central and local Government authorities on the principle of "Work or Full Maintenance at Trade Union Rates"' (NUWCM, 1929, Report of Sixth National Conference, p. 7).

At the same conference, a resolution was passed opposing the abolition of the Boards of Guardians, and outlining a strategy of gaining influence in the new PACs by building alliances with labour movement representatives (NUWCM, 1929, Report of Sixth National Conference, pp. 17–18). Furthermore, there were criticisms of the undemocratic character of the new UAB introduced in 1935 (Hannington, 1936, pp. 4–5). Before the advent of the UAB in the middle of the 1930s, the NUW(C)M had focused much of its collective action on the local state's unemployment relief institutions.

Sources of Finance

The vast part of the finance for the NUW(C)M came from its own membership (NUW(C)M Report of the Sixth National Conference, financial statements for 1926–9). This provided the organisation with a strong incentive for 'mass activity' amongst the unemployed, merely to reproduce itself financially. In contrast, centres for the unemployed in the 1980s are dependent on state funding or donations from trade unionists. However, the NUW(C)M faced perpetual financial problems (Croucher, 1987).

Cementing Discourse and Cultural Resources

One key feature of the organisational resources of the NUW(C)M is the local milieu in which it operated, and a detailed understanding of this is necessary to grasp fully the character of the cementing discourse of the organisation at the local level – both of the membership density of working-class organisations amongst the unemployed themselves, and in terms of the potential allies that would support the NUW(C)M in an area. From research carried out in the 1930s by the Pilgrim Trust (1968), it is possible to calculate estimates of organisational density amongst the unemployed in a small, but critical selection of localities. These are presented in table 4.1.

Table 4.1   *Membership of working-class organisations amongst the unemployed in selected localities, 1936 (percentages)*

Locality	Long-term Unemployed	None	Trade union	Working men's clubs	Orgns. per person
Rhondda	63	19.7	38.5	18.7	1.46
Liverpool	23	48.2	5.3	2.7	0.51
Blackburn	38	32.5	25.8	4.5	0.89
Leicester	11	47.6	11.9	5.9	0.57

SOURCE   Calculated from Pilgrim Trust, 1968, table II p. 13 and table LIX p. 274.

The data show that there is no clear relationship between unemployment and organisational density when comparing localities. Those places with the highest proportion of long-term unemployed (unemployed for over one year), Rhondda and Blackburn, have the lowest proportion of unemployed who are not members of working-class organisations. The highest densities of union membership among the unemployed are also found in the Rhondda and Blackburn, and the Rhondda has by far the highest level of membership of working-men's clubs. Membership of no organisation is highest in those localities with the lowest levels of long-term unemployment. The mean number of organisational membership per person presented in the last column of the table (this includes churches, trade unions, working-men's clubs, unemployed clubs, British Legion and 'other' organisations), shows that the Rhondda again comes top with 1.46 organisations per unemployed compared to, say, Liverpool with 0.51.

These data clearly contradict the conventional wisdom of the effects of unemployment on organisational membership. Jahoda (1982), for example, asserts that unemployment straightforwardly results in a decline in organisational membership. My claim here is that it depends crucially on the locality under consideration, since organisational and cultural resources vary markedly between localities. These variations are usually not taken into account by some writers.

In places such as the Rhondda, then, unemployed individuals clearly demonstrated a stronger attachment to their organisations than the unemployed in many other places. However, it is not just the attachment to organisations that matters, but what kind of cultural resources such organisations wield.

In those places where the NUW(C)M was most successful in organising the unemployed, the local political culture and the cementing discourse of the organisation can be characterised as a form of *messianic communism*. In these places and organisations, Communist Party members and their sympathisers took on a central political role. What characterised their political practices, and the fundamental assumptions underlying them, was *an unshakeable belief in the absolute correctness and righteousness of what they were doing*.

The tiny size of the Communist Party in South Wales, however, did not belie the commitment of the members who joined at this time. The prevailing hostile atmosphere, involving both police and coalowners, intensified *the almost messianic conviction of the party members in the rightness (even righteousness) of their cause.*

They bore their persecution in ways resembling latter day sects or even the early Christians. (Francis, 1984, p. 49)

There are a number of features of this situation and culture which deserve closer attention. First, this was a peculiarly 'modern' outlook, in the sense of having a 'rational', 'scientific' account of events and their actions as communists. They saw themselves not as defending a 'tradition' but rather the gains of working-class progression to the inevitable revolution. The Rhondda itself might be seen as the expression of 'modern' society, having been largely developed in the last quarter of the nineteenth century (Smith, 1980, pp. 170–1). Communists saw themselves at the cutting edge of all that was good and 'progressive' with a boundless optimism for a glowing future.

Communism was the way, the truth and the life. Like earlier belief systems, it put forward a complete scheme of social salvation. In place of fear and doubt – 'the defeatist philosophies of our time' – it offered glowing certainty; in place of evil, a state of shining grace – 'the end of war', 'the final and permanent solution to all the problems created by capitalism', 'limitless social and cultural advance'. It was a cause to which people dedicated their lives, 'a faith' . . . (Samuel, 1985, p. 37)

In South Wales, in the late 1930s, it was a cause for which many gave their lives in the Spanish Civil War. But it was not just a variant of a messianic movement, it had a whole infrastructure of training and education for those who were to liberate themselves through the application of its doctrines (Macintyre, 1986, pp. 66–90). The people who lived in these places had a strong sense of 'rights' which were opposed to those embodied in the institutions of authority with which they came into contact. 'A strong morality pervaded their conception of socialism and informed their conduct. Over and over again in their brushes against the legally-constituted authority we encounter the conviction that when the law was inconsistent with basic human rights, it should be disregarded' (Macintyre, 1980, p. 168).

These conceptions of popular rights, opposed to the central capitalist class state as they saw it, were inscribed in the local political organisations. Where the members of these organisations holding these beliefs were elected to local authorities, such as

Boards of Guardians and PACs, this popular morality was practised to some degree (ibid., pp. 168–73). Further, it was not just the belief of the few, since the politics of those few hegemonised and mobilised whole communities.

> Their influence stemmed from their ability to draw on the spirit of solidarity, the sense of concern that residents felt for each other, and the willingness to defend each other, and against external threat. So it was that the Vale of Leven unemployed could enjoy a measure of support over and above political loyalties... The Communists achieved influence as *they initiated and led the struggle in such a way that their policies were identified with the general interests of the community.* (ibid., p. 179;)

Working-class interests as defined by communists and their organisations became the interests of the 'community'. All local organisations identified with these interests in the organisation of hunger marches, aid for Spain and protests against the new UAB (Francis, 1984, pp. 61–83). These places had the largest and locally most active NUW(C)M branches in the country: 500 strong in Cowdenbeath, 500 in Lochgelly, and 1 300 in the Vale of Leven (Macintyre, 1980, pp. 70–100). A further consequence of this culture of class and 'community' solidarity, this sense of common collective interests, was that unemployment was much less likely to be seen as an individual concern and more a collective one. The Pilgrim Trust, for example, found little evidence of 'a social cleavage between employed and unemployed' in the Rhondda (Pilgrim Trust, 1968, p. 280). The Trust's investigators were at pains to emphasise the distinctive level of 'civilisation' and education amongst South Wales miners, in a quote which reveals as much about the investigators as the investigated. 'A casual conversation among unemployed South Wales miners may be on a point of politics or theology or logic – often indeed very imperfectly understood – where in the Midlands or London it would be a series of monosyllables answered with a series of grunts' (ibid., pp. 276–7).

Against the claims for the distinctiveness of these admittedly 'exotic' localities, it might be complained that many working-class 'communities' expressed similar characteristics of oppositional culture. However, what most characterises the 'Little Moscows' was not simply opposition, but the attempt to construct a different way of life according to the 'rationality' of the oppositional culture of substantive natural rights. As Macintyre (1980, p. 168) summarised their outlook: 'when the law was inconsistent with basic human rights, it should be disregarded.' This relates to the sixth dimension of dialogical organisations. The NUW(C)M and wider working-class politics in these were 'cemented' by a discourse of substantive natural rights, which asserted the primacy of people's needs over the strictures of the formal law. This strong belief in the right to work and equitable distribution of resources is exemplified in the NUW(C)M slogan, 'work or full maintenance'.

I argued that a particular conjuncture of cultural resources favours the political mobilisation of the unemployed. This conjuncture, normally within a particular locality, of a transformative class consciousness and critical transformative beliefs which hegemonise the local community, I contrasted with the more widespread situation of fatalistic class consciousness, associated with critical but fatalistic beliefs and various kinds of ideologies which hegemonise the community. The question of what explains the emergence of the former conjuncture I answered as being the outcome of earlier working-class struggles. However, there are other possible explanations which I shall briefly criticise here, in order to defend my preferred explanation in terms of the consequences and effects of social struggles.

The first of these are what might be termed *labour process explanations*, where the extent and form of workers' control over the labour process broadly determines the political character of their organisations. One version of this is Krieger's analysis of the Nottinghamshire and Durham coalfields. In Nottinghamshire, labour was organised through a method of subcontract labour known as the 'butty' system, where a select group of miners contracted others to perform the work generating competitive and individualistic conditions. In Durham, a form of collective work group control prevailed, and according to Krieger the former leads to right-wing unionism whilst the latter leads to left-wing unionism (Krieger, 1984). The problem here is that others have used the character of work control in Durham to explain political quiescence in that region (Daunton, 1981). Further, the 'butty' system also prevailed in the Kent coalfield, where it was overcome by trade union action (Pitt, 1979, pp. 71–2). Kent subsequently became one of the more 'militant' coalfields. Given this confusion, and the existence of counter examples, labour process explanations of local working-class politics seem to be seriously deficient.

Secondly, local working-class radicalism might be explicable in terms of *proletarian homogeneity*. This is very much of the essence of Lockwood's (1975) traditional proletarian model. The basic idea is of a high geographical density of proletarians combined with occupational uniformity generating a class conscious proletarian outlook. All the emphasis here is on social structure, with little attention to the role of organised collective action (Marshall, 1988, pp. 105–7). Further, deviant cases abound, where what would appear to be workers with Lockwood's deferential image of society have been found in social structural conditions otherwise suitable for the development of proletarian radicalism (Martin and Fryer, 1973; Piepe *et al.*, 1969; Mark-Lawson and Warde, 1987; Waller, 1983).

Thirdly, there are explanations in terms of *local cultural traditions*. Sunley (1986), for example, in his discussion of the 1984–5 miners' strike, emphasises the importance of inter-generationally transmitted cultural traditions in explaining the regional variations in the response to the strike amongst miners. But this begs the question how the 'tradition' originated, never mind how it is transmitted. Further, the detailed content of the tradition is left rather vague. The notion of tradition, implying an attention to history, is remarkably ahistorical, glossing over significant changes over time. In South Wales, for instance, the transition from the least densely unionised region to an almost mythical radicalism is lost (Rees, 1986). Such radical localities are the product of struggles for hegemony over the local community.

Localities with apparently similar economic and social structures seem to have developed, at various times, divergent political characteristics. Precisely the same point applies to comparisons between countries (Gallie, 1983, p. 253). Whilst some degree of structural determination and working-class homogeneity is clearly necessary as an explanation of local working-class radicalism, it is clearly far from sufficient.

It is possible to generate relatively abstract ideal types of cultural resources, as I have done. However, they are only useful in so far as they enable instructive and enlightening empirical comparisons to be made. For it is only at the concrete empirical level that the determination of local working-class radicalism can be established, that is, as the effect of social struggles and organisations in contention (Gallie, 1983; Lash, 1984; Marshall, 1988; Rees, 1986).

I have attempted to demonstrate the importance of organisational and cultural resources for the effective, political mobilisation of the unemployed in this section by examining in some detail the characteristics of those places where the NUW(C)M was strongest. This strength, whether measured in terms of membership, participation in hunger marches or influence over local unemployment relief, I have shown to be based on the characteristic political cultures and organisational resources of these localities. Other places with similar industrial and occupational structures and levels of unemployment did not develop strong local branches of the NUW(C)M. The oppositional culture and organisations did not just emerge out of the underlying economic relations, but were the product of political struggles between groups for the hegemony of the local community. In other apparently equally proletarian places with high levels of unemployment at the same time, the NUW(C)M failed to take root.

4.7 GENDER POLITICS IN THE NUW(C)M

Many of the mainstream discussions of the NUW(C)M, both autobiographical and scholarly accounts (for example Hannington, 1977; Stevenson and Cook, 1977), fail to deal with the gender politics of the organisation. Women's involvement in the NUW(C)M differed from men's in significant ways that should be taken into account when analysing the movement. The NUW(C)M was basically a men's movement, since not only was it numerically dominated by men but often pursued men's interests whilst ignoring women's, as in the example of the NGSW clause. Further, some quite misleading claims have been made about women's involvement in the NUW(C)M. Young (1985, p. 149) for example, claims that women were much more involved in Scotland than in England or Wales. I shall show below that, on the contrary, unemployed women from the Yorkshire textile areas were the core group of women who were most active in the NUW(C)M.

There were two ways in which women were involved in the NUW(C)M which can be examined as two modes of gender politics. First, they were involved in a *marginalised but incorporated* fashion. This was where women were active in the support of their unemployed men, usually their male relatives, or did not see themselves as having any distinctive role in the movement but remained active within it. Secondly, there were the autonomous women's sections of the NUW(C)M which developed after 1929, which can be characterised as a form of *incorporated autonomy*. These sections organised unemployed women specifically in terms of what were seen as unemployed women's interests. However, they were subordinate to the wider organisation's aims and activities.

Women's involvement in the NUW(C)M falls into two phases, in the early 1920s and then in the 1930s. The men who ran the organisation usually ignored women's unemployment, and it was only when women within the organisation pushed women's issues that anything was done.

The early involvement of women in the NUW(C)M was concentrated in London, and the key activists were often former suffragettes who had gone on to join the Communist Party (Bruley, 1980, pp. 65–71). Much of their involvement was against the wishes of the ex-servicemen who felt that women had taken men's jobs (Croucher, 1987, p. 16). More generally there were organisational problems concerning whether or not women should have an autonomous organisation within the NUW(C)M, and there were complaints from women activists that the men's committees tended to ignore women's issues. As Lily Webb argued in 1922:

> If we find that we cannot develop in any way whilst merged into the men's committee it will be necessary to remain affiliated *but* to also have our separate meetings, when we could develop a psychology which would be beneficial to the movement. Men take so long over *their own* committee work that anything peculiar to women is left over. Therefore it is necessary that while assisting the men directly, we launch out on branches of activity where opportunity offers. (Webb quoted in Rowbotham, 1977, p. 135)

However, many of the early women activists left both the Communist Party and the NUW(C)M in the early 1920s, and in the case of Sylvia Pankhurst unsuccessfully attempted to set up an alternative unemployed organisation (Croucher, 1987, p. 33).

The autonomous women's sections emerged as a result of an initiative from women who were active in the NUW(C)M, but who, unlike many activists, were not in the Communist Party. The resolution to set up women's sections with limited administrative autonomy from the main branches came from Mrs Youle of Sheffield. This explicitly recognised the distinctive position women had in relation to the state's unemployment relief institutions.

> This conference, appreciating the special persecution meted out to unemployed women by Labour Exchange officials; due to the present organisational defencelessness of women claimants and recognising the important part that women play in industry under present day conditions, pledges itself, wherever possible, to develop women's sections of the NUWCM in every locality. (Resolution on organisation of women, Report of sixth national conference of NUWCM, 1929, p. 22)

By the 1931 conference, several women's sections were functioning in the north of England and sent delegates to the seventh national congress. Table 4.2 below presents details.

Table 4.2 *Delegates from women's sections to NUWM Seventh National Congress, 1931*

Locality	Number of delegates
Leeds	3
Barnsley	2
Wombwell	2
Hucknall	1
Bradford	4
Sheffield	1

SOURCE   NUWM Report of seventh national conference, 1931.

The women's sections were concentrated in the textile areas of West Yorkshire, and Table 4.2 shows this both in terms of the Yorkshire localities represented and the size and level of activity indicated by the number of delegates. There were also active women's sections in the textile areas of Lancashire, as witnessed by the women's hunger marches that started from there in the 1930s (Kingsford, 1982, pp. 142–4). However, it seems to be clear from the data in Table 4.2, and the numbers of women in hunger marches from different localities, that Bradford and Leeds were the centres of the semi-autonomous women's sections. Why should this be so?

At one level women's participation in the labour market was an important factor. Women textile workers in particular refused to accept alternative employment in domestic service which the employment exchanges were attempting to enforce, alongside the Anomalies Act. They thus had a different relationship to the state from women who were not in the labour market. However, large parts of Lancashire had high levels of women's unemployment in the textile sector, but the women's sections here were by no means as successful as in Yorkshire. There are a number of factors which help to explain this.

First, Bradford in particular had a 'tradition' of women's involvement in 'welfare state' politics concerning the issues of school meals and maternity schemes (Brunt and Rowan, 1982, p. 63). The same could also be said of places in Lancashire, where women had been active in welfare politics and the suffragette movement (Mark-Lawson *et al.*, 1985; Liddington and Norris, 1978). What seems to be the crucial difference is the impact of the Communist Party's unsuccessful attempt to intervene in the woollen textile workers' strike of 1930. As part of the 'class against class' strategy of setting up an 'alternative TUC' it was disastrous (Martin, 1969, pp. 142–9). Nevertheless, it did result in an increase of the CPGB's membership in Bradford from sixty-six to 300, half of whom soon left (Branson, 1985, p. 84). The 'fall out' from this dispute ultimately favoured the NUW(C)M which recruited fifty-eight women in Bradford, in two weeks, at the end of 1930 (Bruley, 1980, p. 222). In West Yorkshire, then, women were active in the NUW(C)M in their own interests in relation to the labour market and the state's unemployment relief system. They were incorporated into the movement, but had their own semi-autonomous sections and distinctive programme of demands which they decided on themselves.

A major problem facing the organisation of women into the NUW(C)M elsewhere was the dominance of the organisation by men. National conference resolutions in the 1930s noted the reluctance of many branches to do any work specifically amongst unemployed women (NUWM, 1931, p. 16; NUWM, 1934, p. 4), and criticised local branches for treating some women's sections as little more than catering organisations (Bruley, 1980, p. 246). Hayburn (1970, pp. 619–21) notes that the movement failed to organise women to the extent that was achieved amongst men, especially in South-East Lancashire where men failed to take the women's sections seriously. In South-East Lancashire, the NUW(C)M was dominated by the notoriously patriarchal engineers (ibid., pp. 452–4). In such places, where women were active, they tended to be part of the main branch rather than a semi-autonomous section, as in the engineering dominated central Manchester branch, for example (ibid., p. 445).

This marginalised incorporation was also typical of women's involvement in the NUW(C)M in South Wales. Here, unlike Lancashire, whilst women may have been *organisationally* marginal, they were quite prominent in *public* demonstrations. Women, for example, were conspicuous in the 'riots' surrounding the introduction of the UAB in 1935 (Francis, 1984). Although a few women from South Wales went on one of the hunger marches, they made it clear they were marching as *wives of the unemployed* not for their own labour market interests (Bruley, 1980, pp. 247–8). They were marginal to the NUW(C)M in South Wales, as witnessed by the lack of women's sections, but incorporated to the extent that they participated in the interests of 'their men'. These interests, furthermore, were seen to be the interests of the whole 'community'.

4.8   CONCLUSION

In this chapter I have analysed the development and organisation of political movements of the unemployed between the 1830s and 1930s. Whilst the general level of unemployment in a very diffuse sense dictates the rise and fall of movements of the unemployed, more than this is required to account for how they take on a more permanent form and to explain where they occur. Protest does not rise and fall mechanically in relation to the level of unemployment nationally, nor does it necessarily occur in those places with the highest level of unemployment. Detailed attention to the character of the relationship between the unemployed and the state, and the organisational and cultural resources wielded by the unemployed at a local level is necessary to explain political protest by the unemployed.

At the most general level, the changing form of the state is centrally important. Unemployed movements need something against which to struggle and from which to wrest concessions. Unemployment relief has changed dramatically over the period discussed in this chapter. In the nineteenth century, the working class was largely excluded from the franchise, whilst relief was controlled through locally elected Boards of Guardians, or took the form of mutualist provision amongst the more regularly employed sections of the working class. The unemployed were all but absent from the political scene until the 1880s. Two things changed this situation. First, all the unemployed came under the state's provisions with the Liberal reforms of the 1900s when mutualist forms of relief were 'nationalised'. Secondly, with the progressive extensions of the franchise, the locally controlled forms of relief came under the influence of the unemployed themselves.

However, these conditions soon changed with the abolition of the Boards of Guardians, and a little later the formation of the UAB. This effectively nationalised all forms of unemployment relief and sealed them off from immediate popular democratic control. Political movements of the unemployed can only occur in anything more than the most marginal fashion when they can influence in some visible, direct and substantial way the levels and/ or forms of unemployment relief, through a combination of the franchise and collective action.

Beyond the changing relationship between the unemployed and the state, organisational and cultural resources are also necessary for the political organisation of the unemployed. A consideration of these factors helps us to understand not only the historical aspect of these movements, but also their geographical patterning and their forms of gender politics. Places with apparently similar economic and social structures and levels of unemployment responded differently. This can largely be accounted for in terms of the different local forms of political organisation and political culture.

5

Political Movements of the Unemployed in the 1980s

5.1 INTRODUCTION

There are a number of ways in which the situation in the 1980s differs from that of the 1920s and 1930s. Principal amongst these is the highly centralised character of the unemployment benefits system. In contrast to much of the inter-war period, decision-making over levels, forms and eligibility for benefits is carried out in centralised bureaucratic Ministries. Decisions by local offices are almost entirely circumscribed by detailed centrally determined criteria. Political influence over these issues works entirely through Parliament, national pressure groups or corporatist bodies. Locally, any political movements of the unemployed can only influence the levels of benefit for individuals *within* the legal criteria set down by central government. They cannot influence the levels and forms of relief for the unemployed of a whole locality as was the case to some extent in the past. The relationship between the unemployed and the state is much more *individualised* than in the past. Any attempts at the political organisation of the unemployed during the 1980s, then, take place in relation to a quite different state form.

The development of TUC centres for the unemployed has occurred against the background of the most rapid rise in unemployment since the 1930s. There have also been other political events which are of importance. It goes without saying that the governments of the day, and the general political situation, have not been exactly favourable to the organised labour movement. In addition, the urban 'riots' of the 1980s were widely attributed to unemployment (Rex, 1982; Benyon, 1984). However, they were not riots about unemployment as some have argued, although unemployment was one of the factors associated with

114

them. Racial and public order issues were what the 'riots' were principally concerned with, according to most authors who have examined them (Gilroy, 1987, pp. 236–45; Lea and Young, 1982; Reicher, 1984; Rodrigues, 1981; Scarman, 1986).

There were also two 'People's Marches for Jobs' in 1981 and 1983 concerned with the issue of unemployment. These were organised by local and regional labour movements, being initiated by the North-West Region of the TUC. Although involving the unemployed as marchers, they were not political organisations of the unemployed in any clear and unambiguous way. The 'organising' was not done by the unemployed themselves, but rather by a range of organisations wishing to express a broad concern about the level of unemployment and its consequences (Benn, Carter and Dromey, 1981). In several crucial ways, they were quite different from the 'hunger marches' of the 1920s and 1930s.

The People's Marches for Jobs were not organised by the unemployed themselves, unlike the NUW(C)M's 'hunger marches', and they had quite general and diffuse goals. The original 'hunger marches' usually had some clearly articulated goal often requiring government action on unemployment benefits, as well as more general features of government policy (Kingsford, 1982). In contrast, the People's Marches for Jobs were conceived in order to mobilise the widest range of political forces against the Conservative government on the issue of unemployment. They had no clear, definable goals over and above this.

> We wanted the March to be a vehicle for the intercourse, the exchange of ideas, because we haven't necessarily got the alternative. There are a lot of people in this world outside the trade unions, outside the Labour Party, who have got ideas and solutions. The idea of the March was to try to tie this together so that the March itself would bring forward some alternative based on a people's alternative. (Carter in Benn, Carter and Dromey, 1981, p. 7)

This vague almost utopian ideal for the marches to produce a new alternative from the bringing together of diverse social forces is what constituted its cementing discourse. The problem was this did not happen. No clearly definable 'people's alternatives' emerged from the marches.

5.2   THE TUC AND CENTRES FOR THE UNEMPLOYED

The first unemployed centre was set up by Newcastle's Trade Council in 1977 (Forrester and Ward, 1986). Controlled by a management committee of delegates from the Trade Council, it employed several full-time workers by 1980. This centre had since 1977 been actively involved in opposing redundancies on Tyneside, and, more controversially, it had also been attempting to set up 'unemployed workers' unions' (TUC, 1980, p. 384). The delegate to the 1980 TUC, who was reporting these events in his speech in favour of the motion that would lead to the TUC nationally supporting centres for the unemployed, also voiced concern that the local grass roots radical potential of such centres should not be stifled by national central TUC decisions.

> We have been doing it for three years. It has been put to us that the TUC has already made up its mind about the form of organisation that will be implemented. We ask the TUC not to reject unemployment centres as a form of organisation. By all means let us have TUC Regional Council sponsored centres. By all means let us have trade unions setting up unemployment branches. *But let us be flexible. Let us allow local areas to develop their own forms of organisation, which while controlled by the trade union Movement can respond to local demands.* (G. Craig, NUPE, in TUC 1980, p. 384; emphasis added)

At the very outset, then, there were tensions over the form of organisation of the unemployed that trade unions should engage in, and a fear on the part of local activists that central decisions taken by the TUC might smother local initiatives. Why did the TUC wish to take such a central role in organising the unemployed? At one level there is an explicit political and ideological desire to maintain some kind of 'working-class unity' in the face of the recession, rising unemployment and the decline in union membership. Clive Jenkins articulated this view most clearly.

> Why should we want to organise the non-employed? I start with a political point. The Government would like to drive a wedge between those who are in work and those who are not. They want to blame the unions for that problem. *We want to look after all those who would like to work. We must ensure that we*

establish a community of interest between all those who have to work for their livelihood or who want to do so. (TUC, 1980, p. 383; emphasis added)

Another theme of Jenkins' speech was that unions should be able to maintain their levels of membership through allowing unemployed members special membership rates. He noted the anomalies of some unions already practising this in contrast to others which did not. There were also fears of the initiative being taken by left-wing parties such as the Socialist Workers' Party, who had already organised 'right to work' marches to the TUC. Other speakers on the issue of unemployment also raised the spectre of fascist organisation of the unemployed if the trade union movement did not organise them (TUC, 1980, p. 482).

The initial outcome of the discussions at the 1980 TUC was the conference in November 1980, organised by the TUC to encourage the development of centres for the unemployed. The general council of the TUC pursued what it referred to as a 'two pronged strategy' in relation to the unemployed (TUC, 1981a, p. 48). The first aspect of this was to encourage unions to enable the unemployed to become members, and the second was to facilitate the development of 'services for the unemployed' through a national network of locally run TUC sponsored centres for the unemployed. The conference of November 1980 led to the nationwide development of unemployed centres during 1981 and 1982. The number of centres grew from only one (in Newcastle upon Tyne), prior to the 1980 TUC, to around 200 three years later. Since 1983 the number of centres has levelled off at around the 200 mark (*TUC Services for the Unemployed Bulletins and TUC Directory of TUC Centres for the Unemployed, 1981–1985*). This must be seen as a major *organisational* achievement.

Besides reaffirming the other aspect of the strategy to recruit the unemployed directly into trade unions, the November 1980 conference also developed guidelines for the running of local TUC sponsored centres for the unemployed. These centres were to be set up with the following goals in mind:

1. To advise, assist and involve the unemployed.
2. The TUC would provide the central coordination of the centres and their relationship with trade union organisations.

3.　The approach should be non-bureaucratic and as flexible as possible to avoid already existing trade union and TUC functions.
4.　The local centres should have secure and stable funding.
5.　There would be an aim for unions to work with rather than just for the unemployed (TUC, 1981b).

More practically, this involved suggestions that centres would provide unemployed people with advice and assistance on other facilities and services available to them, and advice about social security issues. Centres were also intended to function as a general point of contact for the unemployed with each other, providing contacts with other organisations and with trade unions, as well as sponsoring education classes. Finally, the centres were to encourage schemes for the unemployed under the auspices of the MSC's programmes, and to seek concessions for the unemployed in relation to public services such as transport and recreation (TUC, 1981a).

Publicly, the TUC appeared to present the view that there was a unified consensus about the role, organisation and funding of the centres at the conference of November 1980 (for example, TUC, 1981a, pp. 48–50). However, others have pointed to the clear divisions between those who wished to see the centres become a focus for organised opposition to government policies, and those who primarily saw them as advice, counselling, education and leisure centres (Barker *et al.*, 1984, p. 400). This basic division has also been found in relation to whether or not to take MSC funding, given its strings relating to political activity. As the MSC put it:

> The projects must not provide for or encourage: any action to be undertaken to intervene in any industrial dispute; the organisation or participation in marches or demonstrations of any kind, or the use of the project premises for these purposes; the community programme must not be used to restore public expenditure cuts. (MSC, 1983 quoted in *Community Action*, 1986, p. 11)

A further feature of the MSC's involvement was that the centres had to follow a particular organisational model, whereby they would be managed by a joint committee of local trade unionists (usually delegates from the local Trades Council), and local authority appointees. This was done explicitly to maximise the possibility of obtaining MSC funding after the TUC General Council had 'pressed' the MSC into funding the centres.[1]

> It was made clear that applications to the MSC would require strong representation of the trade union Movement and of the local authority concerned on the management committees of the centres, *on the basis of parity between the two*. The General Council emphasised that in cases where the trade union Movement was able to raise the level of finances necessary to set up an unemployed workers' centre *it would be up to the Movement to determine the range of activities undertaken from the centre, and the composition of the management committee*. (TUC, 1981, p. 49; emphasis added)

Subsequent TUC advisory documents on how to set up centres for the unemployed give a central role to the TUC Regional Councils in nominating the trade union representatives on management committees (although the representatives were usually drawn from the local Trades Councils). This occurred after certain local political problems, which I will return to below. Regional TUCs were also given the role of monitoring the activities of centres in relation to both finances and political activities (TUC, 1983b, p. 3).

> Should any trade union body seeking to establish a centre, or any management committee of an established centre, act outside TUC Guidelines in a way that could damage the interests of the unemployed or the trade union Movement, or could put at risk the public funding of centres, it would be for the TUC Regional Council concerned to inform the TUC and the appropriate local authority that TUC guidelines are not being followed. (ibid., p. 4)

The consequence of such a close relationship with the MSC, and the dependence on it for funding, was a peripheral role for unemployed people who actually use the centres to control them, at least on the basis of the formal guidelines of the TUC. The *possibility* of representatives of the unemployed sitting on management committees is only mentioned in TUC documents after priority has been given to appointees of the Regional TUCs, local authorities and local voluntary organisations (ibid., p. 3). It also meant a *centralisation* of authority, with the Regional TUCs in practice having to function as institutions of surveillance over the centres in their regions, to ensure that the guidelines were followed. MSC funding ensured that the effective control over the unemployed centres should lie with the management committees, composed principally of appointees of the local authority and the Regional TUC. The management committees were designed like a kind of local 'microcorporatism' with key corporate interest groups (local authorities and Regional TUCs) guaranteed a place, but with no guarantees of democratic participation and control by those who were supposed to benefit from the centres. The early TUC pronouncements were that the aim was to work *with* the unemployed, but in the event institutions were set up that provided services *for* the unemployed.

The picture that emerged was one of a tight 'interlocking' of access to financial resources with institutional forms, and the political functions and goals of the centres for the unemployed. If funding independent of the MSC can be found, then more democratic institutional forms could emerge with different political functions and goals – a movement *of* the unemployed rather than a service *for* them.

At subsequent TUCs the centres were largely seen as a success except that there remained major problems in financing them. However, speakers at the TUC seem to see this success largely in terms of providing services *for* the unemployed. The rationale appears to be 'charitable' rather than political with centres 'teaching' the unemployed about work and trade unions. It would seem from this that the centres were successfully fulfilling their 'non-political' functions as originally intended. The role of centres in exorcising the spectre of organised fascism is also emphasised.[2]

The centres have been successful in presenting a working life to the unemployed and teaching them what trade unionism is about. We must ensure that there is maximum involvement in the scheme. If we do not give the unemployed, especially those who are young, those in the ethnic minorities and unemployed women, the feeling that they are part of our society they will move. If they do not move towards the trade union Movement and the greater labour Movement, they will be on the streets with the National Front. They will not accept what has happened to them over the past two or three years. They will resist. Let us get out and recruit into the Movement all those who have equal rights in our society. (W. Deal, Fire Brigades Union, in TUC 1981, p. 443)

The financing of centres has remained a major problem, and the almost total failure of efforts by the TUC to raise money through national appeals was one of the reasons why the centres became dependent on the MSC, and then local authority funding. By 1982, there were around 200 MSC CEP funded workers employed in the centres for the unemployed (TUC, 1982, p. 50). The success in obtaining MSC funding contrasts with the failure of the National Appeals, so that by January 1982 only £750 had been allocated to each regional TUC and £500 to the Scottish TUC to fund the centres from the 1981 appeal (TUC, 1982, p. 50). The National Appeal was relaunched in November 1982 with the aim of raising £1 from each member (this would have raised approximately £10 million), and to expand local 'check off' schemes.[3] At the 1984 Congress the General Council reported rather disappointing results from their renewed appeals.

In December, the General Council again urged affiliated unions to renew their efforts among their members in support of the National Appeal for TUC centres for the unemployed. The response so far is still a long way from the target of at least £1 from every trade unionist. At the end of the financial year donations amounted to £52,000 and of this amount £47,500 had been distributed equally among the TUC Regional Councils, the Wales Trades Union Council and the Scottish TUC. (TUC, 1984, p. 65).[4]

In each region the TUC still funded a full-time coordinator of centres, so at any one time there would be eleven or twelve full-time union officials working on the schemes for the TUC.

Despite the high levels of input from full-time TUC officials and the annual appeals for more donations, most centres became, for a time, dependent on MSC funding with 60 per cent being funded by the MSC (*Community Action*, 1986, p. 11). However, there were important exceptions to this. One reason why some centres were not funded by the MSC was that there were limits set by central government on the total number of Community Programme posts that could be funded in any one region (TUC, 1984, p. 65). Furthermore, the MSC decided in 1983 not to fund any new centres, but merely to continue the funding of those it already supported as long as they remained within the guidelines (TUC, 1986, p. 66). Over time the centres became less dependent on MSC funding and more dependent on that from local authorities,[5] but the MSC still remained the most important single source of financial support (ibid.).[6]

Generally speaking, the TUC's centres for the unemployed have taken on a characteristically *monological* organisational form. Collective action by the unemployed themselves was clearly not a goal of the TUC in setting up its centres for the unemployed. The emphasis in the functions of centres was on advice and assistance to the unemployed, and on encouraging unions to work with the unemployed. Whilst some 'rank and file' speakers at the TUC saw a more radical potential in the centres, the TUC, by embracing the MSC's money and the consequent political restrictions, was more interested in providing 'services'. The resulting forms of action were characteristically bureaucratic. This resulted partly from the imposition by the TUC of its 'microcorporatist' model of organisation, and partly from the involvement of the MSC with the TUC's regional full-time officers 'policing' the activities of the centres. One of the principal reasons for the TUC being so keen on MSC funding was probably its historic role in the formation and management of the MSC itself.

> The Manpower Services Commission is the brainchild of the TUC, which explains a lot. Its creation is seen by the TUC establishment as a great historic achievement to be preserved at virtually any cost. For the Commission embodies the aspirations of the movement's top bureaucracy to a formal share in the central structure of the state and recognition as part of the establishment of officialdom. (Jackson, 1986, p. 26)

Whilst the central state in the form of the MSC provided the principal source of funding in the initial years, the local micro corporatist model of representation and the use of council owned property meant that the centres also dealt with local state institutions. This orientation towards the local state increased over time. Activists in the centres were able to obtain, relatively easily, concessions and discounts for the unemployed on council services such as transport and recreation. Furthermore, centres became increasingly dependent on local councils as they began to fund more workers in the centres, but without the political strings of the MSC in some cases. The cementing discourse of the new centres was almost entirely in terms of finding some way of integrating the unemployed into the already existing 'Movement' and its structures of organisation.

However, these generalisations need tempering since there have been significant local variations in the organisation and goals of centres. Many, if not the vast majority have conformed to the TUC/MSC model.

From quantitative analyses that I have presented elsewhere, it seems that the organisation of the unemployed at the regional level, as measured by the number and density of TUC centres for the unemployed, is not simply a function of the level of unemployment. Nor does it seem to be clearly related to the level of trade union organisation in terms of regional union densities (Bagguley, 1989, pp. 268–75). If local and regional labour movements are important in understanding the political organisation of the unemployed, that quantitative analysis implies that it must be something other than mere density of organisation. The crucial factors must lie in the distinctive politics of the respective regional and local labour movements.

The way in which I examined these processes was through a case study of one unemployed workers' centre. It might be objected that since the Brighton centre was not typical of TUC centres in general, it is not a valid case study. However, this would be to misunderstand fundamentally the methodological logic of case study analysis. As Mitchell (1983) has argued, the typicality does not matter. The validity of case study analysis lies in the way in which it throws light on the theoretical claims of the analyst. It is not just an illustration of a theory, but it enables explanations to be developed. The case study reported below was central to the development of the theoretical arguments of Chapter 3.

5.3   THE UNEMPLOYED WORKERS' CENTRE IN BRIGHTON

The Brighton centre for the unemployed deviates significantly from the normal organisational characteristics of most other centres in the south east. Whereas most centres in the region opened in 1982 or later, the Brighton centre opened relatively early, in June 1981; by 1985 Brighton Borough Council was 'hung' with no party having overall control, most other centres were in Conservative controlled local authorities; the Brighton centre did not, like most other centres in the region, have public funds for the employment of workers, the centre being run by volunteers from amongst the unemployed; and, finally, the Brighton example was one of only two in the south east giving effective control over the centre to its unemployed users (Bagguley, 1989, pp. 275–83). Why did Brighton develop its centre for the unemployed to such an 'exceptional' degree?

The political situation in Brighton in the early 1980s is crucial to understanding the events discussed below. Whilst not exactly 'dominating' the local labour movement, people associated with *Militant* were certainly influential within it, and were the most visible and vocal left-wing group within the local labour move-ment for a while. One indication of this influence is that at one stage a *Militant* supporter was a Labour Party parliamentary candidate for one of the Brighton constituencies. Further, it is widely claimed that *Militant* supporters 'dominated' the local Trades Council at this time. Again, it is perhaps more accurate to speak of them being the largest and perhaps most influential group on the TC. It was the case that Brighton Labour Party politics were generally to the 'left' of the party nationally (Interviews with key informants).

The initiative for setting up the centre came during the first half of 1981 from two full-time Workers' Education Association (WEA) tutors, in association with the Trades Council. This was largely a response to the rising levels of unemployment during the first two years of the 1979–83 Conservative government. Both locally and nationally in the TUC there were remarkably vague ideas that 'something should be done'. 'The centre was formed out of the WEA, which needed somewhere to teach, the Trades Council, and people from the Friends Centre were involved as well. It was a response to Thatcher and the recession and rising unemployment. A sort of feeling that we should do something' (WEA Tutor).

Throughout its existence the Trades Council and the WEA have provided the major organisational support and continuity for the centre. Furthermore, Brighton Borough Council, which at that time was controlled by the Conservative Party, under considerable lobbying and pressure provided relatively permanent premises for the centre. The initial work of setting it up, obtaining premises from the council, cleaning and furnishing the building and raising money, was carried out by a management committee. At that time it consisted of representatives from the Trades Council, the WEA and local 'community' organisations such as the Brighton Community Resource Centre (a group providing services and facilities to local community organisations), and the Friends Centre (a Quaker organisation). There were not and never have been during the period under study any representatives from Brighton Borough Council on this committee. Nevertheless, the cooperation of the council was necessary, since there was no other viable source of accommodation for a centre.

Important in obtaining the premises was gaining the 'sponsorship' of a councillor, and it was quite easy to obtain the cooperation of a leading Labour councillor. More problematic, however, was obtaining consent from the Conservative majority. Several interviewees pointed out the electoral weakness of the Conservatives in Brighton at the time, which caused a 'softening' of their policies on social and 'community' issues generally in the early 1980s. This was widely held to be a major reason why they were able to obtain the centre in the first place, and subsequently move into much better accommodation.

A Labour councillor and leader of the Labour group, X, was involved in helping us get it through the council and C the Conservative was helpful as well. He seemed genuinely concerned, but he also had electoral concerns because the Conservatives found themselves in a situation of electoral crisis, and this kind of softened them up. For example, in seventy-eight they wouldn't pay their 25 per cent contribution to Urban Aid, but now several Urban Aid schemes have been supported by them. (WEA tutor)

The factors that enabled the centre to be formed and use local authority premises were: (i) access to the organisational resources of the local labour movement (the WEA, the Trades Council and the Labour Party); (ii) the electoral crisis facing the Conservatives in Brighton; (iii) being able to exert influence over the Borough Council through prominent Labour Councillors. At this stage *there were no unemployed people or organisations of them involved.* When they do become involved, however, the political character and organisational form of the centre are challenged and transformed. Initially, it seemed that the centre was following the usual monological pattern of development for TUC centres. This is evident in the early decision to apply for MSC funding.

The initial aims and objectives of the centre included welfare rights advice, educational courses and other activities organised by the unemployed. Financing these activities was a problem right from the beginning. There were obvious organisations that could reasonably be expected to be sympathetic and to be approached for donations, such as trade unions and local branches of the Labour Party. At this early stage, though, it was recognised that the Manpower Services Commission (MSC) was willing to fund full-time workers in the centre. Even so there were reservations about the possible problems with obtaining money from the MSC. 'MSC – the commission appear keen to provide money. We decided to make an application for full-time workers paying close attention to any strings to be attached to the money' (Management Committee Minutes, 2.5.81).

Even at this early date, over two months before it opened, the basis was being laid for the later problems and conflicts within the centre. The stress on organising in a way that encouraged active participation by the users of the centre, under the general administrative umbrella of the management committee, led to the formation of four user groups in the centre: the 'Unemployed Workers' Union' (UWU), the crêche group, the women's group, and the welfare rights group. A situation developed where there was considerable conflict between certain of these user groups, especially the UWU, and the management committee over the application for MSC funding, its associated political strings and consequently the whole organisational structure of the centre. The UWU activists were typically unemployed students and shop stewards, although it had a membership of over 400 at one time, indicating that more than just these kinds of people were involved. A further factor to be taken into account was the turnover of activists, which meant that the social characteristics changed over time.

A formal application for funding from the MSC was drawn up by early July 1981. In this application were detailed the initial aims of the centre: informal social activities to overcome the isolation of individual unemployed people; welfare rights advice; education courses; raising public awareness of the reality and problems of unemployment; research into specific problems of the unemployed and support for developing unemployed workers' centres in nearby localities. Money for fourteen workers was applied for, covering administration, welfare rights workers, crêche workers and specific project workers. Despite the optimistic rhetoric of the official application to the MSC, there was widespread scepticism about the proposal on the management committee as whole.

> The section on the management of centres was particularly unpopular as it referred to management committees for centres comprising TU reps and Local Authority nominees in equal numbers, and provision for other organisations and the unemployed only as observers. The resultant stink has produced revised or clarified guidelines, which allow for greater flexibility, and for the possibility of 'other groups' and the unemployed having a real voice on the MCs. (Management Committee report on MSC application, 14.7.81)

At this stage the policy committee (PC) enters the fray.[7] The PC proposed a new management committee structure for the MSC application: the new MC would have two representatives from the Trades Council, two from the WEA and two from the local authority. Ironically, the meeting of the management committee to which this proposal was put noted that this new structure would make the PC redundant. Furthermore, the local authority was effectively powerless under the proposed structure. It was hoped that a PC that met only once or twice a year would meet the MSC guidelines for the management of unemployed centres (ibid.).

Meanwhile, a new factor was about to make the situation even more complex for the management committee. A general open meeting of the unemployed people using the centre took place on Tuesday 14 July. The essential logic of the Unemployed Workers' Union that developed from this meeting was to involve the unemployed themselves in organising collective action. 'Well my idea was to organise the unemployed for self action – themselves – which was partially successful for the first two years, we managed to keep goin'...we managed to get enough money from the trade unions to keep goin'' (UWU activist).

With over twenty people present, the first meeting made five recommendations for consideration by the management committee: (i) to hold general meetings to elect unemployed representatives to the MC; (ii) to hold weekly meetings of the unemployed; (iii) to launch a public services concessions campaign; (iv) to produce a regular newsletter for the dole queue; (v) to produce a general leaflet opposing redundancies. The management committee accepted the first four recommendations without comment, but the redundancies leaflet had to be cleared with the MC before it could be printed (Management Committee Minutes, 14.7.81). Furthermore, the MC agreed that: 'There shall be a monthly meeting of unemployed people at the centre to elect nine people to serve on the management committee. *The management committee reserves the right to exclude people it considers not in sympathy with the aims of the centre*' (ibid.; emphasis added).

On both these issues the MC was clearly wary of the demands emerging from the unemployed people using the centre, and saw them as a potential threat to its control. However, by the end of August 1981 the MC consisted of nine Trades Council delegates, nine unemployed people and seven coopted members.

In relation to the application for MSC funding for the Community Enterprise Programme (CEP) workers at the centre events began to move against the application going forward. Given the influence of *Militant* supporters, and the left more generally, on the Trades Council, the MC felt that the TC would find it difficult to accept the new guidelines. 'The last policy committee meeting discussed the CEP scheme. The TUC guidelines give massive power to the local authority. Trades council is unlikely to accept this, even if we did. We should attempt to raise issue with TUC regional rep. at next TC' (Management Committee Minutes, 8.9.81).

The Trades Council had a policy of 'non-involvement' in Local Authority/MSC schemes, and it felt that it needed to be convinced that such a scheme was suitable for Brighton's unemployed centre (Brighton and District Trades Council Minutes, 2.9.81). The Trades Council and the WEA nevertheless continued to pursue the idea of MSC funding to secure the long-term organisational and financial future of the centre. At that time they had good reason to be concerned about the financial future of the centre, as by early September 1981 donations were drying up (Management Committee Minutes, 8.9.81).

Despite the guarded optimism of the Trades Council and the WEA over the MSC application, groups using the centre began to voice more fundamental opposition to the MSC funding plan. Consequently, this began to reveal important weaknesses in the organisational structure of the centre. The UWU in particular opposed the movements towards MSC funding, and they had quite a different model of organisation and goals for the centre from those of the management committee. Ultimately, the UWU was to prevail.

However, the policy committee at this stage was where real power lay, but it had no record of its meetings nor representation of the unemployed (Management Committee Minutes, 20.10.81). Furthermore, half of its membership, the two representatives from the Trades Council, was bound by the Trades Council decision not to be involved in any Local Authority/MSC schemes for the development and funding of unemployed workers' centres. It appeared that during the autumn of 1981 a fundamental organisational and political crisis was developing at the centre, in that it could have developed in either of two ways – under the MSC schemes or outside them. There was quite simply no clear majority consensus on the TC, or the MC, as to which way to go. Nationally, the TUC/MSC guidelines deepened these divisions. Locally, a well-organised and active UWU began actively to campaign against MSC funding, and MSC schemes more generally.

In December 1981, the MC called for the views of the various groups using the centre on the proposal for MSC funding. The welfare rights group was in favour of having two workers funded under the Community Enterprise Programme for their work. The crêche group was opposed to workers for the crêche, but believed that other groups should be allowed to decide for themselves. The office group was in favour of MSC funded workers, not only for its own group but for the centre as a whole (Management Committee Minutes, 1.12.81). The most serious rift was between the management committee and the Unemployed Workers Union.

The UWU does not feel that an unemployed centre is necessary for the running of the UWU. In addition the present centre is too small and far out [from the centre of Brighton]. The UWU is therefore asking the council for a new building for the union. (ibid.)

These events are significant for a number of reasons. First, the MC had encouraged the organisation of the unemployed at the centre in the first place. Secondly, the division between the welfare rights group and the political work of the UWU had become a major source of political difference in relation to the MSC scheme. The political energies of the participants in the centre were turning inwards into a political struggle over the organisational form of the centre. At stake in this struggle are two opposed logics of organisation in terms of the ideal types that I outlined in Chapter 3: the management committee and the groups supporting its proposal pursuing a strategy for developing the centre into a broadly monological form of organisation, whilst the UWU was aiming for a dialogical form. That is, the UWU was seeking to involve the unemployed in locally organised collective action.

Despite the opposition of the UWU, the management committee at its meeting of 1 December 1981 reaffirmed its support for MSC funded workers at the centre. However, the UWU had decided to restructure itself in the light of the developing problems. The aim of the reorganisation of the UWU was to overcome the division between welfare rights work and political work, and to solve the problem of the duality of power that had developed. Both the UWU and the MC had been claiming responsibility for the centre. As a result, the MC asked the UWU to produce a paper on relations between the centre and the union and their future. Furthermore, the policy committee also wished to see the UWU on the same issues, whilst the financial crisis worsened. Meanwhile, the MSC had clarified and hardened its position on the organisation and financing of unemployed centres (Management Committee Minutes, 15.12.81).

The paper produced by the UWU during late 1981 marks a major turning point in the political and organisational trajectory of the centre and the UWU. The report opposed the forms of organisation of the centre and its practices. The document sees two basic alternatives facing the centre. The first is to follow the trend nationally and what the UWU saw at the time developing in the Brighton centre, that is, to become a TUC/MSC centre with political strings attached. The second is to become an independent base for 'radical' organisations of the unemployed. The critique of the centre and the management committee contained in the document is premised on the desirability of following the second path, in order to break out of the political and organisational isolation the UWU saw developing in the centre's relationship to the local community. The users of the centre, according to the UWU, could only exercise any influence through the management committee (Unemployed Workers' Union, 1981).

The UWU proposed that a new centre was required, because of the dilapidated nature of the building in which the centre was then located and its distance from central Brighton. It was proposed that the new centre should cater for cultural, political and welfare rights activities for a wide range of unemployed groups besides the UWU. It should be democratically controlled by those who used it, and the Trades Council should have representation providing it did not disagree with the political platform, which was 'campaigning and class struggle' (ibid., p. 3). Furthermore, it was argued that representatives of the Trades Council should not have an effective veto on decisions taken by the unemployed. It was envisaged that future finance would come from regular contributions from the local labour movement. Certain advantages were seen in this source of finance, specifically, that it preserved the UWU's political independence, and also cemented relations with the labour movement at rank and file level, therefore aiding the opposition to the TUC guidelines for unemployed centres. Additional income might also be raised through the fund-raising activities of the unemployed themselves.

> We are therefore arguing that a new centre should be administered by a new MC ... constituted by elected and recallable reps from the UWU, unemployed TU branches, YOPS's trainees, and reps from those sections of the labour movement who would be willing to sponsor the centre and who would, therefore, be in agreement with its political aims and objectives. The exact composition of the new MC would obviously have to be subject to consultation and discussion within and between constituent groups. (ibid.)

In terms of the ideal types of monological and dialogical forms of organisations of the unemployed developed above, the develop-

ment of the centre in Brighton can be understood as a conflict
between the two modes of organisation.

First, in terms of *goals*, the UWU was interested in the
qualitative transformation of society as instanced in its rhetoric
about commitment to 'class struggle', for example. In contrast, the
MC was principally interested in providing facilities through which
the unemployed could meet each other and share their experiences.

Secondly, in relation to the preferred *forms of action*, the UWU
was primarily concerned to involve the unemployed in local
collective action. Whilst the MC was concerned about develop-
ments amongst the users of the centre that were *outside its control*.
This is evident in its responses to the initial meetings of the
unemployed, its responses to the proposals to produce a leaflet
against redundancies, and a willingness to exclude people who were
not sympathetic to the aims of the centre. The MC is perhaps best
understood in terms of the technocratic aspect of the monological
form of action. The MC preferred to employ people to do things
for the unemployed.

The third aspect of providing services for the unemployed is
perhaps the central characteristic of TUC centres. This particular
relationship of representation of the monological form of organisation is exemplified by the way the MC wanted to run the centre
with a majority of local authority and Trades Council appointees.
In direct opposition to this, the UWU wanted the unemployed
themselves to take the central role in decision-making.

Fourthly, *orientations to the state* might initially seem to be one
of the least relevant aspects of my ideal types. However, the
UWU's campaigning was centred on the local authority to obtain
concessions for the unemployed using public services and to
develop a new centre. On the contrary, the MC wished to use
not only the local authority but that corporatist institution of the
central state, the MSC, to provide facilities as well.

The fifth dimension, *sources of finance*, was clearly a major issue
in the struggles within the centre. The MC was determined at one
stage to obtain MSC funding. The UWU in contrast was totally
opposed to this, suggesting as an alternative, its own fund-raising
activities in the wider labour movement. The central problem with
MSC funding was the political restrictions it would have involved.

Overall, three key factors can be drawn out which account for
the Brighton centre not going for MSC funding. First there was the

strong opposition from within the centre from some of the user groups, but especially the UWU. From the beginning the MC had emphasised the the importance of involving users in the running of the centre, and engaging in 'political' as well as 'welfare' work. The MC, then, was hardly in a position to propose a form of organising the centre that excluded the UWU. Secondly, the Trades Council was opposed to MSC schemes, so a key organisational support for the centre could have been lost if funding were accepted from that source. In the event, the Trades Council supported the application by *one vote*, but the application did not go ahead because of the narrowness of the vote and the depth of feeling about the issue.

> We had enormous debates on the Trades Council about the MSC and X produced an enormous detailed application to the MSC applying for finances to meet the needs of *nine* full-time organisers, ha ha ha ... to finance nine organisers none of which was implemented which is ironical now because the TUC is using that document as an example for all the others. Because of the big debates that went on in the Trades Council for about six months on this MSC money. It was finally agreed to make this application by one vote, in fact the application never got made. Because the movement was entirely divided on the question so it never got made, so we never received any MSC funding at all. (Management Committee member)

Finally, the MSC tightened up its regulations for centres for the unemployed late in 1981 as the MC noted (Management Committee Minutes, 15.12.81). This effectively undermined the MC's case, since the new MSC regulations were now even less acceptable to them. In retrospect, some of those previously strongly in favour of MSC funding changed their minds in the light of the application of the new regulations and the experience of centres of them. 'In retrospect it wasn't a bad idea rejecting the MSC scheme as most centres who've used it have had serious problems of control by the MSC and local councils' (WEA tutor).

I have shown how the Brighton centre moved from a mono-logical to a dialogical form of organisation, emphasising the importance of considering the local processes of how organisations of the unemployed emerge. Only through considering this in some detail is it possible to understand why the Brighton centre became the deviant case in the south east. The fact that it is only a single case study does not matter for the resulting sociological understanding. What *is* important is that we can trace empirically how the process of organisation worked itself out through concrete social struggles.

5.4   THE CAMPAIGN FOR A NEW CENTRE

Early in 1985 the Brighton centre moved to new premises shared with the Community Resource Centre, and which were provided by Brighton Borough Council. These new premises were obtained through a form of action quite different from that which pressurised the Council to provide the initial site. Whilst in the setting up of the centre the MC had used 'insider' tactics, gaining the sponsorship of Councillors, the new centre was obtained after public marches and demonstrations at council meetings. This total change was due to the emergence of the UWU.

> Three or four months after the centre came into existence the Brighton Unemployed Workers' Union was formed. In October we managed to organise a demonstration of 200, mostly unemployed, to demand assistance from the council in the form of free or half price for all council facilities. And we did obtain them and they still exist. We did get quite a bit of support then. (UWU activist)

This kind of action was quite different from the 'insider' tactics used by the WEA and the Trades Council that led to the opening of the centre initially. Those tactics were more characteristic of the forms of action of monological organisations. Now the UWU, operating from within the centre, was attempting to gain generalised collective concessions for the unemployed through the collective action of the unemployed themselves. In this instance, the WEA and the Trades Council are crucial as perhaps 'unwitting' allies, in that they provided the immediate organisational focus through the unemployed centre for the UWU to develop. However, it seems that at this stage the UWU was principally drawing on the organisational capabilities of unemployed students and shop stewards.

After that it all subsided again 'cos different groups of people came in at different times full of enthusiasm. The first lot were mostly unemployed undergraduates or graduates with one or two unemployed tagging along. And of course those sort of groups are given to sudden bursts of activity... if they don't get immediate results or fairly immediate results they fall by the wayside. But on the other hand they are better at organisation, they're better technically. They can type and they can use duplicating machines. They can do all those kinds of things that most workers can't do, so we had some kind of organisation, some kind of effective organisation for the first demonstration. (UWU activist)

Although it was generally easy to attract a strongly committed core of activists periodically, it was more difficult to attract wider groups of people. This was despite the fact that the centre was in what could be described as an 'inner city' zone, a short walking distance from several blocks of council flats and the DHSS office. There was no sense in which the centre was part of this 'community'. It had been imposed from 'outside' by a set of organisations which had a much wider geographical focus. Furthermore, there seemed to be no attempt to forge connections with the people living in the immediate vicinity, or with any organisations that might have been firmly rooted in it, beyond the labour movement.

One particularly problematic group to attract to the centre was women, and this was mentioned by several key informants. They noted, for example, the problem of the need for some kind of structured organised activity to attract women, although the point could be extended to all the unemployed.

Although a crèche group was organised, the idea of women 'dropping in' and using the crèche didn't work, the idea of a women's day or afternoon is probably better and a women and health class was quite successful. Just 'dropping in' without any structured activity seems a bit pointless. (WEA tutor)

The problem of just 'dropping in' was also indicated by a woman who could be described as one of the core activists at one stage. She was sufficiently committed and determined to 'force herself' on the place. 'Nothing was happening when I first came round here a few weeks ago, no one even acknowledged that I was here, so I had to kind of force myself on the place' (Female UWU activist).

Beyond the need for some kind of organised and structured activity to attract people, women with children in particular require access to clean premises, and 'tighter' organisation and activity more generally.

> I feel the centre is too trade union and male oriented, the people down there just don't take account of the specific needs of women with children. You need tight organisation for people looking after children like turning up for meetings on time and a proper crêche. I turned up for one meeting and the place was dirty with nails on the floor, totally unsuitable for small children, and also people turned up late so I had to leave early 'cos of my child. (Female member of Management Committee)

As the previous quote also indicated, the orientation of the place was towards male dominated trade unions and organised left-wing politics – not particularly welcoming for most people, especially women. One consequence of this leaning to organised left-wing politics was that it attracted more of the same, somewhat to the resentment (or perhaps amusement) of those who were active in the centre on a more permanent basis. 'Various political groupings appeared, seeing what they could get out of it, the SWP with their march for jobs, but whereas we wanted something around local demands. So after a few months they disappeared' (UWU activist).

One more important consequence of the turn away from the MSC and towards the UWU campaigning was the opening of the new centre in 1985. It is difficult to convey the inadequacy of the original premises in words. For a start they were far too small, with the largest room able to hold comfortably only about twenty people. Consequently, it was difficult if not impossible to raise money from the hiring out of rooms, for example. The fact that the roof fell in at the end of 1984 perhaps best conveys the state of the place.

The campaign for the new centre largely developed out of the wider campaigning activities of the UWU, despite the periodic lulls in activity. The catalyst for the campaign for a new centre was the rejection of applying for MSC funding by the UWU, as discussed above. The campaign was based around the inadequacy of what the Borough Council was already providing, and it received fairly widespread support, as indicated by the size of the petition to the Council (estimates vary from 6000 to 8500 signatures) and the size of the demonstration that supported it. Again 'outside' political groups, such as the Socialist Workers' Party and some anarchists, tried to exercise some influence, but failed.

The premises we did get at Coalbrook Street were totally inadequate, a dump really, totally inadequate and should never have been accepted in the first place ... so we concentrated on getting better premises from the council. And in spring of '83 we got a demonstration of about 400 people and that was the time the anarchists came down intent on stopping the town. They were mostly from London and they demanded that the whole street be blocked, there was only 400 of us, and they demanded that the whole traffic stop ... they raised a whole hue and cry about blocking the whole street – 'don't walk, spread across the whole street'. They managed to get several of themselves arrested, whereas our main aim was to get to the town hall and put our demands. (UWU activist)

Furthermore, the electoral fortunes of the Conservatives on the Borough Council were worsening, and this again was cited as a reason for the success of the campaign.

On the first demonstration you see the Tories had been very indecisive about what their attitude to it was. Although in the end they came round to granting most of it. But by the second demonstration in '83 the political situation was such that the Tories didn't want to get on the wrong side of the unemployed citizens in the town, and we had produced a petition of 8500 signatures. Of course, they immediately saw what a large number of votes could be lost ... So their attitude completely changed. And the Labour group tabled a motion calling for a decent spacious unemployed centre to be provided by the council free off the rates, with a capital advance to get it off the ground, which they expected the Tories would oppose, but low and behold when the day came the Tories swung behind it. So that there was no opposition at all ... We packed the gallery expecting it to get thrown out. (UWU activist)

Finally, one activist felt that one important reason why many unemployed people and not just the activists had become involved in the campaign for the new centre was that there was some concrete material gain to be had, rather than some more abstract political goal.

We had got a lot of support because British workers I think will respond to something concrete, when there's something concrete to be got out of it. Like May Day demonstrations are too abstract, they're asked to support a principle of international brotherhood or something and it's too abstract. What are they gonna get from it? If there's some concrete purpose, if there's gonna be some tangible outcome in their interests then they'll respond much more and they responded quite well despite all the anarchists and that there were quite a number of genuine unemployed. (UWU activist)

This last point gets to the heart of the problems facing any movement attempting to organise collective action amongst the unemployed in Britain. Whilst more diffuse and abstract discourses may cement the activist component of a social movement, it does seem to be the case that the prospect of more immediate collective gains is crucially important in mobilising larger numbers of people who are not routinely involved in organised politics.

One possible option is welfare rights work. However, this requires expertise in order to provide adequate advice to individuals. The system works in such a way as to *individualise rather than collectivise discontent*. Consequently, welfare rights work tends to be 'depoliticised' (in the sense of collective political action by the unemployed themselves), since only particular individuals benefit from its successes. Some of the early activists in the Brighton centre feared this artificial separation of welfare rights work from political work, and this is precisely what happened. Work in the centre on welfare rights issues focused on advice to individuals, and the WEA running welfare rights courses once or twice a year. Furthermore, the centre was effectively competing with the Brighton Rights Centre, which had Urban Aid funding for full-time workers, in the area of welfare rights advice. This form of action is highly structured by a state form which effectively provides no immediate goals for collective action by the unemployed.

The activists in the unemployed centre were dealing with two levels of the state in quite different forms: the central bureaucratic state for welfare rights work, and the local representative democratic state which was more open to influence through their collective action. Whilst the central state individualised issues, the local state, by providing the unemployed centre and the concessions for council run services, was able to provide in response to locally organised collective action limited collective benefits for the unemployed as a whole.

5.5 CONCLUSION

What many find surprising about unemployment in the 1980s is the non-emergence of an organisation comparable to the NUW(C)M of the inter-war period. This has generated a wide range of largely speculative discussions. However, a comparison of what has actually developed during the 1980s with that of the inter-war period throws some light on this conundrum.

The changing form of the state is central to understanding the differing experiences of the 1930s and 1980s. The NUW(C)M focused its everyday campaigns on locally controlled unemployment relief agencies. Today, the centralised bureaucratic welfare state is largely immune to similar local protests. Local organisations of the unemployed can only achieve gains for individuals within a tightly defined legal framework. There are no collective material gains of any great significance to be had from such forms of action. However, this has not prevented organisations of the unemployed and claimants more generally from extracting certain limited concessions for individuals (Novak, 1988). But these have been small and limited compared to what was achieved by the NUW(C)M.

Organisational and cultural resources have also been restructured. The material and cultural bases of the NUW(C)M have been undermined by forty years of deindustrialisation and economic restructuring. Those places no longer have the potential to produce and sustain an organisation such as the NUW(C)M. Political movements of the unemployed crucially depend on local political and cultural resources. Part of the explanation for the absence of mass movements of the unemployed during the 1980s, and the failure to develop one in Brighton, is the decline of the symbolic communities which sustained the NUW(C)M in its strongest localities. There has also been a major change in the role of political parties in mobilising the unemployed since the 1930s. Then the Communist Party was a key organisational resource for their mobilisation. During the 1980s no political party or grouping has taken a role analogous to that of the Communist Party during the 1930s.

In contrast to the NUW(C)M, the TUC's centres for the unemployed have been part of the 'mainstream' of the labour movement, being actively campaigned for and supported by the TUC. The use by the TUC of MSC funding has meant that they have taken a typically monological organisational form, providing services for the unemployed rather than organising them for collective action.

The Brighton centre eventually rejected the possibility of MSC funding, and a radical Unemployed Workers' Union developed. This dialogical form of organisation was grounded in the already existing politics of the local labour movement. However, it only ever had a membership of 400, and relied on a hard core of activists never numbering more than around thirty or forty and often much less than this. Quite simply, such movements find it difficult to produce, through their collective action, material gains from the state for all unemployed people. Further, the wider organisational and cultural resources are both weaker and different from those found in the past.

6

The Experience of Unemployment

6.1 INTRODUCTION

This chapter is based on material from a series of qualitative interviews with unemployed people that I carried out in Brighton in 1984.[1] This small sample (N 26) was selected around one basic criterion that is central to my theoretical argument, namely, that those who have the requisite cultural, political and organisational resources will develop particular forms of political response to unemployment. Consequently, there are two groups in this sample: those who were involved in the unemployed workers' centre, and those who were not. The interview material will be considered in relation to several of the theoretical issues discussed earlier.

First, I shall show that there are two basic kinds of *dialogical* discourses to be found amongst the activists, but both can be considered to be *substantive rationalities*. The first is a variety of *class politics* concerned with both the immediate practical material interests of the working class and a longer-term socialist vision. This was typical of the, usually middle-aged, former shop stewards involved in the centre. The second is a variety of *post-materialist* politics (Knutsen, 1988) associated most frequently with the former students and younger people involved in the centre. These emphasise issues concerned with individual autonomy and identity, with a rejection of the 'work ethic' which 'class–political' discourses embraced. Whereas in the past, in the case of the NUW(C)M, a 'class–political' discourse was dominant, I shall argue that contemporary political movements of the unemployed draw on cementing discourses which may be in conflict with each other.

Secondly, the interviews with those from the centre enable me to examine in more detail the cultural resources that contemporary political movements of the unemployed may draw upon. It is here where the comparison of the two groups – those from the centre, and those who were not from the centre – is most central. I shall show that not only do those using the centre have distinctive backgrounds (usually former trade union activists or students), but by virtue of this they have perceptions of unemployment and its consequences which are quite different from the other unemployed people whom I interviewed. The most distinctive factor underlying these differences is the involvement of those from the centre in some form of politics prior to becoming involved in the centre.

Rather than use an open-ended question of the form 'what is it like to be unemployed?', which I suspected might produce some blank responses, I attempted to get some impression of people's experience of unemployment and what it meant to them by asking about the advantages and disadvantages of unemployment. These initial questions were then followed by similar open-ended questions about their experience of the Department of Employment (DE) and the Department of Health and Social Security (DHSS), and questions concerning the causes of unemployment and possible solutions. In the following chapter, I shall move on to consider the more directly 'political' issues of Thatcherism and class consciousness, using the interview data.

Initially, I shall consider the views of the two groups around the issue of the advantages and disadvantages of unemployment on three levels: to themselves personally, to unemployed people as a whole and to society as a whole. Throughout the following I shall consider the group of unemployed people who had not been involved with the unemployed centre first, and then consider the group which I had contacted through the centre.

6.2   PERCEPTIONS OF THE DISADVANTAGES OF UNEMPLOYMENT

The group of unemployed people who were not from the centre thought that the disadvantages of unemployment to themselves were principally boredom and lack of money. Of note is the fact that lack of money is seen as an important factor preventing participation in social activities with others. This raises important problems for the simple social psychological models of the latent functions of employment. In the everyday context of the lives of unemployed people social isolation – and any subsequent deleterious psychological consequences – flows from an inability to participate in commodified social and cultural practices at the taken for granted level of simply going to the pub. Whilst some analysts have tended to focus almost entirely on the 'latent functions' of employment (Jahoda, 1982), others have recently challenged this generalisation. For example, Bostyn and Wight (1987) have argued that the income from a wage provides access to goods which are consumed 'symbolically'. That is, goods may be consumed not for their utilitarian value but for their value as expressions of personal identity, such as masculinity or femininity (ibid., pp. 139–46). The low incomes associated with unemployment undermine people's market power as consumers, reducing their symbolic patterns of consumption, and often breaking their former patterns of association with friends.

This might be described as 'forced privatisation' through market forces, rather than choice exercised through the market. There is no sense in which these people, without prompting, related their situation at the level of individual disadvantages to wider social and political processes over which anyone (least of all themselves) might exert some control. Boredom and lack of money were frequent themes.

> To me personally ... er ... I think occasionally a little bit bored. I dunno' I've sort of got used to it in a way quite a few people do. Er ... I suppose money really more than anything else. (Married man, mid twenties, unemployed over one year)

> Er, its just boredom i'nit and lack of money. I suppose you think it's a laugh for the first three months after coming out of work. You think it's great 'n' that, after that ... Cor, it does yer brain in. It's really boring and you can't go out much, not as much as you used to, you can't buy your friends a drink. (18-year-old man, unemployed over one year)

A number of rather different themes emerged, however, from the interviews with those unemployed people who had been involved with the unemployed centre. At the most general level their responses were more elaborate and worked out; they clearly had a better idea, or set of ideas, about the disadvantages of unemployment to themselves.[2] There was no clear 'boredom plus money' theme that ran through their replies, in contrast to those in the first group. Some at least of this group of unemployed were able to construct a partial narrative relating their individual situation to the wider social context, such as government policy, public attitudes or comparisons amongst different groups of unemployed people.

This first quote below exemplifies the views of a former shop steward. He notes a theme that emerges several times from amongst those interviewed from the centre, that people in employment are able to negotiate increases in income, and are able to defend their immediate material interests, whilst the unemployed, due to their relationship to the state, are not able to do so. Further, there is some indication of a 'collectivist work ethic', in the sense of making a contribution to society, and he also relates isolation to involvement in political organisations. For him it is not just general social isolation.

> Financial would be the major [problem]... 'cos I'm still living on finances that basically the state considers to be the absolute minimum. There is no room for negotiation. I mean, surely if I was in the job I had two and half years ago I would have had an increase of wages and an increase in conditions, or at least be in a situation where I would have negotiated those increases. But you're totally isolated, you're kept at a financial minimum. You're demoralised in as much as you feel, er... worthless to society. I think that everybody wants to feel that they can make a contribution, but er... I don't have the attitude that I'm sponging off the society, because I think that my situation, the situation of millions of people, is created consciously by governments and I would dearly like to work and to have a decent wage for a decent day's work, and it's not being made available to me. (Middle-aged married man, former shop steward, unemployed for over two years)

However, not all of those at the centre express such materialist values associated with class politics. The quote below indicates quite well the characteristics of post-materialist views. It also reveals a certain ambiguity or uncertainty, in that employment has disadvantages like unemployment, but if you are unemployed you do have a degree of 'choice'.

> I find it difficult to find things to occupy myself... I think the disadvantages are also automatically balanced against being at work and as I'm not satisfied with being at work... being unemployed is obviously good for me. So if that's the only alternative to being in work, whatever its disadvantages, the only disadvantage I have is the choice. (Single man, under 20, unemployed under one year).

The consideration of perceptions of disadvantages to unemployed people as a whole was to see if there was any identification with the unemployed in general, to see if people identified their individual problems with a wider reference group, without any initial prompting from myself. Only when prompted, however, did the first group of unemployed people make explicit comparisons between groups of unemployed people or make general reference to relationships with the state, 'the dole office', or 'public attitudes' to the unemployed in general. And, of course, there's the attempt to blame the unemployed for their predicament. Overall there is no attempt to relate the issues to any political perspective.

> Well, I think I'm quite fortunate having somewhere decent to live. I think one of the worst things is finding somewhere decent to live. 'Cos once you haven't got a job and you haven't got any money to back you up, you can't afford to put a deposit on a nice place and you end up living in awful accommodation, and I think that affects their whole life really. (Married man, mid twenties, long-term unemployed)

> Well some don't work 'cos they're... well there's a lot of kiddies who just turn to crime, you know. I suppose there's some lazy people about ain't there. (Long-term unemployed 18-year-old man)

Amongst those from the unemployed centre there is a bifurcation of views between those who see major disadvantages to unemployment and expect or hope for a collective political response, and those who have effectively taken an individualist political solution, rejecting paid work as a central goal in life. The first, an instance of the 'class–politics' form of discourse, clearly shows some sense of common interests grounded in a common experience, namely that of 'signing on'. However, he sees that unemployed people's relationship with the state is an isolating rather than collectivising experience.

> I would have thought that the most vocal body against this government would be unemployed people. Er ... because I think you only have to look at your direct conditions that you're living in, that you're forced to face ... But because of the nature of unemployment, the way it makes people sign on the dotted line every two weeks, and then go back into poverty ... away from sharing the experience with other people. (Middle-aged man, former shop steward)

This second quote exemplifies the post-materialist emphasis on individual solutions against the 'system', as distinct from the collectivism of 'class politics'.

> I don't feel any kind of obligation to go out and find a job. I never feel I would fulfil myself much more. I don't feel a job is necessary to prove my masculinity or anything like that. And er ... so I can't really identify with people who think like that. I do understand that if they're like that, then they feel miserable, hopeless and totally useless if they're unemployed ... I'm aware of the fact that I'm part of a small minority on the dole. (Man, student 'dropout', unemployed less than one year)

Two single women both make reference to unemployment being worse for those with children and families. One of these also refers to the fact that unemployment need not be boring, given the range of voluntary activities that people could become involved in.

> ... certain states of apathy, a lack of optimism of seeing the situation ever getting better, and obviously other things, lack of money if you've got a family ... and just basically magnified all over really. (Woman, unemployed less than one year, former student)

I think most disadvantaged are the people who've got children, because they...they get so little benefit for children that they can't really afford things...I think I'm kind of very fortunate living in Brighton, because it's not too bad being unemployed here like other places, there's lots of community things and voluntary work. That takes up a lot of time so I don't really get bored. (Woman, former shop steward)

Another former shop steward contrasted the different structural position of the unemployed compared to the employed when it comes to political organisation. Whilst there is a recognisable *common* experience of unemployment, namely, in relation to the state, signing on, etc., this is not a *collective, shared experience*. Furthermore, in the workplace former shop stewards recognised the sense of power that emerged culturally ('camaraderie') and organisationally through trade unions. For the unemployed there is no 'functional equivalent' to the workplace culture, or, for that matter, a trade union organisation that has, for all practical purposes, permanently been in place. Moreover, this man sees these weaknesses of the unemployed being exploited by the government.

I think in a work situation, er...where we're talking about far far smaller numbers than the unemployed, because the company needs your labour and has to make profit out of your labour, you have a bargaining position, and you have, er...a camaraderie builds up through the socialised aspects of work, and therefore, and this is the history of trade unionism, you're then able to organise and to bring people forward and to gain some control over your life. And that is the great difficulty. I think even at the unemployment centre they would say that to motivate people to feel that they can do something constructive on unemployment is very very difficult. And the government know this. This is why I suppose the unemployed are being so hammered. (Middle-aged man, former shop steward)

At the level of personal disadvantages and the disadvantages of unemployment to the unemployed at large, there is a clear divergence of views between the two groups. The former non-political group do not immediately connect these with a wider political ideology as do some of the second group of political activists. Amongst the second group there is no clear set of views that unifies them. There are both collectivist labour movement themes, associated with a class–politics discourse, and individualist themes associated with post-materialist values.

Those unemployed people who had not had any contact with the unemployed workers' centre had extreme difficulty answering the question about the disadvantages of unemployment to society as a whole. Arguably this is a significant finding in and of itself, since the question presumably asked about something they had not really thought about much, so they could not produce a meaningful answer. Rather than being a poor or irrelevant question, it reveals that those unemployed people who are not politically active do not consider the wider consequences of unemployment very much. In short, there is no cognitive appreciation of the wider consequences of unemployment. It may further reveal their lack of a particular communicative competence. Nevertheless, some did argue that unemployment is highly focused in its effects. People generally, they felt, were not touched by the consequences of unemployment, whilst the government was only concerned about the figures.

I don't think other people that are employed it bothers them about unemployment. I think there's one or two people, but most people sort of don't really think about it, don't consider it or care. I think where unemployment continues, it depends how modern production keeps up with financing it otherwise we run into money problems. (Married man, mid twenties, unemployed for over a year)

Well, the disadvantages are only to the people who are unemployed, to themselves, and to the government I suppose it's bad figures really, that's all they're worried about. (Unemployed man, under 21, long-term unemployed)

These were the most elaborate responses to this question from this group of unemployed people, others were typically short and terse such as, 'No I don't think so' (Middle-aged man), 'Nothing really' (20-year-old man) or just referring to unemployment as a burden on the economy.

Others contacted through the unemployed workers' centre had a more elaborate view of the disadvantages of unemployment to society at large. These views, again, were drawing on, or building upon, a wider political ideology, through which they interpreted not only their own predicament but those of other unemployed people and society at large. These disadvantages were seen principally in terms of the general financial cost to the state, the waste of skills, the use to which the labour of the unemployed could be put if employed in public services, and the consequences of high unemployment for those in work in terms of the weakening of trade union bargaining power. There was both a cognitive and evaluative appreciation of the wider effects of unemployment. In both these instances the individuals concerned were former shop stewards in manufacturing industry.

> Yeah, oh yeah, very much so ... well, for instance, the bill for unemployment runs into billions ... billions of pounds to keep people with potential and skills outside of society where they can't be used...so it seems madness to me that society will allow that situation to develop ... er ... for instance, the government have made this big thing about cuts because they want to save on government spending so they've cut thousands and thousands of jobs in hospitals, education, in all kinds of public services. Now we're having to pay far greater than those cuts would save in keeping those people unemployed ... and ... it's a secret wage that we're all getting in society by the services that those people are supplying, so it's a terrible thing really for society. (Middle-aged man, former shop steward)

> ...certainly for society as a whole we're all at a disadvantage ... look at how unemployment is used to cut people's living standards. Once you've got a mass of poor people out of work you can then turn round, in industries that are making large profits, to the workers in those industries, who would want to see reflected in their wages some of that profit, to say 'now don't get stroppy or if you don't like it we've got people banging at the door who are ready to do your job for less money'. (Long-term unemployed man, former shop steward)

In this section I have shown that there are important differences between the two groups in terms of what they feel are the disadvantages of unemployment. For those who are not from the unemployed workers' centre, unemployment principally results in boredom and poverty. They are unable to afford those things which enable them to participate socially with those they would otherwise normally associate with. They make no wider political connections, unlike those from the centre.

For these unemployed people from the centre, boredom and poverty are not the only problems, but there is a stronger sense of being denied participation in the collective projects of wider society, and the inability to defend their immediate material interests in the ways they had been used to when in employment. However, this only represents the 'class–politics' perspective. Others were more ambiguous about the disadvantages of unemployment. In what I have termed a post-materialist discourse, they can see certain advantages of unemployment. They put more emphasis on the possibilities for choosing to do things other than work while unemployed. Those from the unemployed workers' centre had the communicative competence, and the cognitive and evaluative discourses, to draw upon in providing critical accounts of the consequences of unemployment.

6.3   PERCEPTIONS OF ADVANTAGES OF UNEMPLOYMENT

These questions were designed to act as a further probe about what it feels like to be unemployed, and how the unemployed might relate their situation to other unemployed people and wider 'society'. Amongst the first group of unemployed, who were not involved with the unemployed workers' centre, there were general references to more leisure time and boredom. In other words, for some at least there are no advantages to unemployment for themselves. However, there are those who see the advantages of increased freedom of choice over how they spend their time.

> I suppose in the summer if you like the beach and things like that. I should think the winter isn't such a good time to be unemployed to be an advantage. It's an advantage to be able to on a nice sunny day to go down on the beach. You know it's nice. Besides I prefer to stay at home. (Married man, mid twenties, long-term unemployed)

Well they say you've got a lot of leisure time, but you don't count it as leisure time do yer? It's all right at first, but after a while it's, it gets you down. I dunno'...it's just boring. You can lay in until two and that, but that's no good. People say you can lay in...my girlfriend she works, and she goes out to work all day she says, 'It's right for you, all you do is sit indoors'...they don't understand. (18-year-old man, long-term unemployed)

In contrast to the references amongst the first group, to a vaguely defined boredom, the second group specified certain *political* 'advantages' of unemployment to themselves. Again, two political themes emerge, the labourist and individualist responses to unemployment. The first, highlighting the possibilities of greater involvement in collective labour movement politics, whilst the second emphasises an individual rejection of exploitation at work. Overall they were *more* likely to be able to think of concrete advantages of unemployment to themselves. For example, a former shop steward emphasises advantages to himself in terms of his involvement in trade union activities and political work for 'his class'.

...politically, I think, I read a lot more now, er, have got a greater interest in what happens, you know. I'm lucky in as much as when I was made redundant I didn't drop out of the trade union and I'm in a very good trade union as far as unemployment is concerned. They like to keep unemployed people in the union, to keep their activities within the union and there are a lot of facilities that the union make available to the membership, i.e. weekend schools, I've just been on a weekend school...Also branch activity and divisional activity within the union can really keep you involved and feel that you're doing something for...for your class for your people. (Middle-aged man, former shop steward)

As in the discussion of the disadvantages of unemployment above, those with a post-materialist view, former students, offer quite different accounts. In particular, as the quotes below show, they are more likely to see advantages to unemployment as opposed to the disadvantages of employment.

I don't have to prostitute myself for forty hours a week doing something which, however much I might enjoy at the start, I wouldn't enjoy it at the end because I'd be alienating myself doing something for somebody else. Er...and just spending the time in the evenings that I've got left, just spending the money I've just earned. Er...being pushed around by someone else, doing certain things. I wouldn't completely enjoy doing that. Yeah, it's just the alternatives to that...freedom, ability to live your own life...other than somebody else's. (Man, mid twenties, former student)

The advantages are not really of being unemployed, but not being in a job that you hate. Yes possibly, and that you can still think that you haven't compromised, that what you want to do is look around sort of things in your free time...as an unpaid worker, it depends, I do voluntary work, so it's probably easier for me to find things I find interesting and worthwhile doing. (Woman, former student, mid twenties)

Where a former shop steward did point out disadvantages of employment compared to unemployment, this referred to the specific disadvantages of the shift system of her previous job.

Well, yes, I think there are quite a few. I mean, the fact that you can have some choice over how you spend your time is an advantage, 'cos I used to do sort of shift work, and I find it good to be able to plan to do things without having to worry about whether you're working or not. (Woman, late twenties, former shop steward)

This is another important contrast in the experience of unemployment between the two groups. The former group finds it hard to see any advantages in unemployment compared to the political activists. The activists, furthermore, see the advantages principally in terms of some political ideology, project or activity, either of a collectivist 'class politics' or more individualist post-materialist politics. The latter in particular emphasised the disadvantages of employment compared to unemployment. The first group of unemployed found it difficult to relate in a meaningful way to the question about the advantages of unemployment to all unemployed people, in other words, to generalise from their own situation. Most responses here were fairly bland and short, 'None' or 'No, I don't think so', despite prompting.

The second group from the unemployed workers' centre, however, made clear distinctions between their own predicament and that of other unemployed people, usually making it clear that the others were worse off than themselves. Most importantly, they turned the question round to emphasise again the disadvantages of unemployment, as in the case of the shop steward below. This is counterposed by the views of two former students quoted immediately afterwards, expressing their difference from the 'normal' unemployed person who is incapable of seeing the advantages of unemployment

> I don't think that people have the same relations to...to the same situations that they're sharing. I think some people, especially single people who for instance are in a bed-sitter, would probably react far worse to the situation than I have, because the gap between what they would be getting when they're working and when they're not working in finances is probably far greater. Then the social aspects of it is far more amplified. I mean, I'm lucky that I have got my wife and two kids, and that I'm able to feel part of a group, a family unit. (Middle-aged man, former shop steward)

> I regard myself as an exception...so generalisations are hard to make, er...unemployed people in general don't seem to be prepared to see the advantages of unemployment at all. (20-year-old man, former student)

> It's what you're geared up to...if you've got responsibility of children...it's not the right cultural values if you come from a traditional background to see the advantages...you've been working in a regular job...Well I've said for me...I want a job that's . . . it would have to be something more, that 'n' a basic cash thing. (Woman, former student, mid twenties)

When it came to considering the advantages of unemployment for society at large, the first group had real difficulty in relating meaningfully to this question. Most retorted that there were not any, a few elaborated further on how others saw the unemployed, or did not consider it a problem at all. They feel that for society generally there are no clear advantages of high unemployment.

Rather, they feel that society sees the unemployed as a problem group, reiterating the view that unemployment is highly focused in its consequences.

> I think society in general, in small bands, sort of think they're having a lovely time, but besides that no. I think some people are concerned that they ought to have jobs ... and some people think that they ought to cut their dole money and get them out to work. I think really they're just minority groups and the majority just don't consider it. (Married man, mid twenties)

Such perceptive comments from those who had not been involved in the unemployed centre were quite unusual. Nevertheless, the message seems clear that the question itself is to some degree meaningless, since they see that unemployment does not affect most of society, so there are no advantages, or strongly perceived disadvantages, for society in their view.

On this question there were more similarities between the politically active and inactive groups than on the other sets of issues. Most of those who had been involved in the unemployed workers' centre found this a difficult question to answer, although some were able to elaborate further on what they had already said about the wider political context in relation to unemployment.

> We're living in a very selfish time, we're living under a government that's telling people that we're all right, Jack, er, that at least that's the only thing they should be considering. You know we're not living in a society that wants to look after everybody or have that as a goal at all. It's this great 'let's free the market forces. Let's free the individual ... ' Of course, what it really means is that millions of people who are unemployed, low paid, have had even the most basic freedoms restricted so I think unemployment is a damning indictment on society. Particularly when it conspires like this government has consciously and through obvious policies to create it. (Middle-aged man, former shop steward)

Generally, those unemployed people who were not from the centre saw no advantages to being unemployed, although a few saw advantages of 'freedom of choice'. Similarly, they saw no advantage to unemployed people generally or the rest of society. Those from the unemployed workers' centre, however, saw some advantages in terms of more time for political work. Although they recognised that the unemployed were not in a position to influence their own standard of living. Further, a much stronger view of the advantages of unemployment came from those with a post-materialist view. These people tended to see the disadvantages of employment counterposed to the advantages of unemployment for them personally. More generally, those former shop stewards expressing a class–politics perspective saw no advantages of unemployment for society generally, and reasserted their belief in the waste of talent.

6.4   EXPERIENCE OF THE UNEMPLOYMENT BENEFIT AND DHSS OFFICES

In many ways the unemployed have little day to day contact with the Unemployment Benefit Office and the Social Security Office, despite the tremendous power these bureaucracies have over them. I have already discussed how some former shop stewards from the centre noted that the relationship between the unemployed and the state was an isolating rather than a collectivising experience. In this section I shall be considering the responses when I asked directly about their experience of the DE and DHSS.

The most important finding, contrary to most of the other findings in this chapter, is the similarity of views expressed by the two groups. All these accounts are grounded in people's experiences of these bureaucracies. People cited examples of their problems, and positive features, concerning these institutions when talking about them. Several noted that it was of the character of the work of the DHSS that generated problems for those working there, and the frustrations created by having to deal with other more problematic claimants. Despite these insights, they also felt that some particular civil servants were 'awkward' with claimants in what seemed to them a quite deliberate fashion.

> I think it's an awful job, er, when I've signed on I've come across one or two that've, well have been, er. I don't know why...they can be so awkward, they just don't want to know, but there again you come across others that are OK. I can't understand

anyone really, unless they couldn't get any other form of employment wanting to work in social security. (Man, mid twenties, long-term unemployed)

Oh, I was on the phone to them yesterday. People are all right who work there. It's not their fault, you can't blame them. You have a lot of people who phone 'em up and slag 'em off. It's just the system, like I phoned up yesterday ... to get my money, 'cos I've supposed to have some money Friday and I haven't had no money since ... they take two weeks about it and, er, I phoned up and she said my form's up in Newcastle, so and er, I said, 'What's it doing in Newcastle?' But she said it'll take two weeks to get some money, and you know I'm desperate for money, so they said, 'Do you want some forms?' an' that. It's all complicated. It's the system. The people are all right, but the system they're set on with. (Man under 21, unemployed over one year)

Well ... they have their problems everyday ... People get on their wick, walking in all day grumbling and moaning, so ... But I was talkin' to a bloke on the phone an' 'e was quite helpful, you know what I mean? But some of 'em just really ... just wanna' get you out of sight as soon as possible. Some of 'em are all right and some of 'em ain't. (Middle-aged man)

Those whom I had contacted through the unemployed workers' centre expressed *broadly similar views* about the social security bureaucracies. Again, three broad features stand out: first, the division between the DE and the DHSS; secondly, the 'awkward' individual civil servant; and thirdly, the recognition that it is the system, for example staff shortages, that generates problems for claimants. Further, these views are also strongly grounded in people's experiences of these bureaucracies. There is, however, one important difference. Those from the centre do not mention other claimants causing problems for the staff as the source of poor treatment by the DHSS. They see the problems entirely in terms of the system and the occasional awkward civil servant.

Very good and helpful and understanding, that is the basic general impression I get. And there are exceptions to that, you get the odd individual who really will try and prevent you from getting entitlements that you might be allowed, or would be an obstruction, and perhaps there are certain aspects to their thinking that are biased against unemployed people why they do that. But I would say generally . . . 95 per cent of the people there are very friendly and are probably doing a difficult job. They're understaffed. As I say, I've come across people who've been very obstructive. (Middle-aged man, former shop steward)

Er . . . the people at the Department of Employment are basically all right . . . I'm not terribly fond of the people either at the council and at the DHSS. I'm totally intimidated by the glass screens . . . er, I speak very quietly so I have to put my head right up to the screen to be heard . . . er . . . it's not very pleasant to have to queue up there . . . With the DHSS particularly it's frightening, because you fear they've found something out, or discovered that you shouldn't have been claiming or something like that. I feel intimidated. Most of the people seem to feel like that. (20-year-old man, former student)

They're basically all right, actually, in Upper North Street [the Unemployment Benefit Office]. I find them quite helpful, they have posters up advertising the unemployed centre . . . notices about jobs and prospects . . . that's a different thing from supp. ben. Edward Street, er, there's a different type of attitude up there in terms of any way you look at it . . . they seem to be more, if you like, socialised in terms of not telling claimants anything about supp. ben. and getting it in any situation. (Woman, mid twenties, former student)

These results are broadly in line with quantitative studies, which have also shown a significant degree of dissatisfaction with the DHSS among the unemployed. For example, Marshall *et al.* (1988b, p. 221) found that almost half of the unemployed in their study had complained to some government department. More specifically, research carried out by the National Audit Office (1988) found that the unemployed were much more likely than other Supplementary Benefit Claimants (62 per cent of the unemployed compared to 45 per cent of all claimants), to have experienced 'some' or 'lots' of problems with the DHSS (ibid., p. 10).

This basic similarity of views about the DE and the DHSS, and the two 'stereotypes' of civil servants, supports one of my key theoretical arguments, namely, that unemployed people's relationship to the state is one of the fundamental structuring features of the social relations of unemployment. The evidence above shows that this is indeed the case, and that, by and large, this does give rise to common views about the DE and the DHSS. Even the perception that many of the problems faced by claimants are due to 'the system' or 'understaffing' are found among both groups of the unemployed. Further, there appeared to be less of a difference between the two groups in their communicative competence in answering this question, which lends further support to the argument that these bureaucracies are the basis of common experiences amongst the unemployed. The only important difference being where those unemployed people who were not from the centre felt that some of the poor treatment they received was due to the civil servants having to deal with troublesome claimants. Those from the centre did not mention this at all.

6.5 VIEWS ABOUT REASONS FOR HIGH UNEMPLOYMENT

Questions in this section were designed to see if people made any connections between perceptions of causes of unemployment and political action, either by governments or the unemployed themselves. More specific and direct questions about collective action by the unemployed were also asked, and I consider the results from those questions later. Questions about high unemployment were asked in a logical 'narrative' order. First, a general question was asked about why there is so much unemployment. Secondly, this was followed up with a specific question about whether or not the government could do anything about unemployment. Finally, there was a further specific question asking whether or not they thought that the unemployed themselves could do anything about high unemployment. Those who had not had any contact with the unemployed workers' centre first gave highly fatalistic accounts of the world recession, with some providing elaborations about trade union power, increased population, voluntary unemployment and government policy.

Er, because there ain't no jobs, that's the only answer, in'it?

PB: Why?

I don't know, there ain't no jobs. (18-year-old man)

It's inevitable, in the economy, the world economy. (Middle-aged man)

Er...it's basically, I suppose, the government that's the main reason for it...er...population's higher. There's quite a few people now who want to be unemployed. I'd say that a quarter of it was voluntary, but certainly not all of it. There's certainly a lot of people that do want jobs. (20-year-old man, unemployed under one year)

Some, however, blamed the unions on top of the world recession.

The world recession...and trade unions, they've been too powerful in the workplace, interfering with people's jobs. (Middle-aged man, unemployed over one year)

In contrast, we get more clearly articulated views, by and large, from the group from the unemployed workers' centre, with a strong bias towards blaming the Conservative government for the high rates of unemployment. There was also some account given in terms of a combination of government policies and the world recession. Furthermore, another contrast between this second politically active group and the first group is that some people refer to capitalism as some kind of 'social system' that creates unemployment, or monetarism as the set of policies being pursued by the government. Running through some of these accounts of the reasons for high unemployment is an argument about government mismanagement of the economy. Connected to the perceptions of the causes of unemployment, then, is an ideological critique of both the 'social system' and the government's response to unemployment generated by that system. Among these activists there is little in the way of the fatalistic accounts produced by the first group. Whereas fatalism prevails among those who were not politically active, there are both cognitive and evaluative accounts from those who were involved in the centre.

There are world conditions that the government can interpret differently and have an effect on that unemployment. I think that in the capitalist system that we live in, er, even if you had a Labour government you wouldn't eliminate unemployment, er, but it would probably be far less than it is today, but I don't think eliminate it. I think there is something inherent in capitalism that, er, needs unemployment, even in the 'sixties when people were marvellous, there were still a few people unemployed. (Middle-aged man, former shop steward)

Could have something to do with the policies of the government and our Prime Minister [sarcastically]...er...the world situation...though basically I think it's more to do with the policies of our own government. (Woman, early twenties, former student)

I think a lot of it is deliberate policy on the part of the Tory government. It sort of weakens people's position generally...a large amount of unemployment [and] people are afraid to strike and demand higher wages. It's sort of like a, it's just regarded as a pool of labour really...Well I think it's very bad with the cutbacks in the public sector. Not only does it mean that people aren't getting services that they need such as housing and hospitals and education and so on, it's also very wasteful of human resources. (Woman, late twenties, former shop steward)

Amongst the first group it was thought that little could be done by government about unemployment, which is to be expected given their more fatalistic accounts of the causes of unemployment in the first place. On the other hand, those who saw unemployment as in large part brought about by trade unions felt that the government was doing the right thing by using unemployment to discipline the unions.

No I can't see it.

PB: Not by the government?

No, not really. (18-year old man)

The government?...Not really, they only give people an income and work, but they aren't proper jobs. (Married man, mid twenties)

I think the creation of work is a bit false. I think work's false in the first place, therefore they don't put any effort into it... I think maybe in the long term they could do, but whether people would actually want that to happen I don't know. (Single man, early twenties)

The government's only doing the right thing to try and smash the unions. (Middle-aged man)

The interviews with those from the unemployed workers' centre, however, revealed clearer and more concrete views about government strategies for lowering unemployment. What is most distinctive here, perhaps, is the listing of possible job generation strategies that governments could pursue, from direct public investment and its multiplier effects, to controls over foreign investment, and the encouragement of cooperative ventures to create jobs. A further distinctive feature of these accounts is that they are not abstract ideas, but very concrete practical solutions for meeting human needs in a specific way – through state intervention.

Er... well, first of all I would look at all the public services, I think we should look into public works schemes. Schemes that would be benefiting society on a social level, without demanding profit at the end of it, to put people who are basically receiving from society and not able to give anything back at the moment... we need more hospitals, we need more houses, we need better roads... But we should definitely be protecting our industries, we should be putting controls on finances or monies that are made out of the efforts of working people that are invested abroad. Er, I think our tax system should be completely altered, so that people on minimal incomes are not taxed so that their families can enjoy a better standard of living , 'cos I think the spending power of the people is very important to counteract unemployment. Obviously the more money you've got the more televisions or whatever it is you can buy, which means there's more demand for products and therefore more people can be employed in that respect. (Middle-aged man, former shop steward)

Well, yes, I think they should employ more people in the public sector to try and sort of boost the economy... they ought to encourage small coops and stop money from being invested abroad. (Woman, late twenties, former shop steward)

The final issue considered in this section is the question about whether or not unemployed people themselves could do anything about unemployment. From the first group the responses were typically in terms of the possibility and associated difficulties of the unemployed setting up their own businesses. This also involved a degree of fatalistic reasoning.

Well they can try and make their own business up, but you need money don't yer, and not many do try that, but they can't create jobs can they, if there ain't jobs then they can't ... what they gonna do? How can they make jobs? It's of course government money i'nit, and they don't want to spend that money do they? (Man, under 21)

Well, I think they could set up their own schemes ... things like, er ... self-employment, coops, self-help groups.

PB: How do you see that coming about?

I suppose if someone wants to do that and they have the time, I think you can apply for some money to set yourself up like. (Married man, late twenties)

In contrast, some of the second group from the unemployed workers' centre immediately offered organised political action as a possible step that the unemployed could take to reduce unemployment. However, these views were by no means put forward by all of them, and to varying degrees they were all sceptical about the political power of the unemployed. A stronger argument came from some former shop stewards, who argued mostly in terms of an underlying unity of working-class interests between the employed and the unemployed.

I am against this idea that if you're unemployed you go to an unemployed centre, you relate solely to unemployed people, and you feel an unemployed person ... you're a worker, even if you're unemployed you're a worker, and your unemployment is something you've got to struggle against and organise against, and, er, be motivated to change. But, er, I think there is a tendency, you know, amongst some people in unemployed centres to isolate unemployed people through their unemployment, and just look at issues that affect you in that sense. If you're unemployed you're still part of the workforce, you're just an unemployed worker, you know. (Middle-aged man, former shop steward)

It appears that for these people a wider working-class solidarity takes precedence over a specific political organisation of the unemployed. For former shop stewards, their involvement in the unemployed centre was largely in terms of what they saw as a wider political project of the labour movement. For them the unemployed could do something about unemployment principally through being part of a wider movement of organised labour. Within this wider labour movement, the social and political status of the unemployed is seen as secondary to the project of working-class solidarity, as one of them put it, '... you're just an unemployed worker, you know'.

However, not all those involved in the centre expressed such spontaneous political sentiments. One, for instance, was more immediately sceptical and dismissive, drawing attention to the contrast with the situation of those in employment.

I don't think unemployed people are a very strong group really. I think they can sort of vote against it and have marches. No, I don't think they're in as strong a position as people who are working. (Woman, late twenties, former shop steward)

This woman was a former shop steward, but unlike the previous two did not see any organisation of the unemployed as part of a wider project of class politics. Her former unions were COHSE and NUPE, when she worked as a nurse. The previous two shop stewards were both in TASS (having maintained their membership). The contrast is, in part at least, one between shop stewards in a skilled, male-dominated, manufacturing sector union compared to general public sector unions. For the others from the unemployed workers' centre who had no experience of trade unionism either as members or shop stewards, their views in this context are rather more like the first group who had not been involved in the unemployed centre. This involved ideas about setting up small businesses, although they are treated rather sceptically.

> Very little, I don't see how they could, er, OK we've got these schemes of setting up you're own business, but they're only a drop in the ocean in terms of the scale of things ... and ... a lot of those are going bankrupt themselves. (Woman, mid twenties, former student)

Finally, there are those from the unemployed workers' centre who reject the goal of employment in itself as an individualistic political response to unemployment, and these had not been involved in trade unions. For them there is no clear political project for either government or the unemployed to pursue to reduce unemployment. This expresses most strongly the post-materialist theme of individualistic solutions to the 'oppressions of the system'.

> The problem is that, er ... Labour who would probably say that there is ... they see unemployment as an evil propagated by the current administration, and whatever sympathies I might have with the Labour Party, er, my situation of being unemployed through choice, I don't really find them particularly of use to me. But counter to that, that's one aspect I can't really understand, though I appreciate this ... how miserable the unemployed are ... I can't really identify with them fully. I can't really identify with what Neil Kinnock and Roy Hattersly are saying ... that it's horrible and we've got to put vast quantities of public funds into the British economy in order to get rid of it. (Man, early twenties, former student)

6.6   CONCLUSION

Clearly there is no uniform homogeneous 'unemployed consciousness' or identity, as suggested by some social–psychological models. There is no essential 'experience' of unemployment, except perhaps in relation to the state's social security system. However, this is not automatically translated into an oppositional discourse and associated collective action. People need cultural and organisational resources to draw upon in order to engage in such action, and the other wider differences between the two groups show this quite clearly. Further, the state's unemployment and supplementary benefit bureaucracies are quite impervious to local organisation and action by the unemployed. This is to some degree revealed in the feelings of powerlessness expressed by the former shop stewards, when comparing the unemployed to organised employed workers. Such people would, no doubt, be 'negotiating' increases for themselves, and other unemployed people locally, if it were possible, as former shop stewards did when they became involved in the NUW(C)M in the 1920s and 1930s. They have the organisational and cultural resources, but they do not have the opportunity.

The differences between the two groups are quite striking. However, from an analytical and theoretical point of view the differences within the group from the unemployed workers' centre are perhaps equally important. Here it is most apparent that the unemployed are not homogeneous in terms of political discourses. These variations flow from *prior* political experiences, especially in relation to the trade union movement. It is within the pre-existing trade union movement, particularly amongst its shop-floor activists – shop stewards – that a set of critical cultural resources are to be found. They are thus able to provide an account of the causes of unemployment in terms of economic crisis and government actions to discipline the working class. Consequently, unemployment can be reduced by changes in government policy, although whilst society remains 'capitalist' there will still be some unemployment. Finally, the unemployed can do something about unemployment by organising as a subordinate ally of the trade union movement.

The alternative 'type' of politically active unemployed person is exemplified by their espousal of ideologies associated with 'new social movements'. These emphasise social cleavages and axes of struggle other than class. The essential feature of this type is perhaps the emphasis on an *individual personal rejection of the 'work ethic'*. Now I should make it clear that these form a minority, but the fact that they are politically active makes them an important minority. Paradoxically perhaps, as Offe (1985, pp. 819–20) has noted, these movements share with contemporary 'neo-conservatism' a suspicion of centralising regulatory responses to the economic crisis tendencies of contemporary societies. Hence their inability to give a clear indication of alternative sets of policies to reduce unemployment.

With two quite different kinds of cultural resources and cementing discourses, which articulate different, and to some degree opposing, political projects, the cohesion and support for any organisation cannot be guaranteed. However, it is clear that the class politics paradigm was dominant within the centre. Further, post-materialist political discourses do not lend themselves to taking over in any way organisations such as the unemployed workers' centre, given their individualist emphasis and strong rejection of formal collective organisation (ibid.). Rather, people from such political backgrounds tended to use the centre as a service. In Brighton, none of these discourses was anywhere near hegemonising local communities in quite the same way as the cultural resources underpinning the NUW(C)M did in some places in the inter-war period. This is, therefore, an important factor holding back any further political mobilisation of the unemployed in Brighton. The Brighton unemployed workers' centre and the Unemployed Workers' Union thus tended to remain peripheral rather than mass organisations.

In this chapter, I have been concerned with the fairly general experiences of unemployment of those who were and were not politically active. In the following chapter, I shall consider issues which are more directly 'political' in character, the questions of Thatcherism and class consciousness.

7

Thatcherism, Class Consciousness and the Unemployed

7.1 THATCHERISM

In this chapter I examine the issue of whether or not the unemployed systematically hold a set of views that have been described as 'Thatcherite' (Hall, 1982), and then I shall go on to consider issues of class consciousness. The particular claim about Thatcherism is one conclusion of the research by Golding and Middleton (1982). I criticised their work in theoretical terms earlier. However, given the wider significance of the Thatcherite thesis for explaining contemporary working-class quiescence, and the detailed criticism it has received (Jessop *et al.*, 1984), I believe it also merits empirical assessment. A further reason for considering Golding and Middleton's analysis empirically is that their results have been used entirely uncritically by some authors (for example Alcock, 1987, pp. 118–19). However, others have produced evidence contradicting Golding and Middleton's claims (Taylor-Gooby, 1985, pp. 21–52). Further, the specific features of Thatcherite discourse that I shall be examining below also enable me to develop empirically my arguments relating to the structuring and content of ideological discourses. I have argued that the content of ideologies may have dissimulating (concealing), reifying, legitimising, fragmenting or fatalistic effects with respect to relations of domination. I shall also be further pursuing my general claim about the importance of political organisations in producing and disseminating critical, oppositional beliefs.

The idea of Thatcherism was developed to account for the ideological and political drift to the right in Britain since the early 1970s. One of the putative, distinctive features of the radical right was its reaction to the social democracy of both Labour and Conservative governments since the Second World War. A number of themes were pulled out as being distinctive features of the new right: its criticism of state services as too bureaucratic, wasteful and unproductive; its arguments that taxation and welfare spending were too high; that the unions were too powerful and were distorting, in a monopolistic fashion, the workings of the labour market. As such it was seen as a combination of traditional Toryism – stressing the themes of 'Nation', 'family', 'authority' and 'traditionalism' – and a revived neo-liberalism, which stressed self-interest, competitive individualism and anti-statism. It was seen not only as a dominating set of themes in media discourses, and the speeches of leading Conservative politicians, but also as speaking directly to popular sentiments.

> It works on the ground of already constituted social practices and lived ideologies. It wins space there by constantly drawing on these elements which have secured over time a traditional resonance and left their traces in popular inventories...What makes these representations popular is that they have a purchase on practice, they shape it, they are written into its materiality. (Hall, 1982, p. 39)

It is this notion of the populist elements of Thatcherism that Golding and Middleton considered. Their claim was that they had become the dominant 'public opinion' on welfare, and that the 'poor' themselves were most likely to express these views. From the the work by Golding and Middleton (1982), I 'operationalised' these theoretical arguments as three core themes or items for the interviews. The first of these was the 'scrounger' theme; the second was a combination of the racism and sexism themes; and the third was the anti-trade union theme. They are set up as 'ideal typical' attitudes based especially on the interviews quoted in Golding and Middleton's work, and the actual phrases of Conservative politician's public speeches.

The first of these 'Thatcherite' items was: 'Unemployment benefit is too high and this encourages scroungers and lazy people to stay on the dole rather than find a job.' This was set up as a specific 'test' of Golding and Middleton's conclusion that unemployment was believed generally to be voluntary, and involved no hardship among the unemployed themselves (Golding and Middleton, 1982, p. 177).

Among those who had no contact with the unemployed workers' centre, the data below show that there are those who feel that in general Unemployment Benefit is not too high, and does not encourage people to stop looking for jobs. However, there is an important reservation to this generalisation, in that some believe there may be a few people who won't work as long as benefits are available. This seems to be a weak but critical acceptance of the Thatcherite arguments. Nevertheless, others in this group rejected the argument more categorically. As one of them put it, 'If there ain't no jobs to find you can't 'ave one, can you?' Now, it is quite reasonable not to expect unemployed people to respond positively to the claim that Unemployment Benefit is too high. However, Golding and Middleton argue that most of the unemployed *do* feel that Unemployment Benefit is too high. Nevertheless, what some of the responses below do indicate is a certain fragmentation effect operating through these beliefs. In this quite specific sense, then, Thatcherism does have some consequences, but they are part of quite complex and qualified views. The claims of Thatcherism would seem to contradict their experiences rather than relate directly to them as suggested in Hall's accounts.

> Huh, well that's a cheer isn't it [sarcastically]. I suppose there are one or two people that, er, can benefit out of being unemployed, but they're very few and far between. I just think that's rubbish. (Man, mid twenties, unemployed over one year)

> Well it's not too high, it's too low i'nit? I suppose it does encourage you to find a job, but if there ain't no jobs to find then you can't 'ave one can you? No there's not many people want to live off twenty-six pound a week, but if that's all they're gonna give yer then you've got to try and make it work. (18-year-old man)

> Er...I dunno' if you can say Unemployment Benefit's too high...er...I don't think the people who are so-called scroun-

gers are lazy people actually. I think at the moment there's quite
a large surplus of people wanting jobs anyway, so if some want
to stay on the dole then fair enough, but I wouldn't say
Unemployment Benefit is too high. I don't know how anyone
could come to that conclusion. (Man, early twenties, unemployed less than one year)

A more categorical rejection of these arguments comes from
those who had been involved in the unemployed workers' centre.
One of them, for example, points out how such arguments can be
related to what he sees as small employers' 'class interests'. Among
these there is a bifurcation between the labour movement discourse
of class politics, and an 'anti-work' argument associated with post-
materialist discourses. However, there is not even partial support
given to Thatcherite beliefs by people from the unemployed
workers' centre. Consequently, there is no tendency towards a
fragmentation effect, as instanced in the distinction between the
lazy and the genuinely unemployed, that was found amongst some
of those in the first group.

I don't know how people can relate to that quite frankly. I think
what they're really worried about, the people who make this
claim, is that the wages that they're able to conspire to keep at
an absolute minimum, and it worries them that people are gonna
take the attitude that although they're kept on a minimum of
benefit that there's not that much difference in going out to work
for an absolute minimum, which is, er, the people who I would
say are making this kind of comment are probably people, er,
small employers who are running sweatshops offering the
absolute minimum of wages and conditions who are hoping
that four and a half million unemployed means that there's
hundreds scratching on their doors for the lowest wages and
conditions, and even in their wildest dreams are trying to say
that the Unemployment Benefit they're getting is too much.
(Middle aged man, former shop steward)

The following is a good example of the kind of view expressed by
those utilising a post-materialist discourse. The interviewee makes
a sharp distinction between himself and the rest of the unemployed
who, he believes, do not have the same approach to life as

himself. That is to say, he believes most unemployed people are so concerned with paid work that they cannot see the possible advantages of unemployment.

This idea is abominable because most unemployed people are totally pissed off and spend the day circulating up at Churchill Square until the *Argus* comes out about half past eleven ... and then cross the road to the Job Centre and then home totally miserable because they find themselves at a loss without a job ... It's such an expected comment from some people who write to the *Leader* and the *Argus* all the time and the *Daily Mail.* It's obviously true ... [sarcastically]. Well it's, er, it's true in so far as by their definition I'm a scrounger and a lazy bastard ... but, er, I think the majority of people, the vast majority of people who are unemployed are not sinful ... but just trying to keep their lives together. (Man, early twenties, student 'dropout')

More generally, those from the unemployed workers' centre stressed Thatcherism's lack of appreciation of the material deprivation caused by unemployment.

When you get down to poverty traps for people with children and those sort of things, as I've just said, I don't think that [applies to] an unemployed person looking damned hard for a job, trying to sort out the situation for themselves. Life on the poverty line ... it's bloody hard to get a job. If you're unemployed for two years what are you gonna do, like what are you gonna do, blame the unemployment on the unemployed? (Woman, early twenties, former student)

Well I don't agree with that. I don't think it's too high, and even if it was high it wouldn't be a bad thing, because that would mean people would have more money to spend which boosts the economy anyway. I don't think most people like being unemployed anyway. Even if they were paid the same I think people would prefer to work, because of the sort of isolation of being unemployed. (Woman, late twenties, former shop steward)

The second of the Thatcherite items that I used was: 'Unemployment is so high these days because immigrants and women have taken too many jobs.' Again, this is partly set up as a 'test' of Golding and Middleton's findings of racism being just beneath the surface of people's attitudes to social security benefits and unemployment (Golding and Middleton 1982, p. 171).

However, Golding and Middleton were concerned only with attitudes to welfare benefits, whereas here I am also concerned with two wider issues. First, whether or not there is some sense of blame on ethnic minorities for the high levels of unemployment, which is a central feature of much racist ideological discourse. This is what one would expect from the arguments of authors such as Phizacklea and Miles (1980) and Miles (1982). They have argued that what they call the 'negative racialisation' of colonial immigrants in Britain has occurred partly through the white working class making a causal connection between immigration and the industrial decline of the areas where they live and the country as a whole (Miles, 1982, p. 172).

Secondly, I am also concerned with to what extent there is a patriarchal ideological discourse in relation to women and unemployment. The view that part of the solution to high unemployment was to take women out of the labour market was, for example, an argument of Norman Tebbit's, leaked in 1983 (Campbell, 1987, p. 175), and Thatcherism's more general concerns about the family. Furthermore, I was also interested in the possible relationship between racist and sexist beliefs in relation to unemployment, so the two themes were linked together in one statement.

Amongst some of those who were not from the unemployed workers' centre, there was a general rejection of the basic core of the explicit racism and sexism of the statement. There was a broad commitment to some formal legalistic notion of equality. There was one exception to this quoted below and, interestingly, included strongly racist and sexist arguments. Nevertheless, there is a certain hesitancy or ambiguity expressed by some, for example: 'immigrants...I wouldn't say they've got a good reputation', and '...I suppose they do take jobs'. But in both instances more explicit racist remarks do not follow, rather, there is a degree of sympathy for them. These quotes could be interpreted in other ways. They might, for instance, be seen as racist remarks, but this would have to decontextualise them from the rest of the individuals' comments. They are certainly not suggestive of a virulent racism, especially when compared with the strongly racist beliefs below.

...immigrants...I wouldn't say they've got a good reputation...when England gave up the Empire, then I would say
that was a big mistake...that made them into English citizens,
gave them an English passport and with that came the right to
come over here to England. OK, but if you look at what these
people are doing for jobs. Look at the catering business. How
many English people are there who are, say, proper chefs and
who are doing the washing up, who's doing the cleaning? Yes,
they're all immigrants, foreigners, 'cos the English don't like
doing it, and always the immigrants are doing the worst job...

PB: So what about the women, what do you think?

Er, women, they got the same right to work...females got the
same right to work as the male, but only if you employ, well
what I see is if you employ females they are paid less than males,
and with this they are worse off than the males, and they don't
take away many jobs. (Man, middle aged, long-term unemployed)

Well, women are allowed to work, aren't they, they 'ave equal
rights 'n' all that. Immigrants, yeah, I suppose they do take jobs,
well it's all right for me to say about that in'it 'cos my dad's an
immigrant in 'e...but, er, people who are over 'ere, they can't
do anything about it now, they can't send them back so they got
to work like anyone else. (18-year-old man)

...well I don't really agree with that anyway...er...I mean
generally I think that's pathetic 'cos we should see ourselves as a
whole rather than lots of different countries and to support each
other. I don't think that affects unemployment at all 'cos people
from here can always go to different countries. I think being
people they have as much right to jobs as anyone else, and if they
wanna' take them, all well and good. (Man, early twenties)

The argument against women and blacks quoted below works in
quite different ways. The sexist argument is cast in terms of a
reification of men's and women's capacities to work in particular
jobs, specifically engineering. The racist argument is cast in terms
of nationalism, in the sense that this is a 'white man's country'. The
interviewee also believes that employers and the social security

system are biased in favour of blacks. This is a strongly held virulent racist set of beliefs that contrast sharply with the examples above.

> Well, I'd like to see equal rights brought down. I disagree with women workin' 'cos all the men could do the work then...a lot of women can't do engineerin' jobs in factories. They can't do the job and yet when they do it they get the same pay as men.

> PB: So you think men have more right to a job than women?

> Yeah.

> PB: Well, what about immigrants?

> I lost my job 'cos I wasn't a coloured person, they changed 'cos I didn't like doing it...there was a coloured person working with me...they should get back to their own country, 'n' I know they get more money on social security than what a white person does. (Middle-aged man)

In contrast, what is significant about some of those from the unemployed workers' centre is the spontaneous use of 'class language' and interpretative schemes. The response is in terms of capitalist ideologies that generate divisions of race and gender in an *a priori* unified working class. There were no racist or sexist sentiments explicitly expressed. Otherwise there is little in the way of strong differences between these views and those of the others above. The replies are also largely in terms of formal legal equality being referred to. The references here, then, are structured not so much in terms of a discourse of substantive natural rights, but in terms of a legitimate rational legal rights discourse. This is probably because there is legislation against race and sex discrimination, which those from the unemployed workers' centre might see as a 'gain' for the left. This is, however, seen as being undermined by systematic ideologies, and the practices of employers.

> Yeah, well, this is another stock in trade of capitalism...You see they can only keep people down and keep conditions down and prevent the working class from coming forward if they divide and rule. And what they're inferring by this, and I know

that many working-class people hold this view, is by trying to make, if you look at it most black people we are talking about are working people, certainly women are working people, they're trying to suggest that somehow there's a white male norm in the working class that should be protected, and a black or female abnormality that's competing with this and of course it's not true. Women have a right to work as much as men. Blacks have as much of a right to work in this country as whites. And it's not a question of saying that women are competing with male jobs, or blacks, but having a proper look at the system and the factors inherent in that system which is creating unemployment. (Middle-aged man, former shop steward)

Er, apart from trying to refrain from hitting a person if I'd heard that . . . unemployment is unemployment regardless of who's had the job. That's almost saying there's one class of person who should have a job in the beginning, and I have no idea that that's the way society should be going. I want a right to work, and just that about immigrants and women, it's just prejudice that. (Woman, early twenties, former student)

Among those expressing post-materialist views, there is rather more emphasis on the employer bias against a whole host of 'minorities', rather than some reference to creating divisions within the working class.

I think that's totally untrue, but er . . . I should think it's just as difficult for them to find a job.

PB: You don't think men should have more of a right to work than women?

No. But I think the bias amongst firms will go against women, gays, disabled and for men. (Man, early twenties, former student)

The role of unions in creating unemployment has been a constant theme of 'New Right' theoretical writings since the 1950s, and remains one of the principal rationales for the removal of trade unions' legal 'immunities' (Hanson and Mather, 1988). This claim was part of Conservative politicians' views from the late

1970s onwards about the persistence of relatively high unemployment in the UK, for example, in the case of Keith Joseph (Joseph, 1978, p. 25).

From these themes and debates among 'New Right' theorists and politicians, on the one hand, and the analyses of Hall and Golding and Middleton, on the other, the following item was developed: 'The trouble is that the unions have pushed wages too high so that employers can't afford to pay them. They've priced their members out of work, that's why there is so much unemployment these days.' Among those who had no contact with the unemployed workers' centre there does appear to be some limited evidence of views that approximate to the Thatcherite argument, but none of them unambiguously supported the argument. The first quote below shows an example of the limited acceptance of the argument. Otherwise unemployed people did not think that unions, and the effect that they had on wages, had deleterious effects on unemployment.[1]

I think there's something to that...er...I think some of the unions, er, seem to be just looking for trouble sometimes, and I think it's showing now. Workers want a bit more say in their own union where they haven't done for quite a while. I think it's down to individual cases how much an employer gives, if he's trying to make a big profit in one firm and he could afford to give more wages but in another firm it can't be, you know, it just can't be if there isn't enough money. It depends on the individual firm. (Man, mid twenties)

No, I don't really agree with that... 'the trouble is that unions have pushed wages too high'...I mean you want a decent wage don't yer. You ain't gonna work for something pretty low. No I don't agree with that...(Man, under 20, unemployed over one year)

Well, I wouldn't believe that the unions would do that in the first place. Seeing as the unions are there for the protection of the workers, so I can't understand that the unions would over price themselves. I think that the unions generally do a good job in keeping the standards fairly high...I can't believe that they'd push the wages too high. (Man, early twenties)

Strong disagreements with the Thatcherite view about trade
unions pushing wages too high came from those from the
unemployed workers' centre. There were no instances of even
partial sympathy with the anti-union view. Several of them argued
against it in terms of their own experience of trade unions.

I've heard workers at C say this argument, but I've never come
across a worker who'd say that about his factory or his
conditions. Everybody that I've ever spoken to who is in a
trade union or even those who aren't in trade unions feel that
their pay doesn't reflect the work they do and that their conditions could be improved upon... Now I think that organised
trade unionism allows people through the collective strength of
the membership... allows workers to aspire to higher pay levels
and better conditions, I can't see the situation where this would
go beyond the profits that the company had made. (Middle-aged
man, former shop steward)

Well, the whole role of unions is to protect the workers, and it's
not that... I mean it's like in times of boom when employers can
afford to pay wages and when times are slack... or have
different ideas, they'll just squash them down really. There
aren't the unions pushing them up, they're forced there to make
sure that people just aren't actually exploited... That to me is
like an argument to get away with unions... It's not that unions
push wages too high, OK you've got strikes for certain things. I
would just hate to see the day with society without unions. It
would just all be back in the nineteenth century really. (Woman,
early twenties, former student)

Overall there is little widespread support among those interviewed for the strong Thatcherite sentiments they were asked
about. Some, all of whom had not been involved with the
unemployed workers' centre, did express sympathy with particular
aspects of the radical right items on trade unions, racism and
sexism, and slightly more so on the levels of Unemployment
Benefit/scrounger item. However, all these were highly qualified
responses. More categorical and well argued responses came from
those who had been involved in the unemployed centre. They
seemed to be able to engage more critically with Thatcherite

discourse, drawing upon the wider cultural resources of critical beliefs. This is also a further indication that communicative competence may be a political resource with which to criticise and oppose more effectively dominating ideologies.

However, what is to be made of Golding and Middleton's strong claims about the effects of Thatcherism? One possibility might be that popular attitudes have changed, and there is some evidence for this. 'Public support' for the view that welfare benefits are too high has declined from 50 per cent in 1979 to 19.5 per cent in 1983 (Whiteley and Winyard, 1987, p. 144). Further reasons for Golding and Middleton's unusual results, I believe, are that their attitude measures are poorly worded, and they push their data too far. In particular, they fail to convey the complexity and ambivalence of people's views about unemployment and welfare benefits. The ambivalence of people's views about unemployment and benefits, what I have termed a tendency to express a *fragmenting* ideological view, was found in Taylor-Gooby's work using quantitative data (Taylor-Gooby, 1985, pp. 23–38).

It seems that unemployed people have subtle and qualified criticisms of 'scroungers', for example. The unemployed people I have interviewed expressed no spontaneous support for Thatcherism. Furthermore, I have shown how, in relation to Thatcherism, political socialisation has an impact through involvement in political organisations that are opposed to the government, and which propagate alternative ideologies. People who had been involved in the unemployed workers' centre appeared to have the conceptual apparatus with which to criticise more effectively and more categorically the claims of Thatcherite discourses. Organisations play a major role in developing critiques of 'dominant' ideologies.

7.2　CLASS CONSCIOUSNESS AND THE UNEMPLOYED

I have argued that certain forms of class consciousness can be characterised as cultural resources for collective action. I described the content of these cultural resources abstractly as discourses of substantive natural rights. This is operationalised here as a set of relatively simple claims about the relationships between economic inequalities and power. These are outlined in more detail below.

Further questions about class consciousness followed the standard interview questions common in sociological analyses of class consciousness. However, unlike the usual quantitative approach, these qualitative interviews enable a more subtle account to be given by interviewees. Moreover, this approach also enables me to examine the cognitive and evaluative aspects of people's views in more detail, and to assess whether or not people are using claims about substantive natural rights.

Generally, the questions were designed to examine whether or not people had perceptions of a class bias in the state and the government in a very *diffuse* sense. Hence, these items do not use 'class' language in a strict sense, but more general notions of 'rich and poor', 'working people and big business' and 'employers'. This leaves the items open to interpretation in terms of class language. People were also asked about the political interests of the unemployed, and what people thought about the desirability of collective political action by the unemployed. Finally, I asked whether or not they thought there were classes in Britain today, followed by 'prompts' asking for clarification on 'boundaries', what class they put themselves in (the cognitive aspects) and what effects they thought it had on people's lives (the evaluative aspect).

Those who had not been in contact with the centre generally disagreed with the claim that 'The trouble with this country is that there is one law for the rich and another for the poor', usually arguing that such phenomena would be the exception rather than the rule. Others see a division between 'rich' and 'poor' that may be widening, but do not see it as connected in any way to the actions of the state. Finally, some saw a connection between the poverty of the unemployed and 'having to steal', whereas the rich don't have to break the law in the same way.

No, I disagree with this one. OK they make a little bit of difference, so that really is a special law for the rich and a special law for the poor, no. (Man, middle-aged, long-term unemployed)

Well I don't think that's quite right, but I think there are ... sort of differences and I think they've become more so the way things are going, 'cos the poor I suppose in a sense is the unemployed, and er, in general, but not all, and as sort of technology continues, and the people with skills get larger and larger wages and the people that are unemployed are gonna get more and more unemployable, then I think you will get more of a rich and poor. (Man, mid twenties)

No... unless the rich can bribe the judge, but that's the only way... [or]... say... when a top MP breaks the law or does something wrong, then not a lot happens to him, but, er, I mean the rich don't go out shopliftin', but they do, but not many go out shopliftin'. If you're poor you've got more reason to do it, but, er, otherwise I don't agree with it. (Man, under 20)

Those who had been involved in the unemployed workers' centre, in contrast, frequently made some important 'causal' connection in their views between wealth, or lack of it, and the way that the legal system worked to the detriment of those without wealth. The actions of the state were seen systematically to favour the 'interests' of the wealthy. There is also, in part, an inversion of 'dominant values' in some of the views expressed, for example in the legitimacy accorded to a 'little bit of fiddling on the dole' compared to the large-scale 'fraud' by the rich in the area of taxation. Other themes in the responses included references to the policing of the 1984–5 miners' strike, and the stereotyped attitudes of the judiciary. They were both cognisant of class bias in the legal system, and had a relatively sophisticated critical evaluation of this. The first quote below provides a good example of a substantive natural rights claim in comparing social security fraud to business fraud.

I think that the vast majority of the laws that are enacted in Parliament are there to serve the interests of the wealthy. Er... this in many cases works to the detriment of the dispossessed and the people who can't control their means of production, um, so I would say definitely that there's one law for the rich and another for the poor, er, for instance, if you are unemployed and you do a fiddle, you work for your next door neighbour and you get five pounds or ten pounds for it, the law's calling you criminal. But if you're a multimillionaire your profits in your company that you've set up are millions, and you've found a tax haven, or you're the receiver of a government subsidy that's come purely through your support of that government coming into power. You're a good man, and yet we're talking about one bloke who's trying to provide for his family as best as he can, meeting the situation he's in by doing a little bit of fiddling. You've got somebody else who with impunity is wresting millions of pounds, which should have been paid in taxes, away from the community as a whole, is doing it with state approval. (Man, middle-aged, former shop steward)

It does seem to be true actually... but it's not particularly relevant to unemployment, but there does seem to be legal bias to rich people, it seems legal for the police to hassle people, it seems illegal for Yorkshire miners to travel down the M1 to picket other places. (Man, twenties, single)

Ooh yeah I agree with that... well I think that a kind of ruling class have sort of privileges and freedoms... I mean for example multinational corporations, they get away with swindling their tax returns, but, um, if an unemployed person is caught fiddling on the dole there is a great sort of outcry... Well, the law generally, I think, you know, how you fare in court depends on the solicitor you've got and judges and magistrates tend to have biases towards people. They have stereotypes of how people should behave. (Woman, former shop steward)

In relation to wealth, power and the state there are important differences in the content of the responses from the two groups. Amongst those who had not been in contact with the unemployed workers' centre, the main tendency was to assert that there is no bias in the rule of law. It was seen to operate rationally, legitimately and equally to all. This can be seen as a *dissimulating* ideology, concealing the class bias of the legal system. It is not a case of legitimation, since that would imply cognition of systematic bias that would be *evaluated* as legitimate in terms of some rational or traditional values. This first group had no clear cognition of systematic class bias, rather, where they did refer to it, then it was seen as exceptional and due to the actions or attributes of individuals. However, the second group from the unemployed workers' centre had a strong critical sense of the class bias of the state. For the second group, there was both cognition and a negative evaluation of the class bias of the state. What they saw to be the rights of subordinate groups such as striking miners were seen to be treated with contempt by the state. This negative evaluation of the state was grounded in a sense of 'natural justice', a form of substantive natural rights discourse.

For those who had not been involved in the unemployed workers' centre, government's bias towards big business was often justified on the grounds that it benefits the country as a whole. On the other hand, they also tended to see that the government was in some sense 'even handed', also doing things for working people. Others express a kind of 'fatalistic' view of the way governments just have to take account of the 'needs' of big business, and that working people are being unrealistic to expect much from government. However, this is not an instance of fatalism as I have defined it earlier, since it does not operate on the relationship between the beliefs and actions of the respondents themselves. Rather, it is a complex *dissimulative* ideology. Essentially, what several people argued was that the government favours big business, *because it is in the interests of the country as whole to do so*. That is, being concerned about the success of big business means that the government, in these people's eyes, is also concerning itself with the interests of working people. This is how they evaluate their perception of class bias. This dissimulative effect operates not on the *cognition* of the government favouring big business, but on the *evaluation* of the government's reasons for doing so.

Well, I think in a sense people possibly look at the government, working-class people quite often, and they sort of expect... 'I'll vote for them if you're gonna give me another two quid a week', and I sort of think politics is economics really. People misconstrue what's going on, 'cos they personally don't benefit. I think that you couldn't run a country sort of considering each sort of Joe Bloggs and all that, giving each a few more quid a week. I think they've got to consider big business, well all sorts of businesses, and big business if it's profitable is good for the country. People misconstrue it because they don't directly benefit as they see it. (Man, mid twenties)

Yeah, well, it is always on the side of big business, you know, businesses to do well... Yeah... well, I think it is concerned about what happens to working people 'cos they want everyone to be happy, for everything to go well, I think it is concerned, but it is on the side of big business. (Man, under 20)

I wouldn't say it was always on the side of big business... um... I'd say it looks like that a lot of the time it's helping out big business, but in turn that should help out the worker... If the government helps out the big businesses then it should eventually get down to the workers. (Man, middle-aged)

In contrast, a variety of connections were made by those from the unemployed workers' centre between government and 'big business'. These included arguments about the business interests of leading members of the government to the perceived bias in policies, and the Conservatives being the 'natural' party of business interests. Furthermore, others pointed to the way that they felt the government was 'using' nationalism and 'law and order' issues to obscure or detract from other 'divisive' aspects of their policies. The evaluation here is in terms of the systematic class bias of this particular government.

Most of the government have got shares in big companies, they don't like to talk to working-class people. They should listen to the working-class people and the bosses at the same time. (Man, middle-aged, former shop steward)

I think it's perfectly natural considering the ideas of the government at the moment... business and free enterprise is the way to get things right... I don't think anybody should be particularly surprised at that, so, er, siding with business is the way the government exists, it believes in the stronger and the fitter whoever that is... I just think it's expecting a lot of people generally to look after themselves and not to expect to be looked after from the cradle to the grave... I just think it's natural with this sort of government. (Man, early twenties, former student)

Yes I think it is... it's true... in terms of just like protecting, um, you know, our economy and what is *our* economy, and when it falls down they don't give a damn about state industries and nationalised industries which is *our* economy...and, um, the idea of privatisation it's like big business and private individuals, etc., and if everything is conducted with that in mind then, er, it doesn't really matter about what makes that work or the people who happen to be unemployed. If there's a general reason then that's what it is. (Woman, mid twenties, former student)

There are systematic differences between the two groups in their perceptions of class bias in the government. Although the first group were cognisant of the government doing things for 'big business' and being concerned about its economic interests, this was seen as reasonable since the effects were believed ultimately to help everyone in the country. This is a dissimulative ideological effect operating at the level of evaluation rather than cognition. In contrast, those from the unemployed workers' centre were more critical of the government in the class terms suggested by the question. Generally, the government is not seen to be at all concerned with what happens to working people as a result of their policies.

The group who had not had any contact with the unemployed workers' centre *all categorically disagreed with the statement*, 'This government is creating unemployment to scare people into taking lower wages, so that employers can make more profit.' However, the reasons they gave for this disagreement were somewhat diverse. First, there was total disagreement where the statement couldn't be taken seriously and was effectively meaningless. In contrast, those from the unemployed workers' centre could quite clearly identify the logic of the question; it was quite meaningful to them. Secondly, others found particular aspects of its 'reasoning' contentious, such as picking up on the idea that the government was scaring people through unemployment to accept lower wages. Thirdly, there was the view that this was somehow legitimate in terms of Britain's world economic position where British industry had to be made competitive again. This is a form of legitimising ideology where systematic bias is perceived and seen to be legitimate in terms of the rationality of 'market forces'. Finally, there was the view that the government had no control over economic forces and therefore was not to blame for the high levels of unemployment. Here again we have the 'fatalistic' rationalisation of government actions in the face of insurmountable economic forces, as one of them put it: '...It's just...um...they can't do anything about it.'

> I don't agree with that at all. No, I sort of think the reason this government's doing it is, er, in the hope to sort of cut back all that's wasted in the unprofitable businesses, to make ones that are stronger so that they will keep money coming into this country. On a world basis they aren't viable. I don't think they do that to scare people. You'd have to be a bit paranoid to think that. (Man, early twenties)

> No I don't agree with that...I don't think the government is, yer know creating unemployment. It's just...um...they can't do nothing about it. (Man, under 20)

> I wouldn't say that they were tryin' to scare people into takin' lower wages. If anythin' the employers are takin' advantage of it. I don't think that's the intention...I can't believe a government would intentionally do that. They may do...I think that unemployment does push wages down, but I think that people who are unemployed would take jobs that are badly paid anyway...I think possibly for school leavers, I think they're the only one's down there, the benefits are very low, so they're pushed into jobs with a lower wage. I don't think the government's actually doing it intentionally for that reason. I think if anythin' they are creatin' unemployment by cuttin' their support for some industries, but I don't think they're doin' it intentionally to push wages down. (Man, early twenties)

In the arguments of this first group there is also a dissimulative effect operating, not at the level of cognition but on the evaluation of the government's policies. That is, unemployment and lower wages are seen as an *unintended* consequence of government actions carried out for other purposes. However, there is an economistic fatalism that some also articulate.

The second group, in contrast, *all clearly agreed with the statement*. Various connections were made here with the perception of attempts to break organised labour, or with the wider government strategy of control over the money supply and inflation, where unemployment is seen as a 'convenient' by-product. Other themes to these views were perceptions of attempts to encourage a low-wage labour market. There would appear to be two sets of arguments being put here. The first sees unemployment as *central* to the government's 'strategy', whilst the second sees unemployment as a 'by-product' of the government's anti-inflation policies. The former shop stewards in particular argued that unemployment was more central to the government's strategy, and this was seen as breaking unions and encouraging a low-wage economy. This is a further example of the class–politics discourse.

It's being used to undermine wage scales...to give them the whip hand again...this is it, you see, 'cos when you've got an organised working class you're able to say to the employer, 'We want some control over the factors that we're involved with.' Now you have the employers who can do exactly what they want. So when she talks about being the party of freeing these market forces to sort of rise to maximum freedom, she can only do that if she's got a demoralised and fragmented working class...this is the tragedy of unemployment. (Man, middle-aged, former steward)

I think that unemployment is simply a by-product. I don't think they actually create it...er...if people get lower wages there's gonna be less money in circulation, so this government's gonna press for that, er...it's all to do with the supply of money...lower wages may create more jobs, but people still work forty hours a week for wages only £4 more than benefit. People accept it because they're afraid of losing their jobs. Except the miners, they seem more unified. (Man, early twenties, former student)

Yeah, I think that's true, but it's also forcing young people into badly paid jobs...to make the unemployment situation seem less bad...I do think it has an effect on the people who are working. I mean the whole kind of legislation about trade unions has been changed. I don't really know a lot about the details, but the whole thing about the tresspass law, and secondary picketing isn't allowed and a lot of that wouldn't have been possible without higher unemployment. (Woman, late twenties, former shop steward)

In relation to government policy on unemployment those from the unemployed workers' centre are much more critical than the others. The former group do not believe that the government are consciously creating unemployment, but that it is an unintended consequence of some of their actions and policies, or that the government is powerless to prevent it. There was also some legitimation of government policies in terms of the 'rationality' of responding to 'market forces'. Former shop stewards from the unemployed workers' centre argued that unemployment was being used by the government as part of a class strategy to break the unions and create a low wage economy.

7.3   THE POLITICAL ORGANISATION OF THE UNEMPLOYED

Those who had not been in contact with the unemployed workers' centre had largely negative views about the possibility of collective action by the unemployed, despite agreeing in broad terms with the general idea. The negative arguments were put in terms of people being too individualistic for such a thing to be a success – 'people go their own way', as one of them put it. There was also the view that such things were the creation of people who would find something to protest about whatever the situation was, grounding their argument in a general 'economic fatalism'. Others argued that such actions would not be able to have any significant effects despite the desirability of the consequences.

Since this question bears directly on the issue of possible action by the group of which the interviewees are part, fatalism, as I have discussed earlier, is central to their responses. In some instances the wider ideological effects are used to 'rationalise' the general fatalistic argument. For example, in the first quote below, the perception of the fragmented character of the unemployed is used to support a generally fatalistic account.

> ... there are not many people who want to go together and try to really fight for their rights, but if you do really do a good job, and you are unemployed, then they must have the chance to go forward and say, look, now we must do something. But really, I see a lot of groups, but you must work very hard to bring them

all together, especially to bring them all together underneath one head. This will be very hard... people go their own ways. (Man, middle-aged)

More directly fatalistic are the accounts below, which are partly in terms of the lack of political effectiveness of any putative actions, and simple lack of jobs. A classic example of 'informed' fatalism.

Well, I don't really know... the sort of people I meet who seem to be pretty heavy on these sorts of things, they're the sort of people who'd wave a banner anywhere, even if there wasn't unemployment they'd be protesting about something else, you know. It's just the type of person, and I don't think that would do unemployed people any good... They could sort of, if they pressurised they might get a little something. The government which is quite capable of deceiving especially working-class people... then they're no better. So they'll all protest and they're told this, that and the other and think they've won when they'll actually get nothing. I don't think they'll do a lot of good really. (Man, early twenties)

Well that's not gonna make a lot of difference if they all get together and stand up for their rights. I mean if there's no jobs you can't create jobs can yer. Can't get more jobs. I don't see how you can get more jobs by standing up to the government. (Man, under 20)

Um... I should say unemployed people should get together and create their own jobs, rather than constantly look to someone else... I think it's a good idea to keep wages high, to keep them up, I think, to keep wage brackets fairly decent. But I don't think they'd get any support from the media at all.

PB: Why don't you think there's been more of a reaction happening?

There's no place where unemployed people can congregate and get things together like that. I think most people don't think of doin' anythin' like that, just accept that they're unemployed an' there ain't no jobs. They don't seem to think that if they get together with unemployed people they could create jobs together or push other people into creatin' jobs. But even then they'll be artificial jobs, 'cos it's jobs creation that doesn't work. (Man, late twenties)

The answers from those who had been involved in the unemployed workers' centre were more positive and optimistic overall, in relation to the possibility of collective action by unemployed people influencing the course of events. However, there were two distinct views here. The first, coming principally from former shop stewards, emphasised that unemployed people could only have any political influence by working within the already existing structures of the labour and trade union movement. The second view emphasised more independent action by the unemployed in relation to the social security system, and this was connected to the right *not* to work rather than demands for jobs. This is a further example of where the post-materialist political discourse parts company with the class–politics discourse.

Yes and no, unemployed people ought to get together, stand up for their rights and to organise and bring about a situation where there will be more jobs available, I don't necessarily agree with that, that is to the exclusion of bringing in other bodies, it's the organised working class that are gonna help to achieve that. I actually don't think unemployed people alone will achieve it. I think that the unemployed voice is a minimal voice... at the moment we're being drenched by media coverage of workers fighting against unemployment [the miners]. If those unemployed take place and those 20 000 people are on the dole, you won't be able to hear their voice. And this is the situation unemployed people are in. So I would say, yes, unemployed people should be brought into a collective situation, but they should be made to realise they're only gonna be able to get their jobs and security, and all the things they would wish for for the future by organising within the labour and trade union movement. (Man, middle-aged, former shop steward)

I don't know if it's necessarily the best way to beat unemployment, and I think it sounds like it's creating an artificial division between unemployed and employed people, and I think they ought to get together on equal terms to do that.(Woman, former shop steward)

The following quote in particular is a strong example of the post-materialist perspective. It is strongly anti-statist, stressing individualistic solutions to unemployment, whilst arguing for the unemployed to maximise their state benefits.

Unemployed people certainly ought to get together to work out how much they can screw the system out of, and make sure they get it, because it's there to be had ... er, personally I don't want a job ... I certainly don't think it's a way to get jobs. I think people ought to fight just as much for the right not to work. I'm not sure how they can get more work unless they get together to set up a small cooperative. That's the sort of thing I might get involved in ... Personally I don't believe in collective action ... I don't have any feeling of solidarity ... I think one of the most important things is that people who are unemployed is to try to understand their situation, not to feel sorry for themselves, not to feel grateful to the government for their benefits ... to find something to do ... to get an enjoyable experience. (Man, early twenties, former student)

Those who were not from the centre saw collective action by the unemployed as desirable, but fatalistically argued that it was unlikely to happen. If collective action did occur, they felt it would make no difference to the situation of the unemployed. The unemployed people from the centre were divided into two groups. The first, generally former shop stewards, argued in terms of collective action through class solidarity institutionalised through the trade unions. The second, generally former students utilising a post-materialist political discourse, argued that the unemployed should organise to maximise their state benefits. However, they did not present any coherent ideas on how to achieve this. It would seem that those who became involved in the centre did so for quite different sets of reasons: the first for reasons of 'class solidarity' and the second to make the most of the advantages of unemployment in their 'post-materialist' lifestyle.

7.4   CLASS CONSCIOUSNESS AMONGST THE UNEMPLOYED

Early in the interview some of the interviewees had already made some references to class in their own responses. They had introduced the concept of their own accord to make sense of the things they were talking about. Later, I deliberately introduced class into the interview and followed the question with a series of 'probes' and 'prompts' about boundaries, what class the interviewee would put themselves in, and on how they thought class affected people's lives. The initial question concerned the cognition of class divisions, and then moved on to draw out issues of evaluation.

The responses from those who were not from the unemployed workers' centre were quite varied in their details. The first one quoted below sees class divisions existing, but believes they're quite fluid and not really making much difference to people's lives. Others do see classes as affecting people's lives, and in one instance this is thought to be because people believe in classes, not because they are thought to exist in any 'objective' economic sense. Economic inequalities of wealth, income and education are, however, themes of some of the other accounts below. If anything the data below suggest that for these unemployed people class concepts are not important for the way in which they interpret the social world around them. As one of them says, 'It's hard to say really. It's hard to answer these questions.' In relation to class consciousness, communicative competence can function as a political resource.

The language of 'class' means something to these people, but it is not a key scheme of interpretation for their everyday lives. For example, in the quote below there is a recognition of class divisions in terms of an 'aristocratic upper class' with himself being middle class. The consequences of class are seen not in structural economic terms at all, but in terms of people's individual attitudes towards each other. Class is somewhat negatively evaluated, but in terms of problems for individual interpersonal relations.

Er, yes and no, but I would say everywhere in the world is the same . . . In England if you're in the royal line you got a little bit more...er, they take a little bit more notice of you...it makes a little bit of difference if they are, say, somebody from a high class, but I know a lot of people who really worked themselves up, they are rich. And, er, there it doesn't make any difference.

PB: What sort of class would you put yourself in?

Middle class.

PB: How do you think class affects people's lives?

Not much if at all. I don't really, by myself. I must say now I'm talking about myself. I don't make any difference if he is lower class, he is middle class or he is higher class, or he comes from somewhere on the top. (Man, middle-aged)

The following quote again indicates a spontaneous recognition of class divisions, but also in rather individualist terms. The basis of class divisions is seen in quite complex terms, involving distributive (money) and cultural (education and intelligence) factors which by no means neatly correspond in his view. This partly flows from his own situation where he is unemployed, whilst his wife is a 'middle-class' teacher, and he has problems identifying a putative middle class. He sees class as less 'visible' than in the past, when he felt it had held back the working class culturally.

I think there's always been sort of a working class and there always will be, and there'll always be a really rich class, but this middle class to me, I dunno', I can't really sort of er point it out and say 'middle class', I know people do to me.

PB: What do you think are the boundaries of classes, what makes the difference?

What makes the difference is actually in individuals' lives. When you meet people I think education makes a great difference, and even if someone doesn't have a lot of money, they're, you know, quite well educated, a working-class person can be seen as being middle class. Er, also money, of course, that comes into it. From money comes all the other things like, sort of, accommodation, where you go, the sort of house you've got. I think your actual intelligence makes a lot of difference, because it doesn't matter how much money you've got people might still sort of, they'd

still say, 'There's a working-class bloke with a lot of money.'
Now he wouldn't become you know, middle class or upper class
sort of thing.

PB: What class would you say you were in?

I don't know...I think personally by myself I suppose I'm
working class, but with my wife being a teacher, and I'm running
a home I suppose that would be considered middle class.
Although I don't agree with it, but there again you can't as I
said, you know, 'middle class'...I'd like to think I'd fallen in
between.

PB: How do you think class affects people's lives?

I think it did a lot in the past, I think people do in a way, and
there's still a lot of tradition especially among sort of working
class that they can't do this and you can't do that, because
you've got to remember your position. Although I think it was
actually verbally said years ago, I think it's not actually said any
more, but people feel it's there. Quite often they feel, you know,
that they weren't meant for such things. (Man, late twenties)

The following quote provides a good example of class perceived
in distributive terms, with the man identifying with a working class
between a lower and middle class. His evaluation of class is again
in terms of the extremes of distributive inequality, and its
consequences in terms of criminality.

Well there is i'nt there. You got working class 'n' that 'n' middle
class...Middle and lower, mmm, well there's middle class, they
can get by, they're not poor but they're not rich, but I'm poor,
but my mum and dad get by all right, er, lower class they can't
afford nothing for living...squats and all that, and then you've
got your higher class who've got money and comfortable.

PB: How do you think class affects people's lives then?

Yeah, it does affect people's lives dunne it? I mean...
er...people're lower class 'n' that there people, I mean there's
more crooks, there's more people in the lower class breakin' the
law than there is in the higher class, affects people's lives like
that. You don't see many rich people gettin' nicked do yer. It's

hard to say really. It's hard to answer these questions. (Man, school leaver).

In the following account the 'objective' existence of class is denied, but it is seen to exist only to the extent that people believe in it. People's belief in class divisions is the problem, not its objective existence and consequences.

It depends, if you believe in classes, yeah there's classes, if you don't there isn't.

PB: Do you believe in them?

Erm no, some believe there is a class system, there is but it's only in them, it doesn't exist outside.

PB: Why do you say that?

It's, erm, there's nothing that points out there is a class system it's only been created by us...if you stop believing there is a class system then it therefore stops existin' it's there no longer...er, I think, yeah, some people believe there is a class system, er, people think it's there to be overthrown...I think that's a bad thing. (Man, mid twenties)

Among those who had been in contact with the unemployed workers' centre there is a much more uniform affirmation of class language, but with some important variations. Some located class firmly within the workplace with 'workers' subordination to the dictates of 'the bosses'. Others struggle with the complexity of everyday class processes seeing connections through work, social mobility, education and politics, but here again another former shop steward seems to give priority to relations within the workplace. Another partly rejects the concept of class, seeking to give an equal role to race, gender and sexuality in the structuring of politics. This represents the post-materialist discourse. From his views quoted below he is if anything slightly hostile to traditional labour movement politics. Some feel that class divisions are more clearly visible now than in the 1960s, which contrasts with those who were not involved with the centre who felt that, if anything, class divisions were more obscure now. The former shop stewards stand out in this group, and from those who had not been in contact with the centre, in relating class processes to workplace social relations.

Overall, the unemployed people from the centre felt much more at home using class language, except those who most firmly embraced the politics of post-materialism. This suggests that class concepts for them are much more a part of the way in which they interpret what happens around them. Former shop stewards in particular saw class in terms of production relations and the consequences of unequal power relations at work.

> PB: What do you think in terms of working class makes the difference?
>
> They do the jobs day after day...'n' they do do the jobs 'n' when the boss comes round they sack them next minute.
>
> PB: Do you think that makes the difference between working class or not?
>
> Yeah...too many bosses around.
>
> PB: what class would you put yourself in?
>
> Me? working class. (Middle-aged man, former shop steward)

Others stressed the complexity of class processes, noting both production based features and cultural aspects of class relations as they saw them. Further, in seeing class in terms of 'a state of mind', they are making reference to a class-based political solidarity. In evaluative terms, the cultural aspect of working-class people's lives is believed to be negatively affected by class processes. Class is also seen as systematically related to political organisation and struggle.

> I think it's a very hard one this, but I would say a working-class person is someone who has no means to produce, or has no means of production and who is forced to work for an employer who has the means of production, um, but of course is a self-employed bricklayer working class? Yes he is. Some higher management who haven't the means of production themselves and who work for an employer as higher management are receiving a standard of living that you would question as being working class. So it's middle class...er...What are the traditional factors to make a person working class? Is the fact that

your father has been a busman and you went to a secondary modern school, but you set up a business and have now got £100 000. Are you working class? Or somebody who's father was a doctor who went to a grammar school, but you're unemployed. Are you still middle class? Er...I think that working class is to some extent a state of mind as well. Do you feel solid or solidarity to a body of people who traditionally have, er, seen their struggle in society different from another class of people. I think perhaps that would be the best way to put it.

PB: What other classes would you say are people in?

Well...I would say the middle class fall into this professional category where they are the recipients of a lot of the benefits of the society in as much as they control on a lesser level to the upper class, have the decision-making in a factory or at least responsible positions in a factory, have the professional jobs like a doctor which gives them a great amount of respect or direct decision-making. Have an income which gives them benefits in a society that they are happy about. Um, and are then in a position to give that to their children. They understand the benefits of education and make the most of them...It is very very tricky, because many people who I would consider to be middle class, if you take on a purely financial level, would be worse off than people who I would consider to be working class. Er, if you take somebody like Tony Benn, for instance, who when his father was made a Lord and materially you would have to consider him middle or upper class even, but on the intellectual level, on the level, on the level of how he values those things and how he's neglected those things and how he's seen his role to fight and struggle for something else, does it matter?

PB: What effect do you think class will have on people's lives?

I think that it's...the worst aspect of it is the characterisation that class gives people, particularly in this country that people feel that on a cultural level a lot of working-class people feel that going to the theatre is not something that working-class people should do. It's puffy, it's middle class or whatever, er...But the better aspect of it is that, er, the unity that working-class people have developed, particularly in this century, through the trade union movement to aspire towards a fairer society through experience of having to suffer themselves, but wanting to see a better society, a welfare state, people caring about each other, looking after the disadvantaged and all the rest. That solidarity has come from the working-class, and working class consciousness and pride in all these. Upper class is perhaps easier to sort out. You know, to have power and the wealth to control the lives of other people is something that is quite singular to the upper class. But working class and middle class there is a grey area and it's . . . I don't want to be sort of, you know, have to define a point, you know, this is where something stops and this is where something starts. (Middle-aged man, former shop steward)

Well, there's an upper class and there's a monopoly class too . . . these people who run international corporations rather than class in the sense of the public boy system and that sort of thing, but that's very much still around. And certainly we've got this other enormous class from all kinds of backgrounds but I don't know what you'd call it, not working class but not middle class in terms of limited access to things. Ermm . . . and then there are the people that work, that in their opinion are very smug and regard themselves as, you know, as much more somehow not unemployed and not working class. But there are so many subdivisions that people see themselves as part of a small group. But the major division is between those who have to sell their labour up against those who have the right background, etc., and these are the sorts of people who go into the business class, and a lot of inheritance of things.

PB: What class would you put yourself in then?

Working class . . . I'm unemployed . . . simple class.

PB: What effects would you say it has on people's lives?

Um, well in this situation I think it makes you much more political, much more militant . . . It creates divisions obviously, it creates divisions and depending on which side of the division you are, and realising which side of that division you are can make you bloody angry or otherwise it can make you quite contemptuous and ignore whatever side it may be . . . you either see someone as deprived and that can make you politically aware, more willing to change, more actively political. You've got your Tory MPs trying to get Britain out of its muddle, I think that...they only give lip service to what it must be like to be unemployed and basically they don't give a shit, they can't understand it because being middle class is the whole world in their eyes. (Woman, mid twenties former student)

Well, I think just really the ruling class and the working class really.

PB: What do you think makes the difference? What would be the boundaries?

Well, I would say ruling-class people actually owned capital, and therefore make decisions and people in influential positions, perhaps, for example politicians...I think anybody who sells their labour in order to exist is really working class, even if they're a doctor or something like that.

PB: So what would you put yourself as?

Working class.

PB: How do you think class affects people's lives then?

Well, I think that people generally don't have very much control over major decisions...Um, well, they don't have any access to...they have no means of finding out what's going on, it's only through the media which is so biased...er, education which is often geared to selecting and streaming people rather than developing them. (Woman, former shop steward)

Well, er, I don't think there's really class. I don't think there is a working class, it's once again something I feel alienated from looking at my own circumstances. In my own situation I don't want work, I get the impression that all people want is to look after themselves. My experience hasn't been one of a classic or Marxist working class. I have got very little faith in, er, any kind of proletariat with revolutionary potential existing. The majority of them are quite content to stay at home and watch Coronation Street rather than unite.

PB: Do you think there are any real class boundaries in Britain today?

I think they can always be created as things are but, er, these things are always so grey at least in my experience, which I agree is minimal. The borderline is so grey boundaries are difficult to see... I think there are other networks of oppression which are as important, such as gays, race and gender. They're as important and I don't like to see them played down for the sake of class. (Man, early twenties, former student)

In this section I have shown that those who are not from the unemployed workers' centre understand class in a variety of ways: in terms of a distribution of money and wealth, individual attitudes or of 'cultural capital' such as education. For these people class is not a central feature of political discourse, they do not relate it to political events or their own political beliefs or actions. Whilst class is readily accessible as an identity to many of them, they do not immediately relate the classes they might identify with to politics or collective action. In this sense my results are broadly comparable to those of Marshall *et al.* (1988a, pp. 188–90). People are cognisant of class processes in varying, partial and complex ways that are not easily captured using quantitative techniques. Their evaluation of class processes is similarly complex, and although frequently negatively evaluated are seen, fatalistically, as immutable.

Among those from the unemployed workers' centre there is a polarisation between those articulating a class politics discourse and those articulating a post-materialist politics, which in its extreme forms does not recognise class as a source of political identity. Former shop stewards in particular gave an account of class in terms of relationships at the point of production, which indicates that class is for them an important way of understanding the politics of the workplace and trade unions. Several authors have argued in a variety of ways that radical class consciousness is produced and disseminated by political movements, especially working-class parties and trade unions (Gallie, 1983; Lash, 1984; Marshall *et al.*, 1988a). This broad argument is generally supported by the results here. For many of those active in the centre, class is both a source of personal identity and the principal basis of political action.

7.5   CONCLUSION

The central result of the analysis of this chapter is that those unemployed people from the centre had a more clearly articulated set of beliefs through which they were able to interpret their unemployment, and criticise dominant ideological discourses. Most crucially, it would seem that these people held these views before they became involved in the unemployed workers' centre, and these views were a large part of the reason that they became involved in the first place. These beliefs constitute a distinctive set of cultural resources for political mobilisation.

There remains the question of why that mobilisation is not more widespread. From the analyses of this chapter it is evident that those who are not mobilised hold highly fatalistic views of the contemporary social structure, and of the possibilities of collective action within these circumstances obtaining anything substantial for them. Although fatalism is the most important ideological mechanism operating centrally in the relationship between evaluations of the social structure and collective action to change it, this is buttressed to a limited degree by sets of ideological beliefs. However, such beliefs by no means constitute a 'dominant ideology' that secures quiescence among the unemployed; the vast majority of the unemployed perceive all too well the futility of seeking to influence state institutions from which they are excluded at the bottom of the class structure.

8

Conclusion

I have argued that to understand political responses to unemployment by the unemployed it is necessary to consider their relationship with the state, and their organisational and cultural resources for collective action. Through an analysis of political movements of the unemployed between the 1830s and 1930s, an account of attempts to organise the unemployed during the 1980s, and interviews comparing the politically active and politically quiescent amongst the unemployed, I have examined the changing form of the state's unemployment relief institutions and the organisational and cultural resources of the unemployed.

In relation to the changing forms of state unemployment relief I have argued that it is necessary to consider four dimensions of change: the extent of the franchise and the degree of local democratic control over unemployment relief; the various modes of decision-making (representative-democratic, corporatist, pluralist or bureaucratic); whether or not relief is in the form of indoor relief or cash benefits; and the extent of voluntary and state insurance schemes. I have argued that there are two principal forms of organisational resources that political movements of the unemployed may draw upon. The first, monological forms of organisation, concentrates on short-term quantitative gains through centralised technocratic forms of action. These tend to be organisations *for* the unemployed, and the TUC's centres for the unemployed of the 1980s most closely approximate to this ideal type. Secondly, dialogical forms of organisation have qualitative transformation as their long-term goal, but may seek short-term quantitative gains through decentralised forms of action. These are principally organisations of the unemployed, and I have argued that the NUW(C)M of the 1920s and 1930s most closely approximates to this type, and I have also considered an attempt to create this type of organisation in Brighton during the 1980s.

In the historical account, I showed how the changing form of control of unemployment relief and the development of the political resources of the labour movement explain the rise of protest to a peak during the 1920s and 1930s. The increasing involvement of the state in unemployment relief, the widespread development of cash benefits and, especially, the extensions of the franchise made it easier for the unemployed to improve their material standards through collective action, directed at local unemployment relief institutions.

However, these protests were not simply determined by the level and pattern of unemployment. What was significant about the NUW(C)M was its highly localised character as a movement. The NUW(C)M only became a significant force in those places where the requisite organisational and cultural resources were to be found, not just where there was high unemployment. It was strongest in those places where a radical class consciousness had hegemonised the symbolic communities of local working classes. The material and organisational bases of this local hegemony have since been undermined by many years of deindustrialisation and economic restructuring. Consequently, many of the crucial organisational and cultural resources previously available at the local level for political organisations of the unemployed are no longer in existence.

During the 1980s the TUC has taken a central role in organising the unemployed by providing services through its local centres for the unemployed. Generally, these have been funded by the MSC and local authorities. However, in some places, for example Brighton, centres have chosen to avoid MSC funding, and have attempted to organise the unemployed for local collective action. When compared to the 1920s and 1930s these attempts have largely been unsuccessful. However, like earlier movements the attempts in Brighton have drawn largely upon the resources of the local labour movement, and I have shown that it is not the level of unemployment, or the density of formal union organisation, but the political character of the local labour movement that is crucial in shaping these organisations.

I have also analysed a series of qualitative interviews with two groups of unemployed people, some of whom were involved in the

Brighton centre, and some who were not. Using this material I have probed into the detailed content of the cultural resources of the unemployed. Whilst the politically quiescent unemployed express a series of ideological beliefs to a limited degree, most important is an informed and rationalised fatalism about the efficacy of collective action. This is a major reason for the contemporary quiescence of the unemployed.

In contrast, the politically active group were mostly former shop stewards and students. They had quite sophisticated accounts of unemployment and politics, which I have shown divide into two discrete political discourses. The former shop stewards articulated a discourse of collectivist class politics, which emphasised the importance of the organised labour movement and political solidarity between workers and the unemployed. The former students, in contrast, often articulated a more individualist post-materialist political discourse. This emphasised the advantages of unemployment in terms of individual autonomy, and a range of relations of domination other than class were seen as of equal importance for political action. The political rationale for them of an organisation of the unemployed was to make the most of unemployment, and to maximise one's state benefits.

Above all else the conclusion of this book is that, in spite of the attempts of activists, there has been no mass political movement of the unemployed in the 1980s. This is because the state is immune to collective action for higher benefits, the unemployed generally lack the requisite organisational and cultural resources for mobilisation, and like most people the unemployed are highly fatalistic about the efficacy of collective action. In the past, unemployment relief was locally controlled under conditions of some degree of democratic accountability, so local collective action by the unemployed was able to raise the level of benefits. Furthermore, in some localities there were powerful organisational and cultural resources for the unemployed to draw upon. The disappearance of these conditions during the past fifty years or so has seen a shift in political response amongst the unemployed from protest to acquiescence.

Notes

1 Introduction

1. In May 1985, when the unemployment rate for Great Britain was 13.2 per cent, the lowest rate was to be found in Winchester (4.1 per cent) and the highest in Dingwall, in Scotland (26.4 per cent). Long-term unemployment was highest at that time in West Bromwich, and, surprisingly, lowest in Dingwall. This anomaly is explained by the very recent fall in employment in oil and gas related industries in Northern Scotland (Champion *et al.*, 1987, p. 87).

2 Theoretical Approaches to Politics and Unemployment

1. My claim is not that there are no deleterious psychological consequences of unemployment, but, rather, that one should distinguish those effects from the political beliefs and actions of the unemployed which is what Jahoda fails to do.

3 The Structuring of Political Responses to Unemployment

1. This is not only clear where the 'cohabitation rule' discriminates against women, but also where only men are referred to re-establishment centres to reinstil the habits of work. Buckland and Macgregor (1986, p. 183) have argued that this functions principally to maintain men's 'bread winner' status and the sexual division of labour in the household. At this 'extreme' of the 'disciplinary' aspects of the social security system a distinct class bias is also apparent. In Buckland and Macgregor's sample, 91 per cent of those sent to re-establishment centres were unemployed manual workers (ibid., p. 173). In contrast, unemployed professionals and executives are offered expenses paid 'job search seminars', non-attendance at which does not threaten eligibility for benefits (PER, 1988).

2. Given the normally low level of interest in and attendance at trade union branch meetings, it perhaps remains something of a mystery precisely how this works. However, ethnographic accounts of workplace trade unionism (for example Beynon, 1984) may provide some insights. Perhaps it is in certain 'critical conjunctures' when the immediate practical concerns of workers are closely bound up with the actions and pronouncements of their unions that they are most

effective in influencing their members' beliefs. However, unions can lose as well as retain support in such circumstances, which are in any case comparatively rare.

3. I have in mind here the notion of Giddens (1979, p. 69) that the 'properties of social systems are both the medium and the outcome of the practices that constitute those systems'. However, in my view, Giddens tends to underestimate the role of social struggles and political organisations in this process.

4 Early Political Movements of the Unemployed

1. Kerbo and Shaffer (1986) carried out a statistical analysis correlating levels of unemployment with collective action by the unemployed between 1890 and 1940 in the United States. They found that in the 1890s there was little or no protest compared to the extensive protest in the 1930s, although the levels of unemployment were similar. They conclude that there were 'more social movement resources for the unemployed in the 1930s than in the 1890s' (ibid., p. 1052). This conclusion basically supports my argument here.

2. However, see Hay (1977) on the ideas of the Birmingham Chamber of Commerce for a National Insurance Scheme in the 1900s *before* Beveridge's plans of 1909.

3. As a further, admittedly rather experimental exercise, in examining the relationship between levels of unemployment and protest, I compared the list of NUW(C)M branches attending the 1931 conference (NUWM, 1931, p. 3), totalling sixty in all, with the listing given by Beveridge of those localities which had the highest and lowest rates of unemployment for their county in 1934 (Beveridge, 1960, pp. 324–7, table 36). The obvious limitations prevent a valid statistical analysis, however, only two places were common to both lists – Woolwich with 8.4 per cent unemployment, and Cowdenbeath with 23.7 per cent.

4. Normally, historians put the end of the NUW(C)M as occurring in 1940, when Hannington obtained work as a tool maker. However, Croucher has recently shown that the NUW(C)M continued its casework through a single full-time official and several functioning branches until the spring of 1942. The organisation was only formally wound up in 1946 (Croucher, 1987, pp. 198–200).

5. As far as I am aware Ryan (1978, p. 58) is the only historian to have pointed this out albeit briefly and in an undocumented way. Crucially, he fails to note the role of the British Socialist Party, a direct descendant of the SDF, and of which Hannington was a member, in the formation of the Communist Party of Great Britain (Klugman, 1969, p. 16). There is, therefore, a *direct organisational link between the two periods which goes some way to explaining the similar tactics in unemployed struggles.*

6. For more detailed accounts of these kinds of struggle in the early 1920s see, for example, Garrett on Liverpool (no date); Frow and Frow on

Manchester (no date, p. 23); Croucher on Cardiff and Coventry (1987, pp. 30–1; 44–5); and more generally Hannington (1977, pp. 12–78) and Klugman (1969, pp. 116–25).

7. This kind of democracy was not just found in the exceptional 'Little Moscows' that Macintyre examined, it is also characteristic of the way the NUW(C)M worked in other places such as Birkenhead and Liverpool (Garrett, no date; Kelly, 1987).

5   Political Movements of the Unemployed in the 1980s

1. I have not been able to discover precisely what form this 'pressing' took. However, the TUC is quite unequivocal in its 1981 report on 'Services for the Unemployed' that: 'The General Council pressed the Manpower Services Commission to provide assistance towards the running of local centres...under the Community Enterprise Programme' (TUC, 1981a, p. 49). It seems that despite some popular conceptions to the contrary, the TUC still exercised considerable influence at the top of the MSC. It is frequently forgotten that the MSC was largely the TUC's 'brainchild', and the TUC took a central role in drafting the legislation for its formation in 1973 (Eversley, 1986, p. 201; Jackson, 1986). The TUC's three MSC commissioners probably did the pressing.

2. Another feature of the following quote is that the speaker appears to say that unemployed ethnic minorities will join the National Front. It is not clear if this is what he meant to say or if it was a mistake in the heat of the moment.

3. 'Check-off schemes' are where members of trade unions make a weekly donation to a fund for unemployed centres through a deduction from their wages at source, in the same way that they pay their union subscriptions. This has been much more successful than the national appeals. However, it only really operates properly in Merseyside, where the 'One Fund for All' involves 35 000 trade union members donating 10 000 each month to twelve TUC Centres on Merseyside, but similar schemes are being attempted elsewhere (TUC, 1987, p. 53).

4. The appeal was relaunched in 1987 raising only £15 000 in seven months (TUC, 1987, p. 52).

5. More recently, the dependence on local authority funding has proved to be something of a problem. With the abolition of the metropolitan authorities several centres have faced financial crises. London has lost four of its original fifteen centres as a result (TUC, 1987, p. 52).

6. There is evidence that centres nationally have since become more dependent on MSC funding. In September 1986, there were 1157 CP places in 102 centres for the unemployed, but by February 1987 these figures had increased to 1478 places in 124 centres (Unemployment Unit Bulletins, Winter 1986, no. 22, p. 15; Spring 1987, no. 23, p. 14). The majority of these places would be part time. However, these figures are contradicted by those from the TUC, which suggest that in 1987

only 38 per cent of centres were dependent on MSC funding, compared to the approximately 60 per cent suggested by the MSC figures quoted by the Unemployment Unit. I can find no clear reason for this major discrepancy. According to the TUC local authorities account for 41 per cent of centres with 21 per cent receiving funds from elsewhere in 1987 (TUC, 1987, p. 53).

7. This committee was technically 'above' the management committee, and the MC operated within the PC's guidelines. At this stage the PC consisted of representatives of the WEA, and two representatives from the Trades Council. Its role was to oversee the 'interests' of the WEA and the trades council in the centre.

6   The Experience of Unemployment

1. See Bagguley (1989) Appendix A for details of the characteristics of the samples, and discussion of methodological issues.
2. There is an important issue here of the quite clear differences in *communicative competence* between the two groups, that is, an ability to use the appropriate words, meanings and ways of talking according to context (Frazer, 1988, p. 357). The group from the centre are generally better educated than those who were not, and this is crucial to understanding their communicative competence. I shall discuss the issue of communicative competence as a cultural and organisational resource again below.

7   Thatcherism, Class Consciousness and the Unemployed

1. Some readers might find these results somewhat surprising, however, they are consistent with a general increase in public sympathy towards trade unions in general during the 1980s in public opinion polls. For example, the *Gallup Political Index* shows an increase in the percentage of people who think unions are a 'good thing' from 51 per cent in 1979 to 71 per cent in 1987 (Gallup, 1986, p. 14, table 11; 1987, p. 13, table 9).

Bibliography

Primary Sources

Brighton Unemployed Workers' Centre, Management Committee Minutes, 2.5.81.

Brighton Unemployed Workers' Centre, Management Committee report on MSC application, 14.7.81.

Brighton Unemployed Workers' Centre, Management Committee Minutes, 14.7.81.

Brighton Unemployed Workers' Centre, Management Committee Minutes, 10.8.81.

Brighton Unemployed Workers' Centre, Management Committee Minutes, 25.8.81.

Brighton Unemployed Workers' Centre, Management Committee Minutes, 2.9.81.

Brighton Unemployed Workers' Centre, Management Committee Minutes, 8.9.81.

Brighton Unemployed Workers' Centre, Management Committee Minutes, 20.10.81.

Brighton Unemployed Workers' Centre, Management Committee Minutes, 1.12.81.

Brighton Unemployed Workers' Centre, Management Committee Minutes, 15.12.81.

Brighton Unemployed Workers' Union (1981) *The UWU and the Labour Movement*.

Brighton and District Trades Council Minutes, 2.9.81.

Department of Employment, *Employment Gazette*, various issues.

Hannington, W. (1935) *Work for Wages not Slave Camps*, London, NUWM pamphlet.

Hannington, W. (1936) *Why Do They March?* London, NUWM pamphlet.

NUWCM (1929) *Report of the Sixth National Conference*.

NUWM (1931) *Report of the Seventh National Conference*.

NUWM (1934) *Report of the Ninth National Conference*.

PER (1988) *The Job-hunting Handbook*.

SERTUC (1985) *TUC Centres for the Unemployed in the South East: A Detailed Information Directory*.

The Times 12 April 1870.

TUC (1980) *Report of the 112th Annual Trades Union Congress*, London, TUC.

TUC (1981a) *Report of the 113th Annual Trades Union Congress*, London, TUC.

TUC (1981b) *Services for the Unemployed: Unemployed Workers' Centres Bulletin No. 1,* March 1981.

TUC (1982) *Report of the 114th Annual Trades Union Congress,* London, TUC.

TUC (1983a) *Report of the 115th Annual Trades Union Congress,* London, TUC.

TUC (1983b) *Unemployed Workers' Centres: TUC Guidelines.*

TUC (1984) *Report of the 116th Annual Trades Union Congress,* London, TUC.

TUC (1985) *Report of the 117th Annual Trades Union Congress,* London, TUC.

TUC (1986) *Report of the 118th Annual Trades Union Congress,* London, TUC.

TUC (1987) *Report of the 119th Annual Trades Union Congress,* London, TUC.

TUC Services for the Unemployed (1984) *Directory of TUC Centres for the Unemployed,* London, TUC.

TUC Services for the Unemployed (1985) *Directory of TUC Centres for the Unemployed,* London, TUC.

Unemployed Workers' Union (1981) *The Unemployed Workers Union and the Labour Movement: The Case for a New Management Committee.*

Unemployment Unit (1986) *Unemployment Unit Bulletin,* 22, Winter 1986, London, Unemployment Unit.

Unemployment Unit (1986) *Unemployment Unit Bulletin,* 23, Spring 1987, London, Unemployment Unit.

Unemployment Unit (1988) *Unemployment Unit Bulletin,* 27, Summer 1988, London, Unemployment Unit.

Secondary Sources

Abercrombie, N. *et al.* (1980) *The Dominant Ideology Thesis,* London, George Allen & Unwin.

Abercrombie, N. and Urry, J. (1983) *Capital, Labour and the Middle Classes,* Laven, George Allen & Unwin.

Alcock, P. (1987) *Poverty and State Support,* London, Longman.

Ashton, D. N. (1986) *Unemployment under Capitalism.* Brighton, Wheatsheaf Books.

Ashton, D. N. and Maguire, M J. (1985) *Young Adults in the Labour Market,* Department of Employment Research Paper No. 55, London, Department of Employment.

Bagguley, P. (1989) *Organizing the Unemployed: Politics, Ideology and the Experience of Unemployment,* D.Phil. thesis, University of Sussex.

Bagguley, P. and Walby, S. (1988) *Gender Restructuring: A Comparative Analysis of Five Local Labour Markets,* Lancaster Regionalism Group Working Paper No. 28, Dept. of Sociology, University of Lancaster.

Bagguley, P. *et al.* (1990) *Restructuring: place, class and gender*, London, Sage.

Bakke, E. W. (1933) *The Unemployed Man*, London, Nisbet.

Barker, A *et al.* (1984) 'Trades Unions and the Organisation of the Unemployed', *British Journal of Industrial Relations*, 22(3), 391–404.

Bell, C. and Newby, H. (1971) *Community Studies*, London, George Allen & Unwin.

Benn, T., Carter, P. and Dromey, J. (1981) 'Coming in from the Cold', *Marxism Today*, 25(12), 6–13.

Benyon, J. (1984) 'The Riots: Perceptions and Distortions', in Benyon, J. (ed.), *Scarman and After*, Oxford, Pergamon.

Beveridge, W. (1960) *Full Employment in a Free Society*, London, George Allen & Unwin.

Beynon, H. (1984) *Working for Ford*, London, Penguin.

Blewett, N. (1965) 'The Franchise in The United Kingdom 1885–1918', *Past and Present*, 32, 27–56.

Bostyn, A.-M. and Wight, D. (1987) 'Inside a Community: Values Associated with Money and Time', in Fineman, S. (ed.), *Unemployment: Personal and Social consequences*, London, Tavistock.

Branson, N. (1979) *Poplarism, 1919–1925: George Lansbury and the Councillors' Revolt*, London, Lawrence & Wishart.

Branson, N. (1985) *History of the Communist Party of Great Britain, 1927–1941*, London, Lawrence & Wishart.

Briggs, E. and Deacon, A. (1973) 'The Creation of the Unemployment Assistance Board', *Policy and Politics*, 2(1), 43–62.

Brown, C. (1984) *Black and White Britain: The Third PSI Survey*, Aldershot, Gower.

Brown, K.D. (1971) *Labour and Unemployment: 1900–1914*, Newton Abbot, David & Charles.

Bruley, S. (1980) *Socialism and Feminism in the Communist Party of Great Britain, 1920–1939*, PhD Thesis, London School of Economics, University of London.

Brundage, A. (1978) *The Making of the New Poor Law, 1832–39*, London, Hutchinson.

Brunt, R. and Rowan, C. (eds), (1982) *Feminism, Culture and Politics*, London, Lawrence & Wishart.

Buckland, S. and Macgregor, S. (1986) 'Discipline, Training or Welfare? The Functions of a Re-establishment Centre', in Allen, S. *et al.* (eds) *The Experience of Unemployment*, London, Macmillan.

Bulmer, M. (1975) (ed.) *Working-class Images of Society*, London, Routledge & Kegan Paul.

Burawoy, M. (1979) *Manufacturing Consent: Changes in the Labour Process under Monopoly Capitalism*, Chicago, University of Chicago Press.

Burawoy, M. (1985) *The Politics of Production: Factory Regimes under Capitalism and Socialism*, London, Verso.

Campbell, B. (1984) *Wigan Pier Revisited: Poverty and Politics in the 80s*, London, Virago.

Campbell, B. (1987) *The Iron Ladies: Why do Women Vote Tory?*, London, Virago.

Castells, M. (1976) 'An Experimental Study of Urban Social Movements', in C.G. Pickvance (ed.), *Urban Sociology: Critical Essays*, London, Tavistock.

Castells, M. (1977) *The Urban Question: A Marxist Approach*, London, Edward Arnold.

Castells, M. (1978) *City, Class and Power*, London, Macmillan.

Castells, M. (1983) *The City and the Grassroots*, London, Edward Arnold.

Cawson, A. (1982) *Corporatism and Welfare: Social Policy and State Intervention in Britain*, London, Heinemann.

Champion, A.G. *et al.* (1987) *Changing Places: Britain's Demographic, Economic and Social Complexion*, London, Edward Arnold.

Clark, D.Y. (1987) 'Families Facing Redundancy', in Fineman, S. (ed.), *Unemployment: Personal and Social Consequences*, London, Tavistock.

Coffield, F. *et al.* (1986) *Growing Up at the Margins*, Milton Keynes, Open University Press.

Cohen, A.P. (1985) *The Symbolic Construction of Community*, London: Ellis Horwood.

Community Action (1986) 'Sops on the Dole', *Community Action*, 73, 11–13.

Cooke, K. (1987) 'The Living Standards of Unemployed People', in Fryer, D. and Ullah, P. (eds), *Unemployed People: Social and Psychological Perspectives*, Milton Keynes, Open University Press.

Coyle, A. (1984) *Redundant Women*, London, Women's Press.

Croucher, R. (1987) *We Refuse to Starve in Silence: A History of the National Unemployed Workers' Movement, 1920–46*, London, Lawrence & Wishart.

Daunton, M. (1981) 'Down the Pit: Work in the Great Northern and South Wales Coalfields, 1870–1914', *Economic History Review*, 34, 578–97.

Deacon, A. (1977) 'Concession and Coercion: The Politics of Unemployment Insurance in the Twenties', in Briggs, A. and Saville, J. (eds), *Essays in Labour History, 1918–1939*, Vol. 3, London, Croom Helm.

Deacon, A. and Bradshaw, J. (1983) *Reserved for the Poor: The Means Test in British Social Policy*, Oxford, Basil Blackwell.

Deacon, A. and Briggs, E. (1973) 'Local Democracy and Central Policy: The Issue of Pauper Votes in the 1920s', *Policy and Politics*, 2, (4), 347–64.

Department of Employment (1988) 'Membership of Trade Unions in 1986', *Employment Gazette*, 5, 275–8.

Ditton, J. and Brown, R. (1981) 'Why Don't They Revolt? Invisible Income as a Neglected Dimension of Runciman's Relative Deprivation Thesis', *British Journal of Sociology*, 32, (4).

Economist Intelligence Unit (1982) *Coping with Unemployment: The Effects on the Unemployed Themselves*, London, Economist Intelligence Unit.

Edsall, N.C. (1971) *The Anti-Poor Law Movement: 1834–44*, Manchester, Manchester University Press.

Eversley, J. (1986) 'Trade Union Responses to the MSC', in Benn, C. and Fairley, J. (eds), *Challenging the MSC on Jobs, Education and Training*, London, Pluto Press.

Forrester, K. and Ward, K. 1986 'Organising the Unemployed? The TUC and the Unemployed Workers' Centres', *Industrial Relations Journal*, 17(1), 46–56.

Francis, H. (1984) *Miners Against Fascism: Wales and the Spanish Civil War*, London, Lawrence & Wishart.

Frazer, E. (1988) 'Teenage Girls Talking about Class', *Sociology*, 22(3), 343–58.

Frow, E. and Frow, R. (1976) *To Make That Future Now! A History of Manchester and Salford Trades Council*, Manchester, E.J. Morten.

Frow, R. and Frow, E. (No date) *The Communist Party in Manchester, 1920–1926*, Manchester, North West History Group CPGB/The Working Class Movement Library, Manchester.

Gallie, D. (1983) *Social Inequality and Class Radicalism in France and Britain*, Cambridge, Cambridge University Press.

Gallup (1986) *Gallup Political Index*, No. 313, London, Gallup.

Gallup (1987) *Gallup Political Index*, 325, London, Gallup.

Gamson, W.A. and Schmeidler, E. (1984) 'Organizing the Poor', *Theory and Society*, 13(4), 567–85.

Garrett, G. (No date) *Unemployed Struggles: Liverpool, 1921–22*, Liverpool, Merseyside Writers.

Giddens, A. (1979) *Central Problems in Social Theory: Action, Structure and Contradiction in Social Analysis*, London, Macmillan.

Giddens, A. (1982) *Profiles and Critiques in Social Theory*, London, Macmillan.

Giddens, A. (1984) *The Constitution of Society: Outline of the Theory of Structuration*, Cambridge, Polity Press.

Gilbert, B.B. (1966) *The Evolution of National Insurance in Great Britain*, London, Michael Joseph.

Gilroy, P. (1987) *There Ain't No Black in the Union Jack*, London, Hutchinson.

Golding, P. and Middleton, S. (1982) *Images of Welfare: Press and Public Attitudes to Poverty*, Oxford, Martin Robertson.

Gordon, L. (1988) 'What Does Welfare Regulate?', *Social Research*, 55(4), 609–47.

Gramsci, A. (1971) *Selections from Prison Notebooks*, London, Lawrence & Wishart.

Hall, S. (1982) 'The Great Moving Right Show', in Hall, S. and Jacques, M. (eds), *The Politics of Thatcherism*, London, Lawrence & Wishart.

Hannington, W. (1940) *Ten Lean Years: An Examination of the Record of the National Government in the Field of Unemployment*, London, Victor Gollancz.

Hannington, W. (1967) *Never on Our Knees*, London, Lawrence & Wishart.

Hannington, W. (1977) *Unemployed Struggles: 1919–1936*, London, Lawrence & Wishart.

Hanson, C.G. and Mather, G. (1988) *Striking Out Strikes*, London, Institute of Economic Affairs.

Harris, J. (1984) *Unemployment and Politics: A Study in English Social Policy, 1886–1914*, Oxford, Clarendon Press.

Harrison, R. (1965) *Before the Socialists: Studies in Labourand Politics, 1861–1881*, London, Routledge & Kegan Paul.

Hawkins, K. (1984) *Unemployment*, London, Penguin.

Hay, R. (1977) 'Employers and Social Policy in Britain: The Evolution of Welfare Legislation, 1905–14', *Social History*, 4: 435–55.

Hayburn, R. (1970) *The Responses to Unemployment in the 1930s, with Special Reference to South East Lancashire*, PhD thesis, University of Hull.

Hayburn, R. (1972) 'The Police and the Hunger Marchers', *International Review of Social History*, (17), 625–44.

Hayburn, R. (1983) 'The National Unemployed Workers' Movement, 1921–36: A Reappraisal', *International Review of Social History*, 28(3), 279–95.

Henwood, F. and Miles, I. (1987) 'The Experience of Unemployment and the Sexual Division of Labour', in Fryer, D. and Ullah, P. (eds), *Unemployed People: Social and Psychological Perspectives*, Milton Keynes, Open University Press.

Hobsbawm, E.J. (1974) *Labouring Men: Studies in the History of Labour*, London, Weidenfeld & Nicolson.

Hobsbawm, E.J. (1984) 'Should Poor People Organize?', in Hobsbawm, E.J., *Worlds of Labour*, London, Weidenfeld & Nicolson.

Jackson, M. (1986) 'A Seat at the Table?', in Benn, C. and Fairley, J., *Challenging the MSC on Jobs, Education and Training*, London, Pluto Press.

Jackson, P.R. and Walsh, S. (1987) 'Unemployment and the Family', in Fryer, D. and Ullah, P. (eds), *Unemployed People: Social and Psychological Perspectives*, Milton Keynes, Open University Press.

Jahoda, M. (1982) *Employment and Unemployment: A Social-psychological Analysis*, Cambridge, Cambridge University Press.

Jenkins, J.G. (1979) 'What Is to Be Done? Movement or Organization', *Contemporary Sociology*, 8, 222–8.

Jessop, B. (1982) *The Capitalist State: Marxist Theories and Methods*, Oxford, Martin Robertson.

Jessop, B. (1985) *Nicos Poulantzas: Marxist Theory and Political Strategy*, London, Macmillan.

Jessop, B. *et al.* (1984) 'Authoritarian Populism: Two Nations and Thatcherism', *New Left Review*, 147, 32–60.

Jordan, B. (1973) *Paupers: The Making of the New Claiming Class*, London, Routledge & Kegan Paul.

Joseph, K. (1978) *Conditions for Full Employment*, London, Bow Publications.

Kelly, J. (1988) *Trade Unions and Socialist Politics*, London, Verso.

Kelly, S. F. (1987) *Idle Hands, Clenched Fists: The Depression in a Shipyard Town*, Nottingham, Spokesman.

Kerbo, H. R. and Shaffer, R. A. (1986) 'Unemployment and Protest in the United States, 1890–1940: A Methodological Critique and Research Note', *Social Forces*, 64(4), 1046–56.

Kidd, A. J. (1984) 'The Social Democratic Federation and Popular Agitation Amongst the Unemployed in Edwardian Manchester', *International Review of Social History*, 29(3), 336–58.

Kingsford, P. (1982) *The Hunger Marches*, London, Lawrence & Wishart.

Klugman, J. (1969) *History of the Communist Party of Great Britain: Volume 1, Formation and Early Years*, London, Lawrence & Wishart.

Knott, J. (1986) *Popular Opposition to the 1834 Poor Law*, London, Croom Helm.

Knutsen, O. (1988) 'The Impact of Structural and Ideological Party Cleavages in West European Democracies', *British Journal of Political Science*, 18, 323–52.

Krieger, J. (1984) *Undermining Capitalism*, London, Pluto Press.

Laite, J. and Halfpenny, P. (1987) 'Employment, Unemployment and the Domestic Division of Labour', in Fryer, D. and Ullah, P. (eds), *Unemployed People: Social and Psychological Perspectives*, Milton Keynes, Open University Press.

Langan, M. (1985) 'Reorganizing the Labour Market: Unemployment, the State and the Labour Movement, 1880–1914', in Langan, M. and Schwarz, B. (eds), *Crises in the British State: 1880–1930*, London, Hutchinson.

Lash, S. (1984) *The Militant Worker: Class and Radicalism in France and America*, London, Heinemann.

Lash, S. and Urry, J. (1984) 'The New Marxism of Collective Action: A Critical Analysis', *Sociology*. 18(1), 33–50.

Lea, J. and Young, J. (1982) 'Urban Violence and Political Marginalisation: The Riots in Britain; Summer 1981', *Critical Social Policy*, 1(3), 59–69.

Liddington, J. and Norris, J. (1978) *One Hand Tied Behind Us: The Rise of the Women's Suffrage Movement*, London, Virago.

Lockwood, D. (1975) 'Sources of Variation in Working-class Images of Society', in Bulmer, M. (ed.), *Working-class Images of Society*, London, Routledge & Kegan Paul.

McCarthy, M. (1986) *Campaigning for the Poor: CPAG and the Politics of Welfare*, London, Methuen.

McCarthy, J. D. and Zald, M. N. (1977) 'Resource Mobilisation and Social Movements: A Partial Theory', *American Journal of Sociology*, 82(6), 1212–41.

Macintyre, S. (1980) *Little Moscows: Communism and Working-class Militancy in Inter-war Britain*, London, Croom Helm.

Macintyre, S. (1986) *A Proletarian Science: Marxism in Britain, 1917–1933*, London, Lawrence & Wishart.

McKee, L. and Bell, C. (1986) 'His Unemployment, Her Problem: The Domestic and Marital Consequences of Male Unemployment', in Allen, S. *et al.* (eds), *The Experience of Unemployment*, London, Macmillan.

Mann, K. (1984) 'Incorporation, Exclusion, Underclasses and the Unemployed', in Harrison, M. C. (ed.), *Corporatism and the Welfare State*, Aldershot, Gower.

Mann, K. (1986) 'The Making of a Claiming Class: The Neglect of Agency in Analyses of the Welfare State'. *Critical Social Policy*, 15, 62–74.

Mann, K. (1990) *Organised Labour and Divisions of Welfare: The Social Division of Welfare in England*, forthcoming Ph.D. thesis, University of Leeds.

Mann, M. (1973) *Consciousness and Action Amongst the Western Working Class*, London, Macmillan.

Mann, M. (1983) 'The Social Cohesion of Liberal Democracy', in Giddens, A. and Held, D. (eds), *Classes, Power, Conflict: Classical and Contemporary Debates*, London, Macmillan.

Mark-Lawson, J. *et al.* (1985) 'Gender and Local Politics: Struggles over Welfare Policies, 1918–1939', in Lancaster Regionalism Group, *Localities Class and Gender*, London, Pion.

Mark-Lawson, J. and Warde, A. (1987) *Industrial Restructuring and the Transformation of a Local Political Environment: A Case Study of Lancaster*, Lancaster Regionalism Group Working Paper 33, Dept. of Sociology, University of Lancaster, Lancaster.

Marsh, C. *et al.* (1985) 'Political Responses to Unemployment', in Roberts, B. *et al.*, *New Approaches to Economic Life*, Manchester, Manchester University Press.

Marshall, G. (1988) 'Some Remarks on the Study of Working Class Consciousness', in Rose, D. (ed.), *Social Stratification and Economic Change*, London, Hutchinson.

Marshall, G. *et al.* (1988a) *Social Class in Modern Britain*, London, Hutchinson.

Marshall, G. *et al.* (1988b) 'Political Quiescence Among the Unemployed in Modern Britain', in Rose, D. (ed.), *Social Stratification and Economic Change*, London, Hutchinson.

Martin, R. (1969) *Communism and the British Trade Unions 1924–1933: A Study of the National Minority Movement*, Oxford, Clarendon Press.

Martin, R. and Fryer, R. H. (1973) *Redundancy and Paternalist Capitalism*, London, George Allen & Unwin.

Massey, D. (1984) *Spatial Divisions of Labour: Social Structures and the Geography of Production*, London, Macmillan.

Miles, R. (1982) *Racism and Migrant Labour*, London, Routledge & Kegan Paul.

Miller, F. (1974) 'National Assistance or Unemployment Assistance? The British Cabinet and Relief Policy, 1932–33', *Journal of Contemporary History*, 9(2), 163–84.

Miller, F. M. (1979) 'The British Unemployment Assistance Crisis of 1935', *Journal of Contemporary History*, 14, 329–52.

Mitchell, J.C. (1983) 'Case and Situation Analysis', *Sociological Review*, 31, 187–211.

Moore, B. (1985) *All Out!*, Sheffield, Sheffield City Libraries.

Moylan, S. *et al.* (1984) *For Richer for Poorer? DHSS Cohort Study of Unemployed Men*, London, DHSS.

National Audit Office (1988) *Department of Health and Social Security: Quality of Service to the Public at Local Offices*, London, HMSO.

Novak, T. (1988) *Poverty and the State*, Milton Keynes, Open University Press.

Offe, C. (1984) *Contradictions of the Welfare State*, London, Hutchinson.

Offe, C. (1985) 'New Social Movements: Challenging the Boundaries of Institutional Politics', *Social Research*, 52(4), 817–68.

Offe, C. and Wiesenthal, H. (1985) 'Two Logics of Collective Action', in Offe, C., *Disorganized Capitalism*, Oxford, Basil Blackwell.

Pahl, R.E. (1984) *Divisions of Labour*, Oxford, Blackwell.

Pahl, R.E. and Wallace, C. (1988) 'Neither Angels in Marble nor Rebels in Red: Privatization and Working Class Consciousness', in Rose, D. (ed.), *Social Stratification and Economic Change*, London, Hutchinson.

Parkin, F. (1971) *Class Inequality and Political Order: Social Stratification in Capitalist and Communist Societies*, London, Paladin.

Penna, S. (1990) *Thatcherism, Ideology and State Practice: An Analysis of the 1984 Reviews of Social Security*, unpublished Ph.D. thesis, Department of Sociology, University of Lancaster.

Phizacklea, A. and Miles, R. (1980) *Labour and Racism*, London, Routledge & Kegan Paul.

Piepe, A. *et al.* (1969) 'The Location of the Proletarian and Deferential Worker', *Sociology*, 3(2), 239–44.

Pilgrim Trust (1968) *Men Without Work*, New York, Greenwood Press.

Pitt, M. (1979) *The World on Our Backs*, London, Lawrence & Wishart.

Piven, F.F. and Cloward, R.A. (1977) *Poor People's Movements: Why They Succeed, How They Fail*, New York, Pantheon Books.

Poulantzas, N. (1978) *Political Power and Social Classes*, London, Verso.

Prosser, T. (1981) 'The Politics of Discretion: Aspects of Discretionary Power in the Supplementary Benefits Scheme', in Adler, M. and Asquith, S. (eds), *Discretion and Welfare*, London, Heinemann.

Przeworski, A. (1986) *Capitalism and Social Democracy*, Cambridge, Cambridge University Press.

Raffe, D. (1986) 'Change and Continuity in the Youth Labour Market', in Allen, S. *et al.* (eds), *The Experience of Unemployment*, London, Macmillan.

Rees, G. (1986) ' "Coalfield Culture" and the 1984–1985 Miners' Strike: A Reply to Sunley', *Environment and Planning D: Society and Space*, 4(4), 469–76.

Rees, T. and Atkinson, P. (1982) *Youth Unemployment and State Intervention*, London, Routledge & Kegan Paul.

Reicher, S.D. (1984) 'The St Paul's Riot: An Explanation of the Limits of Crowd Action in Terms of a Social Identity Model', *European Journal of Social Psychology*, 14, 1–21.

Rex, J. (1982) 'The 1981 Urban Riots in Britain', *International Journal of Urban and Regional Research*, 6(1), 99–113.

Roach, J.L. and Roach, J.K. (1978) 'Mobilizing the Poor: Road to a Dead End', *Social Forces*, 26, 160–71.

Roberts, K. (1984a) 'Youth Unemployment and Urban Unrest', in Benyon, J. (ed.), *Scarman and After*, Oxford, Pergamon.

Roberts, K. (1984b) *School Leavers and Their Prospects: Youth and the Labour Market in the 1980s*, Milton Keynes, Open University Press.

Roberts, K. *et al.* (1985) *The Changing Structure of Youth Labour Markets*, Department of Employment Research Paper No. 59, London, Department of Employment.

Rodrigues, J. (1981) 'The Riots of '81', *Marxism Today*, 25(10), 18–22.

Rose, H. (1973) 'Up Against the Welfare State: The Claimants' Unions', in Miliband, R. and Saville, J. (eds), *The Socialist Register*, London, Merlin.

Rose, M.E. (1988) 'The Anti-Poor Law Agitation', in Ward, J.T. (ed.), *Popular Movements, c.1830–1850*, London, Macmillan.

Rowan, C. (1982) ' "Mothers, Vote Labour!" ' : The State, the Labour Movement and Working-class Mothers, 1900–1918', in Brunt, R. and Rowan, C., *Feminism, Culture and Politics*, London, Lawrence & Wishart.

Rowbotham, S. (1977) *Hidden from History*, London, Pluto Press.

Rubery, J. and Tarling, R. (1988) 'Women's Employment in Declining Britain', in Rubery, J. (ed.), *Women and Recession*, London, Routledge & Kegan Paul.

Runciman, W.G. (1972) *Relative Deprivation and Social Justice*, London, Pelican.

Ryan, P.A. (1978) ' "Poplarism" 1894–1930', in Thane, P. (ed.), *The Origins of British Social Policy*, London, Croom Helm.

Samuel, R. (1985) 'The Lost World of British Communism', *New Left Review*, 154, 3–53.

Samuel, R. (1986a) 'Introduction', in Samuel, R. *et al.* (eds), *The Enemy Within: Pit Villages and the Miners' Strike of 1984–5*, London, Routledge & Kegan Paul.

Samuel, R. (1986b) 'Staying Power: The Lost World of British Communism, Part Two', *New Left Review*, 156, 63–113.

Saunders, P. (1986) *Social Theory and the Urban Question*, London, Hutchinson.

Scarman, L.G. (1986) *The Scarman Report*, London, Penguin.

Schlozman, K.L. and Verba, S. (1979) *Injury to Insult: Unemployment, Class, and Political Response*, Cambridge Mass., Harvard University Press.

Seabrook, J. (1982) *Unemployment*, London, Quartet.

Smith, D. (1980) 'Tonypandy 1910: Definitions of Community', *Past and Present*, 87, 158–84.

Smith, D.J. (1981) *Unemployment and Racial Minorities*, London, Policy Studies Institute.

Stacey, M. (1969) 'The Myth of Community Studies', *British Journal of Sociology*, 20(2), 134–47.

Stedman-Jones, G. (1984) *Outcast London: A Study in the Relationship Between Classes in Victorian Society*, London, Penguin.

Stevenson, J. and Cook, C. (1977) *The Slump: Society and Politics During the Depression*, London, Quartet.

Summerfield, P. (1984) *Women Workers in the Second World War*, London, Croom Helm.

Sunley, P. (1986) 'Regional Restructuring, Class Change, and Political Action: A Comment', *Environment and Planning D: Society and Space*, 4(4), 465–68.

Taylor-Gooby, P. (1985) *Public Opinion, Ideology and State Welfare*, London, Routledge & Kegan Paul.

Thane, P. (1982) *The Foundations of the Welfare State*, London, Longman.

Thane, P. (1984) 'The Working Class and State "Welfare" in Britain, 1880–1914', *The Historical Journal*, 27(4), 877–900.

Therborn, G. (1986) *Why Some People's Are More Unemployed Than Others*, London, Verso.

Thompson, J. (1984) *Studies in the Theory of Ideology*, Cambridge, Polity Press.

Thompson, J. (1987) 'Language and Ideology: A Framework for Analysis', *Sociological Review*, 35(3), 516–36.

Tilly, C. (1978) *From Mobilization to Revolution*, Reading, Mass., Addison-Wesley.

Townsend, P. (1979) *Poverty in the United Kingdom*, London, Penguin.

Trory, E. (1974) *Between the Wars*, Brighton, Crabtree Press.

Turnbull, M. (1973) 'Attitude of Government and Administration Towards the "Hunger Marches" of the 1920s and 1930s', *Journal of Social Policy*, 2(2), 131–42.

Urry, J. (1981) *The Anatomy of Capitalist Societies: The Economy, Civil Society and the State*, London, Macmillan.

Van Parijs, P. (1987) 'A Revolution in Class Theory', *Politics and Society*, 15(4), 453–82.

Walby, S. (1984) *Gender Relations in Jobloss*, Lancaster Regionalism Group Working Paper 11, Dept. of Sociology, University of Lancaster, Lancaster.

Walby, S. (1986) *Patriarchy at Work: Patriarchal and Capitalist Relations in Employment*, Cambridge, Polity Press.

Walby, S. (1988) 'Gender Politics and Social Theory', *Sociology*, 22(2), 215–32.

Wallace, C. (1987) *For Richer for Poorer: Growing Up in and Out of Work*, London, Tavistock.

Waller, R.J. (1983) *The Dukeries Transformed*, Oxford, Oxford University Press.

Walton, J. (1987) *Lancashire: A Social History, 1558–1939*, Manchester, Manchester University Press.

Weber, M. (1964) *The Theory of Social and Economic Organization*, New York, Free Press.

Weber, M. (1967) *From Max Weber*, London, Routledge & Kegan Paul.

Webster, C. (1985) 'Health, Welfare and Unemployment During the Depression', *Past and Present*, 109, 204–30.

West, G. (1981) *The National Welfare Rights Movement: The Social Protest of Poor Women*, New York, Praeger.

White, M. (1983) *Long-term Unemployment and Labour Markets*, London, Policy Studies Unit.

Whiteley, P. F. and Winyard, S.J. (1987) *Pressure for the Poor: The Poverty Lobby and Policy Making*, London, Methuen.

Wright, E. O. (1985) *Classes*, London, Verso.

Wyncoll, P. (1985) *The Nottingham Labour Movement, 1880–1939*, London, Lawrence & Wishart.

Young, J. D. (1985) *Women and Popular Struggles: A History of British Working-class Women*, Edinburgh, Mainstream.

Index

Abercrombie, N. 17, 28, 70
advantages of unemployment,
    unemployed's perceptions
    of 142, 150–5
alliances 46–7, 55–6, 74
Althusser, L. 59
anti-Poor Law Movement 72–6
Asians 10–11

Bagguley, P. 207n
Bakke, E.W. 16
Barnsley 110
behaviourism 3, 29–32
Beveridge, W. 205n
Beynon, H. 204–5n
Birkenhead 84, 94, 206n
Birmingham 205n
Blackburn 102–3
Boards of Guardians 20, 72–6,
    79, 83, 86, 88–91, 93–4, 97,
    101, 105, 113
Bostyn, A.-M. 143
Bradford 11–12
Branson, N. 42
Brighton 4, 124–40, 54, 84, 141,
    166
Brown, R. 19
Buckland, S. 204n
bureaucracy 42–3

Campbell, B. 20–1, 46
Cardiff 206n
Carter, P. 115
Castells, M. 26–8
Chartism 75–6
Child Poverty Action Group
    (CPAG) 43–4, 52
citizenship 45

claimants' unions 14–15, 52, 161
class 6–7, 9, 13–15, 16, 18, 19,
    21–3, 41, 76, 81, 116
class consciousness 31, 33–5,
    56–9, 65–70, 106, 141, 166,
    178–87, 191–200
Cloward, R.A. 2–3, 12, 23–9, 38
Cohen, A.P. 64
collective action 3, 21, 58, 86, 12
communicative competence 207n
Communist Party of Great Britain
    (CPGB) 87, 98, 102–9,
    111–12, 140, 205n
community 63–70, 105, 125, 135
Community Programme
    (CP) 121–23, 128, 206n
Coventry 206n
Cowdenbeath 105, 205n
Croucher, R. 86, 205n, 206n
cultural resources 4, 21, 37,
    56–63, 65, 74, 83, 79, 113

Deacon, A. 42, 44, 87–93, 96
Department of Employment (DE),
    unemployed's experience
    of 142, 155–8
Department of Health and Social
    Security (DHSS),
    unemployed's experience
    of 142, 155–8
dialogical resources 49–56, 70, 82,
    141
Dingwall 204n
disadvantages of unemployment,
    unemployed's perceptions
    of 142–50
dissimulation 59, 69, 182, 184
Ditton, J. 19
dual labour market 13
dual state thesis 39

220

fatalism 4, 60–3, 68–70, 114, 158, 167, 182, 184, 187–9, 199–200
Fowler reviews 43
Foucault, M. 44
fragmentation 59, 69, 167, 178
franchise 40–2, 79–80, 88–91
Francis, H. 103–4
Frow, E. and R. 205n

Gallup 207n
game theory 21–3
Gamson, W. A. 28
Garrett, G. 205n
gender *see* women
Giddens, A. 45, 47–8, 58–60, 66, 205n
Golding, P. 16–18, 167–78
Gordon, L. 27, 44
Gramsci, A. 60, 61

Hall, S. 169, 176
Hannington, W. 84, 86, 93, 205n, 206n
Harrison, R. 76–8
Hay, R. 205n
Hayburn, R. 112
high unemployment, unemployed's views about 158–64
Hobsbawm, E. J. 27
Hucknall 110

ideology 4, 16–17, 23, 25, 28–9, 58–63, 65, 167, 178, 182, 184
informal economy 19

Jahoda, M. 15–16, 103, 143, 204n
Jenkins, J. G. 116–17
Jessop, B. 38, 44
Jones, L. 95
Jordan, B. 12–16, 52

Kerbo, H. R. 205n
Kidd, A. J. 82
Kingsford, P. 99
Klugman, J. 206n
Knott, J. 40

labour aristocracy 41, 76, 81

Labour Party 13, 16, 80, 124
Lancashire 73, 112
Land and Labour League 76–8
Lash, S. 58, 60–3
Leeds 110–12
legitimation 59, 69, 167
Leicester 102–3
Liverpool 84, 102–3, 205n, 206n
Lochgelly 105
Lockwood, D. 57, 69, 107
London 87
long-term unemployed 1, 204n

McCarthy, J. D. 46–7
Macgregor, S. 204n
Macintyre, S. 100–1, 104–6
Manchester 82, 84, 94, 206n
Mann, K. 41, 76, 80, 91
Mann, M. 62, 66
Manpower Services Commission (MSC) 21, 118–23, 126–30, 202, 206n, 207n
Marshall, G. 33–6, 46, 56–8, 62, 66–7, 157, 199
Merseyside 206n
Middleton, S. 16–18, 167–78
Miles, R. 172
Miller, F. 44, 95
Mitchell, J. C. 123
monological resources 49–56, 70, 82, 122
Moore, B. 97
Moylan, S. 20

National Audit Office 157
National Insurance 86, 91–3, 205n
National Unemployed Workers' (Committee) Movement (NUW(C)M) 21, 42, 53, 63, 65, 69, 71, 84–113, 115, 139–4, 165–6, 201–2, 205n, 206n
neo-Marxist 3, 23–8, 56, 57
new social movements 50
North 6
North West 6
Not Genuinely Seeking Work (NGSW) clause 92–4, 108

Nottingham   84

Offe, C.   47–51, 53, 165
organisational resources   3, 21, 37,
    45–56, 76, 79, 83, 98–108, 113

Pahl, R. E.   19, 64
Parkin, F.   58, 60
Penna, S.   43
People's Marches for Jobs   115
Phizacklea, A.   172
Pilgrim Trust   102–3
Piven, F. F.   2–3, 12, 23–9, 38
pluralism   41, 43, 98
Poor Law   13, 39–40, 44, 72–6, 80,
    88–91, 97
Poplarism   83, 90–1
post-materialism   141, 144, 146,
    148, 151–2, 155, 170, 189, 194,
    199
Poulantzas, N.   26, 44
psychological effects of
    unemployment   15, 143, 204n
Public Assistance Committee
    (PAC)   91, 94–7, 105

race   1, 10–11, 27, 30–1, 34,
    114–15, 172–3
regional unemployment   5–6
reification   59, 69, 167
Rhondda   93, 102–5
Roach, J. L.   27
Rowbotham, S.   109
ruling class   13, 17
Runciman, W. G.   19–20
Ryan, P. A.   205n

Salford   82
Samuel, R.   104
Sartre, J.-P.   44
Saunders, P.   39
Schlozman, K. L.   2–3, 12, 27,
    29–33, 46
Schmeidler, E.   28
Scotland   6, 84, 87, 204n
Seabrook, J.   18
Shaffer, R. A.   205n
Sheffield   84, 110

Social Democratic Federation
    (SDF)   42, 78–84, 86, 205n
Socialist Workers' Party   117, 136
South Wales   84, 87, 104, 112
state   3, 16, 18, 23, 29, 32, 37–45,
    83–4, 113

Taylor-Gooby, P.   178
Thatcherism   16–18, 166–78
Therborn, G.   5–6
Thompson, J. B.   58–61
Tilly, C.   46
Trades Union Congress (TUC)   4,
    43, 55, 114–24, 201–2, 206n,
    207n

Unemployed Workers'
    Union   126–40, 166
Unemployment Assistant Board
    (UAB)   42, 44, 85, 87–8,
    96–7, 99, 101
urban riots   114–15
Urry, J.   58–61, 70

Vale of Leven   105
Van Parijs, P.   21–3
Verba, S.   2–3, 12, 27, 29–33, 46

Wales   6 (*see also* South Wales)
Webb, L.   109
Webster, C.   95
West, G.   27
West Bromwich   204n
West Indians   10–11
West Midlands   6
West Yorkshire   73, 110–12
Whiteley, P. F.   42, 43, 48–9, 52,
    53
Wight, D.   143
Winchester   204n
Winyard, S. J.   42, 43, 48–9, 52, 53
Wombwell   110
women   1, 7, 9, 11, 27, 30, 34,
    44–5, 84, 93, 108–12, 135–7,
    146–7, 173–4, 204n
Woolwich   205n
Workers' Education Association
    (WEA)   124–5, 128–9, 133

Wright, E. O.   22

Yorkshire and Humberside   6

youth unemployment   1–2

Zald, M. N.   46–7